ETHNICITY IN CHINA ───────

China Today series

ETHNICITY IN CHINA ———
A Critical Introduction

Xiaowei Zang

polity

The right of Xiaowei Zang to be identified as Author of this Work has been asserted in accordance with the UK Copyright, Designs and Patents Act 1988.

First published in 2015 by Polity Press

Polity Press
65 Bridge Street
Cambridge CB2 1UR, UK

Polity Press
350 Main Street
Malden, MA 02148, USA

ISBN-13: 978-0-7456-5360-0
ISBN-13: 978-0-7456-5361-7(pb)

A catalogue record for this book is available from the British Library.

Library of Congress Cataloging-in-Publication Data

Zang, Xiaowei.
    Ethnicity in China : a critical introduction / Xiaowei Zang.
      pages cm
    Includes bibliographical references and index.
      ISBN 978-0-7456-5360-0 (hardcover : alk. paper) – ISBN 0-7456-5360-X (hardcover : alk. paper) – ISBN 978-0-7456-5361-7 (pbk. : alk. paper) – ISBN 0-7456-5361-8 (pbk. : alk. paper)   1. Minorities–China.   2. Ethnic groups–China.   3. Ethnicity–China.   4. Ethnology–China.   5. China–Ethnic relations.   I. Title.
    DS730.Z364 2015
    305.800951–dc23
                    2014025915

Typeset in 11.5 on 15 pt Adobe Jenson Pro
by Toppan Best-set Premedia Limited
Printed and bound in the UK by T.J. International Ltd, Padstow, Cornwall.

For further information on Polity, visit our website:
politybooks.com

Contents

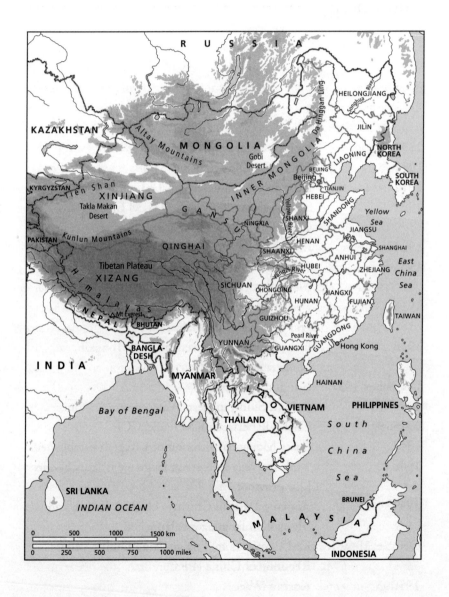

Chronology

1894–5	First Sino-Japanese War
1911	Fall of the Qing dynasty
1912	Republic of China established under Sun Yat-sen
1927	Split between Nationalists (KMT) and Communists (CCP); civil war begins
1934–5	Long March
1935	*Declaration of the Chinese Soviet Republic to the Mongolian Nationality* proclaimed
1936	*Declaration of the Chinese Soviet Republic of the Hui Nationality* proclaimed
1936	Hui autonomous government in Tongxin, Ningxia established
December 1937	Nanjing Massacre
1937–45	Second Sino-Japanese War
1945–9	Civil war between KMT and CCP
1947	Inner Mongolia Autonomous Region established
1948	*Yanbian Daily* in Korean language is launched in Jilin province
1949	*Xinjiang Daily* in Chinese, Uyghur, Kazak and Mongolian languages is launched
October 1949	KMT retreats to Taiwan; Mao founds People's Republic of China (PRC)
1950–3	Korean War
1951	*Qinghai Tibetan Journal* is launched

1951	A seventeen-point agreement between the PRC and representatives of the Dalai Lama is put into effect
1953	First National Traditional Ethnic Minority Sports Meet
1953–4	Ethnic Classification Project
1953–7	First Five-Year Plan; PRC adopts Soviet-style economic planning
1954	First constitution of the PRC and first meeting of the National People's Congress
1955	Xinjiang Uyghur Autonomous Region established
1956–7	Hundred Flowers Movement, a brief period of open political debate
1957	Anti-Rightist Movement
1958	Guangxi Zhuang Autonomous Region established; Ningxia Hui Autonomous Region established
1958–60	Great Leap Forward, an effort to modernize China through rapid industrialization and collectivization
March 1959	Tibetan Uprising in Lhasa; Dalai Lama flees to India
1959–61	Three Hard Years, widespread famine with tens of millions of deaths
1960	Sino-Soviet split
1962	Sino-Indian War
1965	Tibet Autonomous Region established
1966–76	Great Proletarian Cultural Revolution; Mao reasserts power
February 1972	President Richard Nixon visits China; 'Shanghai Communiqué' pledges to normalize US–China relations

September 1976	Death of Mao Zedong
October 1976	Ultra-Leftist Gang of Four arrested and sentenced
December 1978	Deng Xiaoping assumes power; launches Four Modernizations and economic reforms
1978	One-child family planning policy introduced
1979	US and China establish formal diplomatic ties; Deng Xiaoping visits Washington
1979	Sino-Vietnamese war
1982	Census reports PRC population at more than one billion
1984	Law on Regional Autonomy for Minority Nationalities of the PRC issued
December 1984	Margaret Thatcher co-signs Sino-British Joint Declaration agreeing to return Hong Kong to China in 1997
1987–9	Tibetan unrest in Sichuan, Tibet Autonomous Region and Qinghai, and the Tibetan prefectures in Yunnan and Gansu
May 1989	Ürümqi unrest in which Uyghur and Hui Muslims protest the publication of *Sexual Customs* 《性风俗》
1989	Tiananmen Square protests culminate in June 4 military crackdown
1992	Deng Xiaoping's Southern Inspection Tour re-energizes economic reforms
February 1992	Ürümqi bombings resulting in 3 deaths and 23 injuries
February 1997	The Ghulja Incident in which Uyghurs demand independence for Xinjiang
February 1997	Ürümqi bombings resulting in 9 deaths and 74 injuries

1993–2002	Jiang Zemin is president of PRC, continues economic growth agenda
November 2001	WTO accepts China as member
2003–13	Hu Jintao is president of PRC
March 2008	Tibetan riots in which 19 die and more than 380 civilians are injured
March–August 2008	Uyghur unrests in Hotan and Qaraqash county of Xinjiang
August 2008	The Kashgar attack resulting in the death of 16 Chinese police officers
August 2008	Summer Olympic Games in Beijing
June 2009	The Shaoguan incident, which is widely cited as the trigger event for the July 2009 Ürümqi riots
July 2009	Ürümqi riots in which nearly 200 die and more than 1,700 are injured
2010	Shanghai World Exposition
August 2010	The Aksu bombing resulting in 7 deaths and 14 injuries in Xinjiang
July 2011	The Hotan attack in Xinjiang
July 2011	The Kashgar attacks in Xinjiang
2012	Xi Jinping appointed General Secretary of the CCP (and president of PRC from 2013)
February 2012	The Yecheng attack in Xinjiang with 15 deaths and 18 injuries
June 2012	Six Uyghur men fail to hijack Tianjin Airlines Flight 7554
April 2013	The Bachu unrest in Xinjiang in which 21 people die
June 2013	The Shanshan attack in Xinjiang kills 2 policemen and 22 civilians; 11 of the Uyghur attackers are also killed

October 2013   Three Uyghurs drive a 4×4 vehicle into crowds in Tiananmen Square resulting in 5 deaths and 38 injuries

March 2014   The 2014 Kunming attack in which Uyghur attackers kill 29 civilians and injure more than 140 civilians

April 2014   PRC President Xi Jinping makes a four-day tour of Xinjiang

April 2014   Uyghurs attack passengers and detonate bombs at the exit of Ürümqi South Station, killing one civilian and injuring 79 civilians

May 2014   Five Uyghur assailants plough two vehicles and throw explosives into a crowd in a market in Ürümchi, killing 39 civilians and injuring at least 94

July 2014   Uyghur attacks on Shache County in Xinjiang result in a death toll of 37 civilians and 59 people identified as terrorists

Preface

Nationality is arguably a product of state building in the West. No such concept existed in pre-modern China, and it was not until the late nineteenth century that it was introduced to China from Japan. It is often translated as *minzu* (民族) in Chinese, which means 'a people' or 'an ethnic group'. In Chinese, 'minority nationality' is called 'shaoshu minzu' (少数民族). According to the Chinese government, there are altogether 56 ethnic groups in China. This book is about ethnic minorities in China and their relations to the Chinese state in the context of social and political change since 1949, with the emphasis on the post-1978 era, as market reforms have fundamentally changed the institutional arrangements for ethnic relations in the People's Republic of China (PRC). This book insists that the most important aspect of ethnic relations in China is the relations between the PRC state and the ethnic minorities rather than those between Han Chinese, the ethnic majority group, and the ethnic minority groups. The PRC state created the ethnic divide between Han Chinese and non-Han groups, classifying non-Han groups into different nationality groups and maintaining the ethnic identity of each PRC citizen through the state household registration system and personal identity card (Gladney 1996). There would not be 56 nationality groups in China without the PRC nationality policy. Accordingly, this book focuses on the PRC's nationality policy and its impacts on the ethnic minorities to elucidate ethnic relations in China.

Good knowledge of the ethnic relations is a lens through which one can better understand the political system and patterns of government behaviour in China and how the state defines and represents Chinese nationalism, the ethnic identities of Han Chinese, and the ethnic minority groups (Barabantseva 2008; Gladney 1994). Chinese nationalism, together with economic growth, has become a main pillar of political legitimacy for the Chinese Communist Party (CCP) in the post-1978 era. There are other reasons why the study of ethnic relations in China is important. Firstly, given recent ethnic unrest in some minority regions in China, the Chinese state's capacity for governance has been called into question. The ethnic minority groups were previously seen as vulnerable and subject to dominance or even acculturation by Han culture; today they represent one of the most powerful challenges to the Chinese government (Gladney 1996). Secondly, ethnic relations are no longer an issue solely related to domestic politics in China. Concerns over religious freedom and minority rights in China are presently receiving attention from the international community. This not only raises the profile of such issues within the PRC, but also between and among China and other countries on her borders and with which she does business. For example, China's handling of Uyghurs in Xinjiang has had significant implications for her relations with Muslim majority countries in Asia and the Middle East. Thirdly, China has become an economic superpower and is playing an increasingly important role in international affairs, and there is little doubt that its foreign policy towards minority rights has affected how ethnic conflicts in other parts of the world are resolved.

Thus, how the PRC manages ethnic relations has attracted widespread interest in the West. So far, opinions about ethnic relations in China have varied greatly. It is quite popular among some scholars, commentators and politicians in the West to condemn China's nationality policy and to accuse the PRC of suppressing minority rights and persecuting 'the ethnic and democratic consciousness of minority

nationalities'. Others have asserted that Beijing has paid lip service
to minority group rights (Sautman 1999, pp. 283–4). The US
Congressional-Executive Commission on China (2005b, p. 2) states
that 'The Chinese Government systematically denies some minorities
their legal rights and arbitrarily arrests their members for exercising
legally protected freedoms.' Unsurprisingly, Beijing has categorically
rejected these accusations and has tirelessly publicized its efforts to
reverse the traditional pattern of marginalization and subordination of
ethnic minority groups in China. Former senior Chinese leader Deng
Xiaoping claimed with confidence that 'there has never been any ethnic
discrimination' in China. So did other top Chinese leaders. To them,
major ethnic frictions should not exist in China as its nationality policy
is benevolent, and if bad things happen, they must be caused by 'foreign
instigation' or 'a handful of splittists' (Sautman 1997, p. 3).

To help readers find a balanced portrait of ethnic relations in China,
a series of questions are asked and answered in the course of this book:
What is the guiding ideology for Beijing's nationality policy? What has
Beijing done to protect minority cultures and languages and how has
it done this? Has the PRC earnestly promoted multiculturalism or
actively pursued the assimilation of its ethnic minority groups?
Economically, have the minority nationality groups become better off
or worse off after 1978? Are equal opportunity programmes effective
in reducing ethnic gaps in schooling, employment and income? Is
ethnic inequality growing or declining in the post-1978 era? What
does regional autonomy mean to the ethnic minority groups in the
PRC? How much executive, legislative and judiciary power do ethnic
minority groups have in minority areas under the jurisdiction of
regional autonomy? Why have ethnic tensions in Tibet and Xinjiang
been growing in the post-1978 era? What has the PRC done to reduce
ethnic tensions, and are these measures sufficient and effective? What
does the PRC think of minority rights when it engages with the outside
world? Why is there a gap between Beijing's nationality policy and the

international minority rights regime? Will the PRC modify or change its nationality policy and move closer to global norms on minority rights?

In this book, I address these questions using insights from both historical and cultural perspectives on ethnic relations in China, particularly the impact of Confucian assimilative legacies on the PRC nationality policy. I find it productive to conceptualize pre-modern China as a cultural sphere when discussing ethnic relations. Drawing on the hierarchal relations between Han civilization and those of non-Han peoples, and the age-old distinction between cooked (i.e., acculturated) barbarians and raw or uncooked (i.e., unacculturated) barbarians in the pre-1949 era, I emphasize continuity in the evolution of the sinocentric relations between Han Chinese and non-Han groups, from Confucius to Dr Sun Yat-sen and all the way to Mao Zedong, Deng Xiaoping and current Chinese leaders. A central theme that links China's past with current PRC nationality policy in this book is the Confucian ideology of *ronghe*, which promotes and celebrates minority acculturation and eventual assimilation into Han society (see chapter 1).

Chapter 1 examines the basic facts about ethnic demographics in the PRC before discussing the political origin of the ethnic labels which ethnic minority groups are given by the state. Next, it offers an account of the Ethnic Classification Project conducted in 1953–4 and explains that although the PRC government followed the USSR in initiating this project, it relied on the Chinese scholarship on ethnicity rather than Stalin's nationality criterion. The Ethnic Classification Project took place mainly to address Beijing's need to form a multi-ethnic National People's Congress in an attempt to show off its political legitimacy and mandate to govern China. The PRC's political considerations dictated the process of the classification project, and the input from ethnic minority groups in their identification was minimal. Some existing minority groups were officially recognized, some different minority groups were combined under a single group name through administrative fiat despite vast inter-group differences in language, customs, etc., and some groups were arbitrarily denied the status of minority ethnicity. The ethnic labels that were created in the early 1950s are still used by the PRC state to determine the ethnic identities of the people in China, demonstrating the power of the state over ethnic relations in China.

Chapter 1 also discusses the central theme in Beijing's nationality policy – acculturation and assimilation of the minority nationality groups into Han culture and society despite its effort to promote the image of China as a multicultural country to the outside world. It discusses how the notion of nationality was developed in China at the end of the nineteenth century, how the CCP dealt with the nationality question before 1949, why the CCP regarded the nationality question as an issue of class struggle before 1978, and why the official rhetoric and nationality policy worked in the pre-1978 era. The chapter then outlines drastic changes in China's nationality policy in the post-1978 era and the major efforts the Chinese government has made to reduce inter-group inequality as the means of improving ethnic relations. Finally, it draws attention to the impact of Beijing's assimilation stance on ethnic inequality, the protection of minority cultures, and regional autonomy in the PRC.

Chapter 2 evaluates Beijing's efforts to reduce ethnic inequality. This is an important topic, as Beijing believes that all minority problems can be satisfactorily resolved by promoting economic development. For historical reasons, ethnic minority groups have lived in remote and economically backward regions of China and lagged behind Han Chinese in schooling and labour market outcomes. The CCP has pursued a twofold strategy for the reduction of ethnic inequality in China. Firstly, it has attempted to reduce ethnic inequality between Han Chinese and people of ethnic minority status by reducing socioeconomic gaps between Han regions and minority regions.

Secondly, it has implemented affirmative action programmes to improve the life chances of individual members of minority nationalities, regardless of whether they live in Han regions or minority regions. The chapter shows improvements in economic outputs, educational infrastructure and schooling, and general well-being in minority regions since 1949. Beijing has played a major role in promoting economic growth in minority regions, providing aid in the form of labour, material and financial resources to minority regions. This chapter also examines Beijing's policies in the promotion of ethnic tourism and environmental protection in minority areas.

Chapter 2 then outlines Beijing's affirmative action programmes in the areas of education, employment, political careers, legal protection, etc. However, empirical data provided in this chapter show growing inequalities between Han Chinese and the minority nationality groups in the post-1978 era. This development is disappointing as the Chinese government has put so much emphasis on the reduction of ethnic inequalities in China, and there are good reasons to have faith in the government's sincerity in attempting to promote national unity through economic growth and affirmative action. There is little doubt that although the government has enacted many policies to reduce ethnic inequalities, more efforts by, and resources from, the government are required to narrow the gap in status attainment between Han Chinese and the ethnic minority groups in the PRC. If the Chinese government is not willing or able to do more in other areas of ethnic relations, such as regional autonomy and promotion of minority cultures and languages, it can and should do more in the area of economic inequalities between Han Chinese and ethnic minorities.

Chapter 3 assesses Beijing's policy towards the preservation and promotion of ethnic minority cultures and languages. China has often been seen as the home of Confucianism, with an extensive dynastic history and a writing system at its core. Yet before 1949, some ethnic minority groups managed to maintain their own cultures and languages, a historical fact that has not been taken seriously by people in the West. After 1949, the PRC has made some efforts to promote minority cultures, including their languages. However, the PRC has no intention of hiding the fact that the protection of minority rights in China is not the outcome of high court decisions or public debates and discourse, or contestation between the state and society or between the ethnic majority group and ethnic minority groups, but rather is the result of 'gifts' bestowed by the paternalistic Chinese state. Unsurprisingly, the Chinese government has managed minority cultures without much input from ethnic minority groups, and has unilaterally decided what aspects of minority cultures it wants to protect and what aspects of minority cultures it will not take care of. For example, the Chinese state has paid inadequate attention to the collective or communal goods of ethnic minority groups. In particular, since 1978, China has been experiencing rapid economic growth at a scale and pace that is unprecedented in human history. This development has inadvertently placed great pressure on China's cultural diversity and the survival of minority cultures and languages, as a common thread and a general case for all ethnic minorities is concern over the willingness among minority youth in educational settings to learn their own mother tongues and other aspects of their cultural heritage. Beijing has recognized the importance of ethnic minority education and has implemented a bilingual policy in some minority regions. Yet in seeking secular success and upward mobility in Han-dominated society, many minority youth have mastered Mandarin at the expense of their own mother tongues. It appears that the Chinese government has done a poorer job in protecting minority cultures than in reducing ethnic inequalities in status attainment.

Chapter 4 reviews Beijing's efforts to promote regional autonomy from the perspective of its nationality policy. It first outlines the historical origins and post-1949 development of the system of ethnic autonomy in China. This outline describes what regional autonomy in

China should be rather than what it actually is. China has perhaps the most extensive system of ethnic autonomy in the world, which includes some 155 autonomous regions, prefectures, counties, and ethnic townships within its territory. In theory, the system of ethnic autonomy has provided a modicum of special political, legislative and economic rights to territorially concentrated minority people in China, including the rights and power of self-government of ethnic autonomous areas. But the leaders of local government in autonomous regions perform the same functions and maintain the same relations to central authorities as local governments in Han areas do, although in theory they are to be selected in accordance with the wishes of the nationality or nationalities and should act differently. This chapter also includes a discussion of Han migration into minority areas and the changes in Beijing's policy towards regional autonomy, as some government officials and scholars have begun to discuss the possibility of abolishing regional autonomy in China.

Chapter 5 provides an analysis of the intra- and inter-group differences among minority peoples and how Beijing's nationality policy treats the minority nationality groups differently. Chapters 1 and 4 discuss the relationship between the state and ethnic minority groups as if there is no variation among the latter. Chapter 5 shows intra-group differences in the levels of acculturation and status attainment among minority peoples and outlines how these differences affect the political orientations of minority elites in the PRC. Next, it examines inter-group differences among ethnic minorities in family behaviour, levels of acculturation and status attainment. The differences among the minority nationalities in terms of demographics, culture, etc., may be as large as or larger than the aggregate Han–minority differences.

In addition, chapters 2–4 discuss the relationship between the PRC state and minority nationality groups as if the former did not treat the latter differentially. Chapter 5 raises three questions: Does the Chinese state treat the minority groups equally? Do its perceptions of different minority groups affect the distribution of public goods among ethnic minority groups in China? What are the plausible reasons for the state's perceptions: favouritism or discrimination? This chapter argues that state attitudes are driven by political interests. The state is motivated to treat a minority group preferentially if it is useful for it. The state is also likely to treat a minority group favourably if it has the potential to pose a threat to national interests. The PRC state has used force to suppress separatist attempts, and at the same time it has also tried to accommodate some members of the 'threatening' minority to divide and rule. It is less likely to do the same for a minority group that does not pose a serious threat to the status quo. This chapter compares Uyghur Muslims with Hui Muslims to show this likelihood.

Chapter 6 is a case study of ethnic relations in Tibet and Xinjiang. In this chapter, I focus on the Tibet Autonomous Region (TAR) rather than the Greater Tibetan areas of the Qinghai-Tibet Plateau that include TAR, Qinghai and parts of Sichuan, Gansu and Yunnan. Both Uyghurs and Tibetans have attracted a great deal of international attention due to recent ethnic conflicts. Chapter 6 asks: Why has the Chinese state faced challenges of separatism from Tibet and Xinjiang despite rapid economic development in these two regions since 1978? To answer this question, this chapter first outlines the historical contexts of Tibet and then Xinjiang. It then discusses what the CCP did to implement the social transformation of Tibet and Xinjiang between 1949 and 1965, and how the CCP raised new elite groups that supported socialist construction in Tibet and Xinjiang during this period. Next, this chapter examines how the Cultural Revolution of 1966–76 created inter-group antagonism between Han Chinese and Tibetans and between Han Chinese and Uyghurs. Beijing promoted various measures to repair ethnic relations in these two regions after 1976, which included policies for greater religious freedom and expression of ethnic consciousness. At the same time, Beijing has actively promoted economic growth in Tibet and Xinjiang as the means of reducing ethnic inequality and maintaining social stability in these two regions. This chapter then explains why rapid economic development in Tibet and Xinjiang has been accompanied by rising ethnic tensions, contrary to the expectations of the Chinese government. Finally, this chapter explains why the current nationality policy is ill-equipped to cope with the nationality question in Tibet and Xinjiang.

Chapter 7 accesses Beijing's nationality policy from the perspective of the international minority rights regime. In the era of globalization and multiculturalism, nation states have been increasingly judged by their efforts to protect ethnic diversity and self-determination. This chapter asks: Has the Chinese state accepted the international standards of minority rights in designing its ethnic policy? Has it changed its ethnic policy to meet the international standards? What are the possible developments in China's ethnic policy in the years to come? To address these questions, this chapter first discusses the origins and development of the international minority rights regime and provides an account of a major paradigm shift in minority rights in global governance since 1989. This change has been inconsistent with Beijing's way of thinking on minority rights. Next, this chapter examines some key aspects of Beijing's policy of protecting minorities and identifies the areas of improvement in the minority rights regime in the PRC. There is also a discussion of Beijing's foreign policy towards minority rights in international politics. This chapter then reviews Beijing's progress in its socialization into the international norms on minority rights, and explains why there is a gap between Beijing's nationality policy and the international norms on minority rights. This chapter ends with an optimistic note that Beijing may move towards a universal human rights regime that celebrates and promotes diversity, multiculturalism, autonomy, and self-determination as the PRC is further integrated into the international community, extreme Han nationalism loses its appeal to Han people in the face of growing concerns on individual liberality and well-being, and the ideas of human rights and democracy become everyday words in China.

In sum, this book provides readers with an accessible introduction to some of the important themes in ethnic relations in China, including ethnic demographics, economic development and ethnic inequality, ethnic minority languages and cultures, regional autonomy, ethnic minority groups and the state perception of minority threat, ethnic relations in Tibet and Xinjiang, and Beijing's nationality policy from the perspective of the international minority rights regime. As noted above, the analytic framework in this book focuses on the role of the state in ethnic relations (i.e., the impact of the government nationality policy on the ethnic minority groups) in the PRC, with the goal of plunging readers in the West into a political world very different from the one in which they live and are familiar with, thereby developing a good understanding of ethnic relations in the PRC.

Like many other scholars outside China, I have relied on existing documentary sources, including scholarly articles and books on minority nationality groups; official sources such as government white papers, Chinese and Western websites; and relevant PRC regulatory instruments (Ghai and Woodman 2009, p. 31). Also, given the difficulty in gathering data about minority nationality groups in China, I have used some government statistics from the PRC for this book. Readers should bear in mind that official statistics are released mainly to support state views. They should not be understood as normative because of PRC propaganda imperatives, flawed data collection, manipulation, and so on. The statistics support the government claims, not mine. I did my best to cross-check these sources of information, and urge caution regarding the quality and reliability of these official data and how to interpret them. For example, if the Chinese government issued a report that it had invested $1 million in a minority region, readers should not take it for granted that the investment was $1 million. Nor should they uncritically assume that the investment was made for the minority group's benefit. After mentioning all these negative possibilities, I am confident that this book offers a broad contour of ethnic relations in the PRC. Finally, findings from research done by scholars in the West were very important for me in developing my arguments in this book, although I am solely responsible for any possible errors.

Acknowledgements

I would like to thank Emma Longstaff and Jonathan Skerrett at Polity Press for their interest in my research and for inviting me to write this book for the China Today series. I appreciated the opportunity to write this book because it gave me the chance to rethink many of the broad issues related to ethnic relations in China, and to learn insights from other scholars of minority ethnicity in the PRC. I thank Ian Tuttle of Godiva Publishing Services for his wonderful job in copy-editing my manuscript. It took me almost four years to complete this project amid a busy schedule of other academic, professional and administrative commitments. It was hard for me to find time for research, especially after I moved from the University of Sheffield to City University of Hong Kong in 2013. I appreciated every minute I had in the course of writing this book. This appreciation turned into a source of satisfaction when I completed the project. I would like to thank two Polity Press reviewers for many criticisms and encouragements, which have helped me turn this book into a better work. While I did not agree with everything they said, I did appreciate their efforts and time very much. One of them wrote his/her comments, single-spaced, on 28 pages. What a dutiful reviewer he/she was! In addition, I was enlightened by queries, constructive criticisms and challenges from the audience when I presented part of the manuscript in seminars at Peking University and Sun Yat-sen University in China and delivered a distinguished lecture at the East Asian Institute of the National University of Singapore.

David Goodman and William Jankowiak, two fellow contributors to Polity's China Today series, have for many years been a major source of intellectual inspiration for me. I also thank Dr Suisheng Zhao, editor of *Journal of Contemporary China*, for giving me permission to reproduce parts of an article I have previously published in that journal (Zang 2012). Research leave from the University of Sheffield in 2013 gave me much-needed time to complete the draft of this manuscript. I spent part of the research leave in Los Angeles and am grateful to Stanley Rosen, Clayton Dube and Catherine Gao in the US-China Institute at the University of Southern California as they provided me with all the help I asked for. Finally, this book would not have been written without the support of family, friends and associates. It is to them that this book is dedicated.

Abbreviations

CCP   Chinese Communist Party
NGO   Non-governmental organization
NPC   National People's Congress
ROC   Republic of China
PLA   People's Liberation Army
PRC   People's Republic of China
TAR   Tibet Autonomous Region
US(A)   United States (of America)
USSR   Union of Soviet Socialist Republics

1 | The People's Republic of China as a Multinational Country

Who are ethnic minorities in the People's Republic of China (PRC)? What are their demographics? Why are they identified as ethnic minorities? What historical legacies has the PRC inherited when developing its nationality policy? Is assimilation or the promotion of multiculturalism the guiding principle of the nationality policy? Has the PRC modified its nationality policy in recent decades? This chapter addresses these important questions, to which many people in the West have seldom given much thought. They instead have either regarded citizens in China as a homogeneous nation (Fei 1980, p. 95) or associated Chinese with the Han people (Mackerras 2011a, p. 114). Yet in fact there are 56 state-recognized nationality groups (*minzu* 民族) in the PRC. The ruling party of the PRC, the Chinese Communist Party (CCP), is a political machine controlled by Han Chinese, the majority nationality group that accounts for 91.6 per cent of the total population in China. The other 55 groups, classified by the PRC as the ethnic minorities (see below for a discussion of the classification project), make up the remaining 8.4 per cent (Mackerras 1994, pp. 233–59; Yang and Wall 2009, p. 77). While the combined percentage of China's minority nationalities seems small, their combined population is large (about 105 million), outnumbered only by the peoples of Bangladesh, Brazil, India, Indonesia, Nigeria, Russia, Pakistan, the United States, and the Han people of China. Four minority nationalities in China (Zhuang, Hui, Manchus and Uyghurs) number more than 10 million each and four other minority nationalities

(Miao, Yi, Tujia and Tibetans) boast a population of more than 6 million each. In comparison, the population size of each of 48 per cent of the countries in the world in 1999 was less than 5 million (Wong 2000, p. 53).

Although perceived as a unified culture by some people in the West, Han Chinese are not a monolithic entity, nor are they necessarily representative of the PRC state (Tapp 2010, p. 102). They differ among themselves in many ways, speaking eight mutually unintelligible languages: Mandarin, Wu, Yue, Xiang, Hakka, Gan, Southern Min and Northern Min, and there are many mutually unintelligible dialects in different parts of China. Mandarin was imposed as the national language in the early twentieth century and has since become the lingua franca, but is not always used in everyday life in some parts of the country. Even in metropolitan cities such as Shanghai and Guangzhou, local residents prefer to communicate in their dialect, which Han Chinese from other parts of China find totally unintelligible. Cultural perceptions among Han Chinese involve broad stereotypical contrasts between north and south and among different regions in both north and south, and the contrasts are partly based on vastly different customary practices on birth, marriage, burial, etc., carried out by subgroups among northern Chinese and southern Chinese in different parts of China (Olson 1998; also Wong 2000, p. 54).

There are good studies of subgroups among Han Chinese (e.g., Constable 1996; Hansen 2005; Pasternak and Salaff 1993; Xu et al. 2009). This book is about the Chinese government nationality policy, the ethnic minority groups, and the impacts of the nationality policy on the ethnic minority groups residing in both minority areas and Han areas in China. An ethnic minority is a group numerically inferior to the rest of the population, in a non-dominant position and with a distinctive ethnic, religious or linguistic characteristic (Henrard 2001, pp. 41–3; Pentassuglia 2005, p. 9; Vermeersch 2003, p. 1). Minority areas refer to China's five minority autonomous regions, Yunnan,

Guizhou, Qinghai provinces, and sub-provincial units that have large ethnic minority populations (Guo et al. 2010, p. 201; Mackerras 2011a, p. 112). Chapter 4 provides detailed information on minority areas in China. This chapter offers some basic information about the 55 minority nationality groups (table 1.1) and explains how ethnic nationality groups in China are identified and recognized by the PRC state. It also outlines Beijing's assimilation stance in its nationality policy.

This book selectively examines some ethnic minority groups (often large ones) as they are more important than other ethnic minority groups (often small ones) with regard to the discourse on ethnic relations in China. For example, frequent references are made to Tibetans, who numbered 6,282,187 in 2010, and Uyghurs, who numbered 10,069,346 in 2010, in various parts of this book. In comparison, the Daur people, who numbered 131,992 in 2010 and live in Inner Mongolia and Xinjiang (Fei 1980, pp. 100–2), are not mentioned often in this book. The ethnic minority groups such as Tibetans and Uyghurs are selected for detailed discussions in this monograph partly because they are the focus of the global interest in minority rights in China. The relations between these ethnic minority groups and the PRC state provide good case studies of the strengths and inadequacies of Beijing's nationality policy. Moreover, many scholars in the West have carried out detailed research on these ethnic minority groups, and the findings from their studies are vital for a good understanding of minority ethnicity in the PRC.

For convenience I use 'minority nationalities', 'minority peoples', 'ethnic minorities' and 'ethnic minority groups' interchangeably. They all refer to non-Han people in China. Similarly, I use 'the CCP', 'the government', 'the Chinese government', 'the PRC', 'the PRC state', 'the Chinese state' and 'Beijing' interchangeably in this book. They should be distinguished from Han Chinese, the majority nationality group in China, despite the fact that they are essentially the political instrument

Table 1.1: List of the 56 State-Recognized Ethnic Groups in China (2010)

Name	Population	Name	Population
1. Han/汉族	1,220,844,520	30. Mulao/仫佬族	216,257
2. Zhuang/壮族	16,926,381	31. Xibe/錫伯族	190,481
3. Hui/回族	10,586,087	32. Kyrgyz/柯尔克孜族	186,708
4. Manchu/满族	10,387,958	33. Jingpo/景頗族	147,828
5. Uyghur/维吾尔族	10,069,346	34. Daur/达斡尔族	131,992
6. Miao/苗族	9,426,007	35. Salar/撒拉族	130,607
7. Yi/彝族	8,714,393	36. Blang/布朗族	119,639
8. Tujia/土家族	8,353,912	37. Maonan/毛南族	101,192
9. Tibetan/藏族	6,282,187	38. Tajik/塔吉克族	51,069
10. Mongol/蒙古族	5,981,840	39. Pumi/普米族	42,861
11. Dong/侗族	2,879,974	40. Achang/阿昌族	39,555
12. Buyei/布依族	2,870,034	41. Nu/怒族	37,523
13. Yao/瑶族	2,796,003	42. Ewenki/鄂温克族	30,875
14. Bai/白族	1,933,510	43. Gin/京族	28,199
15. Korean/朝鲜族	1,830,929	44. Jino/基諾族	23,143

16. Hani/哈尼族	1,660,932		45. Déang/德昂族	20,556
17. Li/黎族	1,463,064		46. Bonan/保安族	20,074
18. Kazak/哈萨克族	1,462,588		47. Russian/俄罗斯族	15,393
19. Dai/傣族	1,261,311		48. Yugur/裕固族	14,378
20. She/畲族	708,651		49. Uzbeks/乌孜别克族	10,569
21. Lisu/傈僳族	702,839		50. Monba/門巴族	10,561
22. Dongxiang/东乡族	621,500		51. Oroqen/鄂伦春族	8,659
23. Gelao/仡佬族	550,746		52. Derung/独龙族	6,930
24. Lahu/拉祜族	485,966		53. Hezhen/赫哲族	5,354
25. Va/佤族	429,709		54. Gaoshan/高山族	4,009
26. Sui/水族	411,847		55. Lhoba/珞巴族	3,682
27. Nakhi/納西族	326,295		56. Tatars/塔塔尔族	3,556
28. Qiang/羌族	309,576		Undistinguished/未识别民族	640,101
29. Tu/土族	289,565			

Source: http://www.chinesefolklore.org.cn/forum/redirect.php?tid=34020&goto=lastpost; also see http://en.wikipedia.org/wiki/List_of_ethnic_groups_in_China

of Han Chinese in the governance of ethnic relations and minority regions in the PRC.

ETHNIC DEMOGRAPHY

The CCP has tirelessly proclaimed that China has enjoyed a long-standing existence as a unified multi-ethnic state. Chinese legend has it that there were many non-Han groups in addition to Han, in what is now the PRC territory, some 5,000 years ago. Heberer (1989, p. 18) claims that starting with the Han dynasty (206 BC–220 AD), Han Chinese classified non-Han peoples as the Yi (east), Rong (west), Man (south), and Di (north) barbarians, and much of pre-modern Chinese history consisted of intensive interaction between the Han people and these non-Han peoples. The most memorable historical events of this interaction are perhaps the epic war the Han dynasty fought against the Hun between 133 BC and 89 AD and the fact that the Tang dynasty (618–907), the Yuan dynasty (1271–1368) and the Qing dynasty (1644–1911) were all founded by non-Han groups. Due to wars, migration, intermarriage, etc., some non-Han groups such as the Rouran, Tangut, Tujue and Yuezhi faded away during the course of history, while other groups have survived into modern times (Information Office of the State Council 2010a, pp. 223–5; Mackerras 2004a, p. 305).

The 55 ethnic minority groups are scattered in areas that cover some 60 per cent of the PRC's territory, much of which is located in China's border regions and strategically important for Beijing's relations with its neighbours (Potter 2011, p. 2), including Afghanistan, Burma, India, Kazakhstan, North Korea, Kyrgyzstan, Mongolia, Pakistan, Russia, Tajikistan and Vietnam. Many minority areas are rich in natural resources. For example, Qinghai is well known for its oil, natural gas, potassium, salt, nonferrous metals, coal and iron resources. Xinjiang is a major producer of grain and cotton and has large reserves of petroleum, natural gas, asbestos, salt, beryllium, iron ore, muscovite, gemstones, etc. Tibet boasts large reserves of chromite, copper, boron and isinglass, etc. There are alkali reserves and other mineral products such as coal, asbestos and mica in Inner Mongolia. Much woodland and hydropower in China is found in Tibet, Qinghai, Inner Mongolia, Yunnan and Guizhou. Minority areas such as Guangxi, Guizhou and Yunnan are renowned for tourism thanks to their natural environments, time-honoured history and diversified ethnic cultures (see chapter 2).

Many minority nationality groups are concentrated in Inner Mongolia, Xinjiang, Ningxia, Guangxi, Tibet, Yunnan, Guizhou, Qinghai, Sichuan, Gansu, Hubei and Hunan. Of all China's province-level administrative units, Yunnan has the highest number of state-recognized minorities (25 ethnic groups). Almost one in three persons in Yunnan province belongs to one of the state-recognized minority nationalities (Mackerras 2004a, p. 305). Some of the 55 ethnic minority groups, such as Koreans, Mongols, Russians, Uyghurs, Kyrgiz, Kazaks, Uzbeks and Tajiks, in Xinjiang have ethnic counterparts in neighbouring countries, as do Zhuang, Miao, Dai and Shui in Yunnan and Guangxi.

In terms of population size, the Zhuang people constitute the largest ethnic minority group in the PRC, with a total population of nearly 17 million in 2010. They are related to the Tai family found throughout South East Asia. The Zhuang has its own language, but many Zhuang people do not know Zhuang characters. Most Zhuang people live in the Guangxi Zhuang Autonomous Region. The rest can be found in Yunnan, Guangdong, Guizhou and Hunan provinces. The Zhuang are one of the most acculturated ethnic minority groups in China (Kaup 2000; 2002, p. 868; Poston et al. 2006, pp. 75–6).

Some other minorities have been similarly assimilated into Han culture and their status as separate, unique peoples is nearly lost (Chang 2003, pp. 14–15), if not publicly questioned. One example is the She people, who numbered 708,651 in 2010 and live in Fujian, Zhejiang, Anhui, Jiangxi and Guangdong provinces. The She language is a Hmong-Mien language, but many She people speak Chinese dialects such as Hakka. Another example is the Tujia people, who are the seventh largest ethnic minority group in China, with a total population of nearly 8.4 million in 2010. Tujia is a Tibeto-Burman language. Yet there are few speakers of this language, as many Tujia people use a local Chinese dialect or Mandarin (Brown 2002; 2007; Shih 2001). The Tujia people share territory with the Bai people, the Miao people and the Yao people in Yunnan and Sichuan provinces. The number of Bai people was estimated to be more than 1.9 million in 2010. The Bai language is thought to be part of the Sino-Tibetan language family. The Miao people (Poston et al. 2006, pp. 73–4) are a large ethnic group of more than 9.4 million people. The Yao people (Alberts 2007; Jonsson 2000; Litzinger 1998; 2000) were estimated to number nearly 2.8 million in 2010. The ethnic costumes these minority groups have inherited have become perhaps the single most important ethnic marker which distinguishes them from Han Chinese.

Manchus are more assimilated than these minority groups as they are almost indistinguishable from Han Chinese in terms of food, language, religion, costumes, etc. They are the third largest ethnic minority group in China, with a total population of nearly 10.4 million in 2010. They were an Altaic people who were herders and hunters and conquered China in 1664. Unlike the above non-Han groups who had been historically marginalized, repressed and exploited by Han Chinese, the Manchu were the rulers of China between 1664 and 1911. Despite their ruling class status, the Manchu ethnicity was gradually acculturated into Han society before 1911, and the acculturation was accelerated after the demise of the Qing dynasty in 1911. Today, many Manchus speak Mandarin and are found in all trades across China, with little remaining of their ethnic markers, and only a small number of Manchus can speak their mother tongue (Durrant 1979; Fei 1980, p. 96; Huang 1990; Rhoads 2000).

Another acculturated minority nationality group is Hui Muslims with a population of nearly 10 million in 2010, the second largest ethnic minority group in China. They are the descendants of foreign Muslim merchants, militia and officials, who came to China from Arabian and Central Asian countries between the seventh and fourteenth centuries and intermarried with Han Chinese. In spite of cultural, economic and social differences among Hui groups in different localities, they were subsumed into the 'Hui' category during the 1954 Ethnic Classification Project (to be discussed below). The Chinese state has 'ignored the fact that the Hui had no common territory, common language, common "psychological makeup", nor common mode of economic production in favour of simplicity and political expediency' (Caffrey 2004, p. 257; see also Caffrey 2004, pp. 247–9, 262; Poston et al. 2006, p. 76).

Some minority nationality groups have managed to achieve a degree of success in maintaining their cultures, including mother tongues and customs. One example is the Mongol people, who were estimated to have a population of nearly 6 million in 2010. The name 'Mongol' first appeared in the eighth-century record of the Tang dynasty as a tribe of Shiwei. In the thirteenth century, it grew into an umbrella term for a large group of Mongolic and Turkic tribes united under Genghis Khan that conquered Eurasia, China and part of Europe (Chang 2003, pp. 34–5; Ratchnevsky and Haining 1993, p. 7). The Mongolian language is the best-known member of the Mongolic language family, yet an increasing number of Mongols speak Mandarin (Bulag 2003; 2004; Jankowiak 1993).

Tibetans are much less acculturated than Mongols. They speak the Tibetan language, which has been thought to belong to the Sino-Tibetan family of languages. This idea has recently been challenged as fictive, or politically based, or at least highly debatable. It is argued that just because the Tibetan language has many loan words from early Chinese does not necessarily mean that it belongs to the Sino-Tibetan family, since syntax, structure and everything else are different. In terms of religion, many Tibetans practise Tibetan Buddhism, though some observe the indigenous Bön and others are Muslims. The Dalai Lamas belong to the Gelugpa school of Tibetan Buddhism, believed to be an emanation of Chenrezig, the Buddha of Compassion. The present Dalai Lama was awarded the 1989 Nobel Peace Prize. Another important Gelugpa figure is the Panchen Lama. Tibetan medicine, which uses plants, animals and minerals, has enjoyed increasing popularity among Han Chinese in recent years (Blondeau et al. 2008; Henry 2001; Kapstein 2006; Stein 1972).

Other less assimilated ethnic groups in China include the Kazak people, the Kirgiz people, the Ozbek people and the Tajik people. They are Muslims residing in Xinjiang. Uyghurs are not only unassimilated but also known for their demand for independence for Xinjiang (Mamet et al. 2005, p. 191; see also Dautcher 1999, pp. 54–5, 337–9; Kaltman 2007, p. 2; Millward 2007, pp. 348–51; Rudelson and Jankowiak 2004, p. 311). They are Sunni Muslims and ethnically Turkic, who display Indo-Iranian facial features, speak Turkish languages and use Arabic script, eat Islamic foods, wear ethnic costumes, and celebrate their own festivals. Many Uyghurs hold on to Uyghur ways of life and do not read, speak or write Chinese (Dillon 2004, p. 24; Rudelson and Jankowiak 2004, pp. 302–3, 307, 313; Smith 2000, pp. 199, 217).

In addition to the 56 state-recognized ethnic groups mentioned above, there is a list of groups that include the Bajia people (八甲人), who live in Yunnan with a population of 1,106; the Deng people (僜人), who live in Tibet with a population of 1,391; the Gejia people (亻革家人), who live in Guizhou with a population of nearly 60,000; the Khmu people (克木人), who live in Yunnan with a population of 3,300; the Kucong people (苦聪人), who live in Yunnan with a population of 30,000; the Mang people (莽人), who live in Yunnan with a population of 680; the Sherpa people (夏尔巴人), who live in Tibet with a population of 2,000; the Yi people (羿人), who live in Sichuan and Guizhou with a population of some 300; and some others. These peoples have tried for decades to be officially recognized as separate ethnic groups in the PRC (Fei 1980, pp. 102–7; Caffrey 2004, p. 257; Tapp 2002a, p. 69; 2010, p. 100). For undeclared reasons, Beijing has been unwilling to add any further groups to the list of 56 nationalities in China (Mackerras 2004a, p. 304).

THE ETHNIC CLASSIFICATION PROJECT IN THE 1950S

The concept of nationality did not exist in traditional Chinese literature and philosophy. The term '*minzu*' was first introduced into China from Japan by combining the notion of people ('min') and the notion of descent ('zu') in the second half of the nineteenth century. At that time, China was perceived by Han people to be about to be colonized by foreign powers. Leading intellectuals such as Liang Qichao and Kang Youwei advanced the notion of a Chinese nation to unite Han people to save China from foreign dominance (Barabantseva 2008, pp. 569–70; Gladney 1996, pp. 16–17, 85; see also Huang 2002). Yet until 1949, other than Han Chinese, there existed Manchus, Mongols, Tibetans, Huihui and a few loose ethnic categories such as Baiyi (百夷), Miao (苗), Tong (僮), Yao (猺) and Yi (夷). Han–minority boundaries in minority areas were more or less fluid, mobile and ambiguous due to Han–minority interaction and long-term sinicizing processes (Brown 2001, p. 56; Fei 1980, p. 95). The 56 nationality groups that we know in China today did not exist as such.

For example, 僮 people (i.e. Zhuang) were not recognized as a unique nationality group by the Nationalist government that ruled China between 1911 and 1949. Nor did they perceive themselves as a unique nationality group before 1949 (Kaup 2002, p. 869). As another example, many residents in the Enshi region of Hubei province identified themselves as Han Chinese and were identified by the Nationalist government as Han Chinese. Some local men who had been conscripted by the Nationalist government and fled to Taiwan in 1949 were surprised, upon their return to Enshi in the 1980s, to discover that their relatives were now classified by the PRC as Miao or Tujia (Brown 2001, pp. 57–8).

Soon after the CCP came to power in 1949, it started to form a National People's Congress (NPC), a nation state building endeavour to demonstrate its mandate to govern China and to draft a constitution for the PRC (Mackerras 2004a, pp. 308–9; Tapp 2002a, pp. 67, 73–4). To showcase its legitimacy and widespread support from society, and as a strategy of governance (i.e., incorporation of local and non-Han elites into state structures under the United Front policy), the CCP deemed it necessary to allocate congressional seats to deputies from different social groups such as women, intellectuals and non-Han groups (Fei 1980, p. 94; Mullaney 2010a, p. 327). According to the 1953 Election Law, at least one seat in the NPC should be awarded to each non-Han group, regardless of its population size (Mullaney 2004, p. 211; Howland 2011, p. 15). However, in the inaugural census in which individuals were permitted to register their ethnic identities at will, over 400 ethnonyms were recorded (Fei 1980, pp. 94, 97; Gros 2004, p. 277; Mullaney 2004, p. 211; Tapp 2010, p. 100). Thirty-eight groups appeared in the census with populations of between 100 and 1,000 people, and another 92 groups with populations of less than 100. Twenty applicant groups were recorded with populations of only one. This result, if followed by the CCP, would have produced an NPC swollen with minority representatives standing on behalf of a vast mosaic of tiny groups, and would not help demonstrate the CCP's mandate to rule (Mullaney 2010a, p. 327). Thus, if *minzu* was truly going to be one of the axes of Chinese citizenship, the state could not permit people to choose their own designations at will. There would have to be a predetermined set of authorized *minzu* categories from which each person would select. These categories would have to be mutually exclusive, limited in number, of a reasonably large size, but also sufficiently grounded in local realities so as to elicit popular support.

It was with this realization, and not because of any preexisting plan, that the Ethnic Classification project was initiated. (Mullaney 2010a, p. 329)

The CCP was apparently inspired by a campaign of 'nationality recognition (identification)' engineered by Stalin in the 1930s, which recognized over 100 'nationalities' in the Soviet Union. The members of the nationality groups received an official 'nationality status' and republics were formed for large nationality groups in the Soviet Union (Ma 2007a, pp. 16–17; 2009). Heavily supported and influenced by the Soviet Union, the CCP showed interest in Stalin's fourfold criteria of ethnic nationality proclaimed in 1913: a nationality is a group of people with 'a historically constituted, stable community of people, formed on the basis of a common language, territory, economic life, and psychological make-up manifested in a common culture' (Stalin 1953, p. 307; Sautman 1999, p. 288; Howland 2011, pp. 2, 8–9). But later the CCP found it difficult to apply the Stalinist model of classification to ethnic groups in China (Brown 2001, p. 56; Gros 2004, pp. 279, 281–5; Mullaney 2004, pp. 226–7). For example, how could Hui be classified as an ethnic group when they did not have a common language, territory and economic life? Should they be one nationality group or many different nationality groups? What about the descendants of Han Chinese who had settled among non-Han groups and become practically assimilated by those groups (Brown 2001, p. 58; Fei 1980, p. 95)?

The CCP eventually decided not to use Stalin's fourfold criteria of 'nationality' in the Ethnic Classification Project (Gros 2004, p. 278), and pragmatically turned to Republican-era scholarship for conceptual and methodological inspiration in its effort to develop a strategy for identifying nationality groups in the PRC. Although Soviet experts were initially invited to join the Project and give advice, they soon withdrew. Chinese ethnologists such as Fei Xiaotong and Shi Lianzhu led a 'scientific' survey as the basis for a policy on identifying non-Han peoples as minority nationalities (Mullaney 2004, p. 207; 2010a, pp. 329–33; 2010b; see also Mackerras 2004a). This was the beginning of the Ethnic Classification Project, which marked an important departure from Stalin's approach, in that it placed among other considerations an emphasis on the self-consciousness of a group. Identities were not located purely according to the so-called objective, scientific criteria, 'but people's statements about their identities, their desired identifications and their actual ones, were listened to, taken into account, recorded and considered together with other factors such as economic type and stage of social development, history, language and religious affiliation' (Tapp 2002a, p. 67; Mullaney 2004, p. 230; see also Gros 2004, pp. 278, 291; Harrell 1995b, p. 83). In other words, *minzu* as identified in the Ethnic Classification Project focused on, among other criteria, cultural distinctiveness (US Congressional-Executive Commission on China 2005b, p. 10).

Of course, local subjectivities were not the only determinant of ethnic identity, and occasionally they were ignored, as in the case of ethnic classification in the Enshi region of Hubei province mentioned above. Many local Enshi people were culturally Han, thought of themselves as Han, and claimed ethnic identity as Han. Nevertheless, they were officially designated as Tujia because their customs appeared to have served as ethnic markers to Han officials, who came from other parts of China and were in charge of the Ethnic Identification Project in the region (Brown 2001, pp. 58–60).

According to Mullaney (2004, pp. 208, 213), the CCP sent work teams to adjudicate the claims of over 400 aspiring applicant groups in different localities in China. 'They did so either by recommending particular groups for state certification as official minorities or, in the far more likely case, by recommending that they be taxonomically consolidated with other *minzu* groups.' In Yunnan province, for example, only four of the original 260 applicant groups were recognized as standalone minorities: Achang, Bulang, Nu and Xifan. The rest were taxonomically merged with one of the existing four ethnic groups or categorized as Zhuang. According to this classification model, Yunnan was home to only 19 nationality groups (Mullaney 2010a, pp. 329, 340).

This model played a major role in the Ethnic Classification Project, yet its outcomes were not necessarily straightforward and unproblematic. For example, the Mosuo people (摩梭), who lived in Sichuan and Yunnan with a population of 40,000, were not recognized as an ethnic group. Instead, Mosuo who lived in Sichuan province were classified by the government work team as Mongols and those in Yunnan province as the Naxi people despite major differences in customs and lifestyles between the Mosuo people and the other two ethnic groups. The Mosuo group has requested that it be recognized as an independent ethnic group (Harrell 2001, pp. 218–19; Tapp 2002a, p. 66) but their request has yet to be granted. As another example, the speakers of Yao languages on Hainan Island were classified by the government work team as Miao although they identified themselves as Yao, whereas other people who spoke Dong or Miao languages and did not identify themselves as Yao were categorized as Yao (Tapp 2002a, p. 72).

Why did the government work teams make these arbitrary and problematic decisions? One plausible reason is that in many locations the Ethnic Classification Project work team gave voice to some people at the expense of others. Tapp suggests the possibility that only the most clamorous local voices were heard by the work team, the voices that insisted on their rights to define a certain local identity, historical origins, cultural affiliations and the boundaries of ethnic exclusion and inclusion. The outcomes of the Ethnic Classification Project might reflect and privilege the views of certain elite groups in the minority region. Other possible reasons included the government policies on regional autonomy and the fixing of provincial and other boundaries to break up larger groups who might develop sentiments of nationalist unity (Tapp 2002a, p. 71).

Much of the Ethnic Classification Project was completed in six months (Caffrey 2004, p. 253), producing 38 nationality groups in 1954. For unknown reasons, this figure increased drastically to 53 after the second PRC census in 1964. Lhoba was then recognized as the 54th minority nationality group in 1965, and the Jino of Yunnan were designated as the 55th minority group in 1979. In 1990, it was offi-cially confirmed that China had 56 nationalities. Despite the arbitrary and problematic nature of the Ethnic Classification Project, most people in China have accepted the official categories of minority nationalities and many scholars both inside and outside China have used the official categories in their research on ethnic minorities in the PRC. Lipman (1997, p. xxiv) claims that Beijing has been 'remarkably successful in imposing the language of the *minzu* paradigm on its entire population, including scholars and intellectuals of the "minority nation-alities" themselves'.

When the Ethnic Classification Project was conducted in 1953, it was estimated that there were 35.3 million minority people in the PRC. During the period 1953–64, the annual growth rate was 1.59 per cent for Han Chinese, as compared with 1.11 per cent for the ethnic minority groups. This fertility pattern was reversed during the period of 1964–82, when the total population of Han Chinese grew by 43.8 per cent, while that of the ethnic minority groups grew by 68.6 per cent. In 1990, the total fertility rate was 2.9 for the ethnic minority groups, as compared with 2.2 for Han Chinese. The minority population reached 91.2 million in 1990 (Hsu 1993, pp. 280–1). More importantly, from 1982 to 1990, the Manchus, a group long thought to have been assimilated into Han society, increased their population by 128 per cent from 4.3 million to 9.8 million; the population of the Gelao people in Guizhou reported a 714 per cent increase in just eight years; and the Tujia people more than doubled its population from 2.8 million to 5.8 million (Yan 1989, p. 79). Other minority groups reported similar population growths.

This 'minority population explosion' reflected more than a high birth rate; it was also the outcome of 'category-shifting' as people redefined their nationality status from Han to ethnic minority. During this period of time, 14 million newly identified minority persons were reported, which accounted for 59 per cent of the total growth of the minority population (Hsu 1993, pp. 281–2; Tapp 2010, p. 103; see also Cultural Survival 1997). The identity change by these individuals has been viewed partly as an effort to retrieve their cultural roots and partly as a pragmatic response to equal opportunity programmes in education and employment for minority groups (Caffrey 2004, pp. 260, 263; Gladney 1996, pp. 261–78; Sautman 1999, p. 286; Tapp 2010, p. 103). It has become popular to be 'ethnic' in China (Mackerras 2011a, p. 113; see also Cultural Survival 1997). In a research project conducted in the Enshi region in Hubei, it was found that local people thought of themselves as Han Chinese although they were officially designated as part of the Tujia people. They took Tujia status anyway because of the benefits associated with minority status (Brown 2001, p. 59).

The magnitude of the minority population explosion came as a surprise to some Han Chinese, who began to argue that 'the fraternal nationalities' population explosion should be curbed' (Yan 1989, p. 79; see also Chang 2003, p. 28). In November 1989, the PRC State Ethnic Commission and the Ministry of Public Security together issued a directive to impose a temporary moratorium on requests to change ethnic status, with immediate effect, until after the 1990 census (A Directive from the State Ethnic Affairs Commission 1989).

Currently, a person's ethnic status appears on his or her identity card, and his or her ethnic status depends on his or her parents' ethnic status. Ethnic status can be changed from Han to minority or from minority to Han. An individual who wants to change his/her ethnic status can apply for permission from relevant local government offices if he or she meets official criteria (Ma 2007a, p. 14; Leibold 2010, p. 6). I once met a woman in Beijing who had decided to be classified as Han when she was 18 although her parents were Hui. She said that she wanted to be classified as a Han and did not need equal opportunities programmes to get what she wanted. In inter-ethnic marriages, parents can decide the nationality of their children, and then the children themselves can choose their nationality at age 18, which is their final choice of ethnic status (A Decree from the State Ethnic Affairs Commission 1990). I once met a scholar in Xinjiang whose father was a Uyghur and whose mother was a Tajik. He chose to be a Tajik when he was 18.

BEIJING'S ASSIMILATION STANCE

Although the CCP has implemented an affirmative action policy (see chapter 2), there is no guarantee that it intends to promote multiculturalism in China. In fact, its nationality policy has been heavily influenced by Dr Sun Yat-sen (1866–1925), who in turn was heavily influenced by Confucian legacies. Confucianism specifies that anyone can be a member of the Han community if he or she accepts Han culture. A Confucian cultural community can embrace different political communities, and the state should be impartial towards all nationalities as parents are towards their children. Big ethnic groups should love and have a duty to look after smaller ones, as elder brothers do their younger ones (He 2004, p. 113). This partly explains why some specifications of minority rights existed in the imperial era (Sautman 1999, p. 287). In essence, Confucianism celebrates the idea of cultural, economic and political intermingling among ethnic and cultural groups, in order to promote assimilation and unity into a harmonious Han community (Dreyer 1976, p. 1; He 2004, pp. 114–15; Mackerras 1984, p. 188). In other words, Confucianism does not provide a melting pot, but is the result of a cultural system where cultural outsiders can dispose of their uncivilized behaviour and thoughts and partake in Han society by learning, understanding, adopting and incorporating Han ways (He 2004, p. 113; see also Barbour and Jones 2013, pp. 102, 110; Bruhn 2008, pp. 1–3; Wong 2000, p. 54). The Confucian concept of cultural community plays down ethnic criteria and encourages acculturation and eventual assimilation of minority nationalities into Han society. This approach is in sharp contrast with the current international norms on minority rights that promote multiculturalism, group collective guarantees, national self-determination or even secession (chapter 7).

Heberer (1989, pp. 18, 131) argues that historically, Confucianism 'despised these so-called "barbarians", but called for a policy of non-violent assimilation through the imposition of Han-Chinese values rather than through a policy of extermination' (see also Wong 2000, pp. 53–4). Assimilation took place after military conquests. Eberhard writes (1982, p. 8) that in 1500 BC, China as we know it today did not exist, and there were no Han Chinese. The area that is now China was 'inhabited by a great number of tribes with different cultures' (see also Zhu and Yu 2000, p. 45). Some of them gradually merged and formed a Han people, who became stronger than other tribes and expanded from their original territory in middle China to the periphery of the current PRC territory (Chang 2003, pp. 8–9). This expansion involved conquering other tribes and subjecting them to the rule of the Han imperial kingdoms, and resulted in the assimilation of minorities into the Han population such that some non-Han groups gradually lost their traditional cultural practices and ultimately adopted Han culture, including Han language (Chang 2003, p. 10; Hansen 2005, pp. 16–17, 98; Mackerras 1994, pp. 19–45; Poston et al. 2006, pp. 69–70; Wong 2000, pp. 53–4; Zhu and Yu 2000, pp. 45–6). He (2004, p. 112) points out that the key notion in this process of interface is called 'ronghe' (融合), i.e., the amalgamation or fusion of the Han majority and the non-Han minorities in a process of Confucian cultural diffusion (see also Sautman 1999, p. 300).

Dr Sun Yat-sen was influenced by Confucian *ronghe* ideology. To instigate mass support from Han Chinese to overthrow the Qing (i.e., Manchu) dynasty, he championed Chinese nationalism based on Han culture. He claimed that China had been developing a single state out of a single Han race since the Qing (221–207 BC) and Han dynasties, that Manchus were a barbarian race that had conquered China and usurped power illegally, that they must be driven out of China, and that Han sovereignty must be restored. While this line of argument was instrumental in the mobilization of Han support to the revolutionary cause, it became problematic after the demise of the Qing dynasty in 1911: Dr Sun's racially exclusive model alienated not only Manchus but also other non-Han groups such as Uyghurs and Tibetans, which posed a potential danger to China's territorial integrity and national unity. Subsequently, Dr Sun and his comrades proposed a new term 'zhonghua' (中华) by combining the 'middle kingdom' (zhongguo 中国) with 'brilliant xia' (huaxia 华夏), and called the newly established Republic of China (ROC) 'Zhonghua minguo' (中华民国), which included five main *minzu*: Han, Manchus, Mongols, Tibetans and Hui (i.e., Muslims). A five-colour national flag was adopted, in which stripes of red, yellow, blue, white and black symbolized the 'harmonious cohabitation of five ethnic nationalities' (五族共和) (Barabantseva 2008, pp. 571–2; Gladney 1996, pp. 83–4; Huang 2002). Dr Sun argued that the five groups were the offshoots of a Chinese people (*Zhonghua minzu* 中华民族), and called for 'unifying the territories of the Han, Manchu, Mongol, Hui (Xinjiang) and Tibetans as a state, and unifying the Han, Manchu, Mongol, Hui (Muslim) and Tibetans as one people, that is the unification of the Chinese nation'. He insisted that the non-Han groups were the sub-branches of the Chinese nation, which would be assimilated into a 'single cultural and political whole' dominated by Han Chinese (Barabantseva 2008, pp. 570–2; Gladney 1996, pp. 79–85; Hyer 2009, p. 259; Mackerras 2011a, p. 114; Smith 2004, p. 7), and the non-Han groups would enjoy the right of self-determination as long as it did not involve secession from China (Barabantseva 2008, p. 570; He 2004, p. 104). Dr Sun proposed to use both *ronghe* and *tonghua* (同化) to achieve national unity via assimilation. *Ronghe* assumes relatively equal status between the Han and non-Han peoples, while *tonghua* assumes a superior position of the former over the latter (Barabantseva 2008, pp. 571–2; Dreyer 1976, p. 16; He 2003, p. 226; Leibold 2008, pp. 113–75; Wang and Phillion 2009, p. 2).

Dr Sun's successor, the leader of the Nationalist Party Generalissimo Chiang Kai-shek (1887–1975), similarly defined non-Han peoples as sibling branches of Han Chinese (Chiang Kai-shek 1943; Barabantseva 2008, pp. 569–70; Fei 1980, p. 94; Gladney 1996, pp. 16–17; Hyer 2006, pp. 76–7; Liu and Alatan 1988, p. 144), injecting a 'strident and sinocentric tone' into his nationality policy (Hyer 2009, p. 260). Mackerras (2005b, p. 3) notes that in March 1929, the Third Nationalist Party Congress declared Mongolia, Tibet and Xinjiang to be part of the Chinese nation, not merely part of the ROC, reinforcing Dr Sun's idea that these regions were both part of the Han cultural sphere and the sovereign territory of the Chinese people. In addition, Chiang replaced Dr Sun's principle of 'harmonious cohabitation' with an 'amalgamating' (*ronghe*) policy that promoted assimilation of non-Han groups to Han society to form a 'great Chinese nation' (大中华民族). Like Dr Sun, Chiang rejected the right of national self-determination to non-Han people, arguing that 'there is no area that can be split up or separated from the rest (of China), and therefore, no area that can become an independent unit.' He claimed that 'the differentiation among China's five peoples is due to regional and religious factors, and not to race or blood' (Chiang Kai-shek 1943; also Hyer 2006, pp. 76–7; 2009, p. 291).

Although the CCP ousted Chiang and the ROC government from mainland China after the brutal civil war of 1946–9, its nationality policy has continued Dr Sun's (and Chiang's) *ronghe* approach and promoted measures of acculturation and assimilation in the name of an encompassing Chinese nation in the post-1949 era. During the 1950s and the early 1960s, the CCP relied on socialist transformation to promote the *ronghe* policy that all the national minorities formed the Chinese nation. It insisted that Han Chinese had formed a coherent nationality long before 1949, whereas non-Han peoples had remained at feudal or pre-feudal levels of development, had been kept from becoming modern nations, and were 'weak and small nationality' (*ruoxiao minzu*) and 'backward nationality' (*luohou minzu*). This storyline justified the leadership of Han Chinese in the Chinese nation (Barabantseva 2008, p. 585; Hyer 2006, pp. 76–7) and the official rhetoric that non-Han peoples wanted to follow the CCP because they were members of the Chinese nation and were economically and culturally drawn to Han society (Hyer 2006, p. 78). The CCP thus would want to carry out socialist transformations in an effort to lead them to emerge from socioeconomic backwardness to achieve modern nationhood (Ghai and Woodman 2009), which, according to the CCP, predetermined the uniformity of interests of Han Chinese and non-Han peoples in the socialist transformation of ethnic minority groups and minority areas.

But how could a successful socialist transformation be achieved? The CCP argued that the key was class struggle, stressing that non-Han people had been taken advantage of by exploiting classes, which accounted for why they did not become modern nations. Thus, the urgent task for non-Han peoples was to carry out class struggle to eliminate the exploiting classes and establish a socialist system under the CCP's leadership. A socialist revolution would wipe out classes, promote economic growth in minority regions, and reduce the socio-economic gap between Han Chinese and non-Han groups. In other words, class struggle was the driving force for non-Han groups to achieve socialist transformation and modern nationhood (Barabantseva 2008, pp. 576–8; Hyer 2009, p. 271).

It is important to observe that before 1966, the target of class struggles was limited (old ruling classes) and its mission was mainly political rather than social and cultural transformations. This did not mean that the CCP did not make an assimilation effort. Indeed, it promoted Mandarin among citizens as a concrete step for non-Han peoples to acculturate into Han society, and claimed that it carried out development projects in minority regions to help non-Han peoples catch up with Han Chinese and then move together with Han Chinese towards assimilation (*minzu ronghe*). The PRC's Premier Zhou Enlai claimed in 1957 that 'assimilation would not be welcome if it were achieved by force. Assimilation should be promoted if it were the outcome of mutual efforts of the majority and minority peoples. Successful examples of assimilation include the Hui people and the Manchu people' (He 2003, p. 226; Leibold 2008, pp. 113–75; Zhu 2012).

This relatively mild approach towards acculturation and assimilation was suddenly replaced by political extremism and radicalism that favoured outright, forced assimilation during the Cultural Revolution of 1966–76: it was officially denied that China was a multinational country, and regional autonomy to minority nationalities was regarded as an institution that would lead to 'nationalism to the exclusion of patriotism', and create a national schism (Mackerras 1995, p. 152; Sautman 1999, p. 288; Zhu 2012). Class struggle was pursued vigor-ously, and minority cultures and religions were attacked. The minority issue was declared settled, nationality policies were no longer needed, and forceful measures were taken in an attempt to assimilate minorities (Clothey 2001, p. 9; Heberer 1989, p. 26; Leibold 2010, p. 17; Sautman 1999, p. 300). As late as 1978, the CCP declared that "'interracial" adds to unity among nationalities . . . "interracial marriage" expands and strengthens economic and cultural exchanges among fraternal nationalities in our country' (Banister 1992, p. 561).

The radical policy of the Cultural Revolution was abandoned after 1978. The CCP has instead stressed economic development as the major theme in its nationality policy (see chapter 6). But *ronghe* has still guided policy making on minority rights in China to date. The CCP has used the term 'Chinese person' (*Zhongguoren* 中国人), as opposed to Han Chinese, to include all nationality groups within the 'Chinese nation' and has stressed that 'all "minority problems" can be partly resolved by increasing propaganda on the interdependence of the country's nationalities and on the "correct interpretation of ethnic histories"' (US Congressional-Executive Commission on China 2005a, p. 14). The CCP has claimed that China is a united nation of many nationalities due to the 'outgrowth of the historical development of the past several thousand years', that China is a 'big fraternal and co-operative family composed of all nationalities', and that the ethnic minorities 'formed with Han Chinese a single, unbreakable unit' due to historical, cultural and economic reasons (Hyer 2006, 76–7; Mackerras 2011a, p. 114).

Zhu Weiqun, executive deputy minister of the State Ethnic Commission, asserted that Tibetan culture had been part of Chinese culture since the Yuan dynasty (2011, p. 14). China's Ethnic Unity Textbook Compiling Team (2009, pp. 17, 37, 79) similarly maintained that '*Minzu* extinction is an inevitable result of *minzu* self-development and self-improvement . . . It is the final result of *minzu* development at its highest stage . . . in this big *minzu* family every *minzu* group has a higher level of identification – *Zhonghua Minzu*.' The party-state's ideology of historical materialism theorizes history and identity as a progressive flow towards the formation of national community and modernization which entails the disappearance of ethnicity and its symbols. Officially, the constitutional right to 'maintain and develop' minority languages is said to remain unaffected. However, the reduction of the number of languages in the world is considered to be an 'inevitable outcome' of the increasing connections between regions and the expansion of Mandarin use an inevitability of modernization (Xinjiang Education Press 2009, pp. 94–5).

Ronghe has also dominated the scholarly discourse on minority rights in post-1978 China, partly because it has been officially defined by the Chinese government as a key research topic in ethnic studies in China. It is impossible to do research and publish in China without government funding and approval. Unsurprisingly, the term *minzu ronghe* has appeared in many textbooks and research papers published in the PRC, and a number of Chinese scholars have criticized China's affirmative action policy and national autonomy, demanding that public policy must focus on promoting Chinese culture and identity through acculturation rather than the protection of individual minority rights. In their opinion, 'Minorities should agree to assimilate, align their identities with Han, and learn standard Chinese' (Leibold 2010, p. 19; Sautman 2012, p. 19). Some Chinese scholars have claimed that there were numerous examples of *ronghe* in Chinese history; for example, many ancient nomadic peoples no longer exist because they were 'sinicized' into Han people, and there will be an eventual *ronghe* leading to the total disappearance of minority nationalities in China in the future (China's Ethnic Unity Textbook Compiling Team 2009, pp. 17, 37, 79).

Some top PRC officials have concurred that *ronghe* has been a frequent and common phenomenon in Chinese history, and questioned the institutionalization of the boundary between the majority and minority nationalities. In their opinion, it is wrong to achieve assimilation today, but it is similarly wrong not to make efforts to move towards eventual assimilation. Zhu Weiqun (2012) writes that 'While assimilation will not be achieved by administrative fiat, the government has to guide, promote, and lead the assimilative trend. One immediate measure the government must adopt to promote assimilation is to abolish the ethnic identity in personal ID, stop setting up more ethnic autonomous areas, and promote the mixing of students of different ethnic groups' (see also He 2003, p. 226; Leibold 2008, pp. 113–75).

Finally, as noted, Confucianism encouraged the acculturation and assimilation of the 'barbarians' both inside and outside China partly because of China's superpower status in pre-modern times. *Ronghe* became an inward-oriented policy after China lost its hegemonic power in the Opium War of 1840–2. The sense of repeated humiliation at the hands of Western powers and Japan since 1840 has motivated Chinese normative thinking about international relations and China's position in the world (Chin and Thakur 2010, p. 122; Mushkat 2011, pp. 57–8). Instead of acculturation and assimilation of the 'barbarians', national survival has been a major concern in China's modern diplomacy. As expected, the CCP built its diplomacy on the Five Principles of Peaceful Coexistence codified in treaty form between China and India in 1954. The principles include mutual respect for each other's territorial integrity and sovereignty, mutual non-aggression, mutual non-interference in each other's internal affairs, equality and mutual benefit, and peaceful coexistence. These principles are based on the Westphalian norms of state sovereignty and international behaviour (see chapter 7). The CCP has consistently adhered to these norms in its diplomacy, at least theoretically (Chin and Thakur 2010, p. 127; Kent 2002, p. 347; Mushkat 2011, p. 42; Prantl and Nakano 2011, pp. 211–12). Yet these norms do not meet the demands of current international norms on minority rights, especially with regard to the protection of minority cultures and self-determination. The CCP has relied on respect for national sovereignty and non-interference to justify its poor record in supporting minority rights both in China and abroad. This is partly because these minority rights are inconsistent with its *ronghe* policy (see chapter 7), which promotes acculturation and assimilation at the expense of diversity and multiculturalism.

DISCUSSION

Beijing has aggressively promoted the PRC as a multicultural country and publicized its support for minority nationality groups in China (Information Office of the State Council 1996; 2005; 2010a; Xinhua 2008; McCarthy 2009). To a large extent, ethnic groups are the outcome of state intervention in the PRC. The state is the most influential force in institutionalizing ethnic boundaries and the meanings of ethnicity in the PRC, and this power has manifested itself by officially placing individuals in different ethnic group categories and incorporating nationality categories and rewards for minority ethnicity into the politico-bureaucratic system in China (Mullaney 2004, p. 208). For the PRC state, *shaoshu minzu* (i.e., ethnic minorities) has replaced 'barbarian' or 'savage', and to a certain extent performed the function of the tributary trade in imperial China that had shown the ordered humanity arranged along a civilization–barbarian spectrum to confirm the superiority of Han culture (Fairbank 1942; Kang 2010; Wang 2005). The Ethnic Classification Project served as a sign of a bureaucratic state of multi-ethnic composition (Caffrey 2004, pp. 255–6), undertaken with the belief that 'backward' non-Han peoples required the CCP's leadership and 'advanced' Han socialism, and that the presence of non-Han deputies in the NPC highlighted the popular mandate of the PRC. The *minzu* system set up after the Ethnic Classification Project has been a key institution in governance and in the maintenance of the PRC's legitimacy, and at the same time has transformed the relationship between ethnic minority groups and the PRC state: 'By way of their status as a full-fledged *minzu*, they have been able to reinforce their local identity, while also establishing a strongly held faith, among most, in the development and improvement of their social conditions.' This is a kind of contractual acceptance that has been hinged on the state's promise to ethnic minority groups of better integration and improved access to resources (Gros 2004, pp. 291–2).

Nevertheless, it is important to note that Beijing's nationality policy is ultimately driven by Confucian *ronghe* ideology, and the ethnic classification scheme and minority entitlements have been implemented to serve the CCP's long-term goal, i.e., acculturation, integration and eventual assimilation of the non-Han groups into Han society. The path dependence generated by this institutional task has shaped China's domestic nationality policy (Caffrey 2004, p. 261) and foreign policy towards minority rights in international politics (see chapter 7). In essence, China's nationality policy is consistent with Confucian *ronghe* ideology as it supports the enterprise of expanding the Chinese cultural sphere (He 2004, pp. 119–20; Mackerras 1994, pp. 7–10), and is also consistent with Marxism, which looks forward to the elimination of all national differences and eventual assimilation of all peoples (He 2003, p. 229). China's nationality policy is not designed to celebrate diversity and multiculturalism (Bruhn 2008, p. 4; Wang and Phillion 2009, p. 2), and has dictated how much Beijing has honoured its promise to the minority nationality groups in terms of equality (chapter 2), the preservation of minority cultures (chapter 3), regional autonomy (chapter 4) and the promotion of minority rights in international politics (chapter 7).

RECOMMENDED READING

Colin Mackerras (ed.), *Ethnic Minorities in Modern China*, Vol. I (London: Routledge, 2011).

Thomas Mullaney, *Coming to Terms with the Nation: Ethnic Classification in Modern China* (Berkeley, CA: University of California Press, 2010).

2 | Ethnic Inequality ————————————

There is a broad consensus among China experts that with certain exceptions, ethnic minority groups trail Han Chinese in status attainment by a large margin, and minority areas are less developed than Han areas (Gustafsson and Li 2003; Hannum 2002; Hannum and Xie 1998; Poston and Micklin 1993; Poston and Shu 1987). But what exactly is the general situation of ethnic inequality in China? What has the CCP done to reduce inequalities between Han regions and minority regions? What efforts has the CCP made to narrow socioeconomic gaps between Han Chinese and ethnic minority groups in the PRC? How effective are Beijing's efforts? Is ethnic inequality growing or declining in the post-1978 era? These are the main questions this chapter seeks to address. This chapter also explains why more efforts by, and resources from, the government are required to narrow the gap in status attainment between Han Chinese and the ethnic minority groups in the PRC.

The causes of inter-group differences in socioeconomic status have always been at the heart of the intellectual inquiry about ethnic inequality. Chinese leaders have never agreed that ethnic inequality is related to Han prejudice and discrimination against non-Han groups. Sautman (1999, p. 291) wrote that Deng Xiaoping stated in 1987 that 'since New China was founded in 1949, there had never been any ethnic discrimination in the country.' In 1988, the then CCP chief Zhao Ziyang claimed that racial discrimination was common 'everywhere in the world except China'. Nevertheless, Chinese leaders have agreed that inter-group disparity is a major issue in ethnic relations in China and that ethnic tensions result primarily from the uneven levels of economic development between Han Chinese and non-Han groups. They are confident that "all minority problems" can be resolved by promoting socialist development' (US Congressional-Executive Commission on China 2005a, p. 14; Elmer 2011, p. 8; Zhu 2012). Indeed, since 1949, the CCP has regarded common prosperity of all ethnic groups as 'the fundamental stance of China's ethnic policy' (Information Office of the State Council 2010a; Gladney 1996, pp. 91–2). Article 122 of the PRC Constitution proclaims that 'the state gives financial, material and technical assistance to the minority nationalities to accelerate their economic and cultural development' (http://english.peopledaily.com.cn/constitution/constitution.html). Thus, it is a legal obligation that Beijing supports minority areas in speeding up their development (Information Office of the State Council 2005; Xinhua 2008). Some academics in China have agreed that economic development 'is a starting point for minority policies and the key to solving current problems and issues in these minority areas' (Guo et al. 2010, p. 201; Zheng 2009, p. 41).

Generally speaking, the CCP has pursued a two-fold strategy for the reduction of ethnic inequality in China. Firstly, it has attempted to reduce Han–minority inequality by reducing socioeconomic gaps between Han and minority regions. Secondly, it has implemented affirmative action programmes to improve the life chances of individual members of minority nationalities in both Han and minority regions. Thus, this chapter proceeds within two registers of description and analysis. In the first, it outlines the trends in socioeconomic development and highlights the state support for the reduction of poverty in minority areas, followed by a critical assessment of Beijing's policies to promote ethnic tourism and environmental protection in minority areas. In the second, the descriptive and analytic lens shifts to focus on the government's affirmative action policy for individual members of ethnic minorities in family planning, education, employment, political representation, etc.

SOCIOECONOMIC CHANGES IN THE POST-1949 ERA

When the CCP came to power in 1949, the level of socioeconomic development in minority areas was low, with the vast majority of non-Han peoples living in 'pre-feudal' society. Some non-Han groups in Southwest China such as the Yi were still engaged in slash and burn farming, those in remote areas in Northeast China such as the Daur people and the Oroqen people or the Li people on Hainan Island relied on traditional barter trade in which certain goods were exchanged for other goods without using money as the medium of exchange. Few people in non-Han regions were literate, had access to running water or electricity, or visited a hospital (Yang and Wu 2009, p. 117). Modern industry was basically non-existent, only few obsolete handicraft work-shops operated in minority areas, and many essential articles for daily life and agricultural production were imported from Han regions (Information Office of the State Council 1999a; 2009; 2010a).

Significant changes in minority regions have taken place since 1949. Over a thirty-year period (1952–82), the total output of steel in minority regions increased from 103,000 tons to 2,324,500 tons; of cast iron production, from 9,000 tons to 2,581,200 tons; of raw coal, from 1,780,000 tons to 88,912,000 tons; and of crude oil, from 52,000 tons to 8,048,600 tons. Correspondingly, the total value of industrial and agricultural output in minority areas rose from 3,660 million yuan in 1949 to 80,096 million yuan in 1985, an increase of nearly 20 times (Liu and Alatan 1988, p. 159). The pace of economic growth in minority regions was accelerated after 1982. As a result, the number of impoverished ethnic minority people was reduced from 45 million to 14 million in the period from 1994 to 1999 (Information Office of the

State Council 2005), and there has emerged a middle class among ethnic minorities in the post-1978 era (Mackerras 2005a, pp. 814, 821–2).

More recent data show that the gross domestic product (GDP) of the minority areas grew by an impressive average of 9.87 per cent annually from 1994 to 2003. During this period, the total investment in fixed assets in the minority areas increased 3.7 times, the local revenue of the minority areas 3.3 times, and the per capita net income of rural residents in the minority areas 2.31 times. The total value of imports and exports of the minority areas reached $13.6 billion in 2003 (Information Office of the State Council of the PRC 2005). In 2006, the combined GDP of Guangxi, Guizhou, Inner Mongolia, Ningxia, Qinghai, Xinjiang, Tibet and Yunnan exceeded 2 trillion yuan, representing an annual increase of 13.2 per cent from 2002.

Concurrently, there have been major improvements in general well-being in the minority regions since 1949. 'By the end of 2003, the ethnic autonomous areas had 15,230 medical institutions, 13 times the number in 1952; 380,000 hospital beds, nearly 67 times the number in 1952; 460,000 medical technicians, almost 26 times the number in 1952' (Information Office of the State Council of the PRC 2005). 'From 1995 to 2006 there were 2.3 to 2.4 hospital beds per 1,000 residents in the ethnic regions, almost the same as the range of 2.3–2.5 for the nation' (Lai 2009a, p. 10). The number of doctors, nurses, pharmacists and other medical workers in minority regions increased from 3,531 in 1949 to 423,733 (out of whom 105,616 were of minority origin) in 2003. The development of medical services has increased the life expectancy of ethnic minority people: the life expectancy of 13 ethnic minorities in 2003 was higher than the national average, which was 71.40 years, and those of seven of them were higher than the average of Han Chinese, which was 73.34 years (Lai 2009a, p. 10; Liu and Alatan 1988, p. 152; see also Information Office of the State Council 2005; Xinhua 2005a).

The minority areas have witnessed major improvements in schooling and educational infrastructure in the post-1949 era. It is estimated that more than 80 per cent of the ethnic minority population were illiterate in 1949 (US Congressional-Executive Commission on China 2005a, p. 14; Mackerras 2003, p. 66; Yang and Wu 2009, p. 117). The number of primary school pupils of ethnic minority origin increased from 943,000 (2.2 per cent of the national total) in 1951 to 9,528,200 (7.1 per cent of the national total) in 1985, and the number of primary school teachers of ethnic minority origin increased from 59,800 in 1953 to 397,800 in 1985. There was similar progress in secondary school education between 1951 and 1985: minority students at middle schools, technical schools and normal schools increased from 45,507 (0.4 per cent of the national total) to 2,360,000; and the number of middle school teachers of ethnic minority origin went up from 2,708 to 125,560 (US Congressional-Executive Commission on China 2005a, p. 18; Liu and Alatan 1988, p. 151; Yang and Wu 2009, p. 117).

According to Xinhua (2005a), there were 83,726 schools at all levels and of all kinds in minority areas with a total enrolment of 29.43 million in 2004, representing an increase of fivefold from 1952. The fifth national census, conducted in 2000, showed that 14 ethnic minorities, including Koreans, Manchus, Mongolians and Kazaks, had more years of schooling than the national average. By 2009, 686 out of 699 counties in the minority regions implemented nine years of compulsory education and met the target of basically eradicating illiteracy among the young and middle-aged minority population. By 2010, over 10,000 schools with a total of 6 million students had used 29 minority languages in classroom teaching (Information Office of the State Council 2005; Xinhua 2008; 2010b; 2011b).

Tertiary education for ethnic minority groups has performed equally well. University students belonging to minority nationalities accounted for 0.93 per cent ($N = 1,285$) of all university students on campus in 1950. This figure went up to 4.2 per cent by 1978 and then to

5.3 per cent ($N = 94,095$) by 1985. University faculty from minority nationalities increased from 623 or 1.85 per cent of the national total in 1953 to 12,775 or 3.7 per cent of the national total in 1985 (Wang 2007, p. 150). Special preparatory classes for minority students requiring remedial assistance before they attend university have been operated by the government, and more than 9,000 students attended such classes in 2001 alone (US Congressional-Executive Commission on China 2005a, p. 18; Leibold 2010, p. 6). Some minority regions have set up universities or specialized colleges (Liu and Alatan 1988, p. 151) to cater for students of ethnic minority origin.

STATE SUPPORT FOR SOCIOECONOMIC DEVELOPMENT IN MINORITY AREAS

Beijing has played a major role in promoting economic growth in minority regions, providing aid in the form of labour, material and financial resources to minority regions (Information Office of the State Council 1996). Examples of central government financial aid included the educational subsidies for minority regions programme (1951), the subsidy for ethnic minority regions programme (1955), the stand-by fund for ethnic minority regions programme (1964), the subsidy for minority regional border construction programme (1977), and the special fund for ethnic minority region development (1992). In 1994, 257 of 592 impoverished counties officially designated as key recipients of state financial aid were in the minority areas, which accounted for 43.4 per cent of the national total. The corresponding figures for 2001 were 267 of the 592 and 45.1 per cent of the national total. While these figures indicate major inequality between minority regions and Han regions (especially with regard to the fact that 92 per cent of China's population is Han Chinese), they also show how much the central government is willing to support the minority regions, as it is not always an easy task for a county to be listed as a key recipient of state financial aid. In 2003, the central government appropriated special funds totalling 1.37 billion yuan for health services in Inner Mongolia, Xinjiang, Guangxi, Ningxia and Tibet (Information Office of the State Council 2005; 2009; see also Barabantseva 2008, p. 583; Lai 2009a, pp. 10–11). The total amount of central government investment in minority areas in 2009 alone reached 1.24 billion yuan (Xinhua 2010b).

In addition, the central government has decided that the proportions of taxes and profits retained in minority regions should be higher than those in Han regions. It promulgated tax exemptions and loans with discounted interest for the construction of trade networks in the minority regions in 1997, and gave preferential treatment to 1,378 designated manufacturers of necessities for ethnic minorities in 2003, which included special loan rates and the reduction of or exemption from taxes.'Taxes on agriculture, manufacturing, and commerce including cross-border trade in ethnic areas are much lower than those in the regions dominated by the Han. In particular, new ethnic enterprises in these areas are exempted from tax in their first three years of operation' (Information Office of the State Council 1996; US Congressional-Executive Commission on China 2005a, p. 17; Lai 2009a, p. 10).

Beijing launched a grand strategy for the development of Western China in 2000, and invested 850 billion yuan to construct 60 key projects in the western region between 2000 and 2005 (Information Office of the State Council 2005). The share of the Western region in the central government's budgetary funds for capital construction increased from 22.9 per cent in 1998 to 34.2 per cent in 2002 (which was 13 per cent higher than that of China's coastal regions) (Information Office of the State Council 2005; Lai 2009a, pp. 11–12). The aid from the central government accounted for 38–94 per cent of the total budget of the five minority autonomous regions in 2002 (US Congressional-Executive Commission on China 2005a, p. 17; Ma 2007a, p. 17). Some 34 per cent of local government expenditures of western provinces, where many ethnic minority groups live, rely on transferred funding from the central government, while the percentage in eastern provinces, where the majority of the population is Han Chinese, is 7.83 per cent (Wang 2007, p. 154).

The central government has arranged for Han regions to support economic growth in minority regions since the late 1970s. For example, Shandong was to assist Xinjiang; Fujian, Ningxia; and Guangdong, Guangxi. Tibet has received assistance from all other areas of the country (Information Office of the State Council 2005). In March 2010, Beijing announced a ten-year partnership assistance programme, designating 19 provinces and municipalities in Han areas to provide aid of financing, technologies and management expertise to Xinjiang. For example, Liaoning Province was asked to assist Tacheng in north-west Xinjiang, Hunan Province funnelled its aid to central Turpan, and Shenzhen was paired up with Kashgar City and Taxkorgan County. Guangdong province planned to invest 1.078 billion yuan on 73 projects in its partner regions in Xinjiang in 2011 alone (Lai 2009a, p. 11; Yin 2011; Yue 2010).

Finally, Beijing has invested in and maintained school infrastructure and recruited teaching staff for minority regions. Specifically, it has provided allocative resources such as the 'Ethnic Minority Education Aid Special Fund', set up boarding schools in minority regions, funded selected minority students to study in schools in major cities in Han areas, and established universities for minority students. In some minority regions, local governments have established special middle schools for ethnic minorities or minority classes in ordinary middle schools (Clothey 2001, pp. 16–17; Mackerras 2003, pp. 127–8; 2005a, p. 823; Sautman 1999, p. 295; Yang and Wu 2009, pp. 120–2; Zhou 2000). The US Congressional-Executive Commission on China (2005a, p. 14) acknowledged that Beijing's investment in minority regions had raised overall educational levels and trained a corps of minority cadres. Some scholars in the West, however, are cynical about

Beijing's efforts to support economic growth in minority regions, regarding its investment in communication and transportation in minority regions as meeting the need to facilitate its direct administration of, and exploit the natural resources present in, frontier territories (Smith 2004, p. 2).

ETHNIC TOURISM

Beijing has considered ethnic tourism as an efficient way of promoting economic growth in minority regions. From 1949 to the late 1970s, ethnic minorities were regarded in the mass media in China as primitive and in need of all sorts of assistance in order to catch up with 'advanced' Han Chinese (Baranovitch 2001, p. 363; Johnson and Chhetri 2002, p. 148; Harrell 1995a). The matrimonial customs of some ethnic minorities were described by government officials as 'backward' and to be reformed (Barabantseva 2008, pp. 584–5; Yan 1989, p. 79). Since the 1980s, the image of minorities has changed: 'China's minority nationalities, once the objects of pity and disparagement, have recently become objects of admiration' (Xu et al. 2006; Hillman 2003). Both the central government and local governments have taken advantage of this change to promote ethnic tourism in minority regions (Bai 2007, p. 255; Baranovitch 2001, p. 376; Yang and Wall 2009, p. 78; see also Chow 2005; Xu et al. 2006), which is perceived by government officials as being able to bring about economic benefits and serve the CCP's agenda of building an image of the PRC as a multicultural nation state (Bai 2007, p. 246). Dondrub Wangben, a vice-minister of the PRC State Ethnic Affairs Commission, claimed that although ethnic minority regions suffered from backward economies, they possessed rich cultural resources for the tourism industry (Feng 2007; Guo et al. 2010, p. 201). There have been 'new calls to preserve their "unique customs and culture" in the manner of museum antiquities and, of course, for the purpose of attracting tourist revenues . . . A new exoticisation and sexualisation of minority representations has flourished following the "culture fever" (*wenhua re*) in China of the early 1980s as forms of cultural consumption challenge and vie with economic consumption' (Tapp 2010, p. 103; see also Lundberg and Zhou 2009, p. 284).

Since 2000 Guangxi has developed many ethnic tourism projects, including a grand song and dance performance titled *Liu Sanjie Impressions* about the Zhuang people, directed and produced by renowned director Zhang Yimou. Yunnan made similar efforts to forge ethnic cultural brands including the construction of Shangri-la, Lijiang and Dali tourism routes. Yang Liping, one of the best-known dancers in China, acts as the director and choreographer of *Dynamic Yunnan*, a dance musical that depicts the life of ethnic minorities in Yunnan (Bai 2007, pp. 246–7; Guo et al. 2010, p. 204; see also Chow 2005; Yang 2011). 'Local festivals have been entirely reinvented by officials to attract tourists, ritual forms, such as the Dongba pictographs and shamanism of the Naxi people, have been revived as objects of academic study and tourist attraction' in Yunnan (Tapp 2010, p. 103; see also McKhann 1995). The Lugu Lake in Yunnan Province, the home of the Mosuo people mentioned in chapter 1, has become a well-known tourist destination because of Mosuo's matrilineal custom: their brides do not leave their parents to form a new family after marriage. Instead, the husband visits the wife at night-time (Feng 2007; Johnson and Zhang 1991; Hua 2001; Shih 2010; Stacey 2009). Mosuo people and their walking marriages have been the selling point of Lugu Lake tourism.

Lhasa in Tibet has also become a major tourism destination. Guo et al. (2010, p. 203) write that

> There are more than 100 tourism sites in the Lhasa area, four of which are among the best in the nation (national 4A-class) . . . Also, contributing to the grandeur of this area are the fantastic murals, statue art of

Tangga, the ancient sites of the lasting tribute Qu Gong, the Zhala road caves, and the unique charm of Tibetan songs, dance, and opera. These are just some of the colorful customs of the minority people.

Ethnic tourism has brought some positive impacts to minority regions, especially in terms of income generation. In 2003 alone, the tourism revenues for minority regions in the PRC from domestic and international tourism reached 56.3 billion yuan and $600 million, respectively (Information Office of the State Council 2005; Mackerras 2005a, p. 823). A successful example is the Kanas Nature Reserve in Xinjiang, where the vast majority of the villagers are members of the Tuvan minority people, one of the oldest peoples in Central Asia. It started tourism business in 1993 and received over 976,000 visitors by 2006. Tourism revenues from the Kanas Nature Reserve amounted to 1,330 million yuan in 1997–2006 and the annual average growth rate in tourist expenditures reached 81 per cent by 2006 (Wang et al. 2010, p. 760).

Some minority people have made money and hold positive attitudes about ethnic tourism. There are other benefits associated with ethnic tourism. Bai (2007, p. 256) claims that ethnic tourism can both strengthen awareness of ethnic difference and contribute to the sense of minority ethnicity. Other scholars do not agree, arguing that ethnic tourism has brought about cultural and environmental destruction and economic exploitation (Studley 1999, p. 13; Yang and Wall 2009, pp. 78, 85–7). In their opinion, some minority regions have embarked on massive property development driven by commercial interests, at the cost of the destruction of indigenous culture, and minority people 'are mainly involved in providing entertainment for tourists while being paid low wages. They are commonly excluded from the planning and management of tourism' because ethnic tourism is often operated by companies owned by Han Chinese or local governments (Feng 2007; Yang and Wall 2009, pp. 80–1, 93; see also Swain 1989; Xie 2003).

Lundberg and Zhou (2009, pp. 284–5) find that 'In the case of Luoji Mount in Liangshan Yi Autonomous Prefecture, the tourist exploitation did not only fail to give any economic benefits to local Yi villagers, but also caused worsening surroundings, restriction on customary rights, loss of cultivated land and increased poverty among the local people.'

ENVIRONMENTAL DEGRADATION AND PROTECTION

In China, Han regions are more densely populated and industrialized than minority regions, and partly for this reason, the vast majority of government projects to protect forestry and pasture have been heavily concentrated in minority regions. Beijing has carried out large-scale ecological migration (i.e., moving pastoralists off the grasslands to peri-urban settlement villages aiming at the sedentarization of herders) to minimize the environmental degradation of the pastureland in Inner Mongolia (US Congressional-Executive Commission on China 2005b, p. 6; West 2009), set up national nature reserves in minority areas such as the Xishuangbanna Nature Reserve in Yunnan and the Zoige Wetland Nature Reserve in Sichuan, and made efforts to improve the environment of the Tarim Basin in Xinjiang and protected the source of the 'Three Rivers' in Yushu Tibetan Autonomous Prefecture of Qinghai (Information Office of the State Council 2005).

But not everything the government or its officials do is eco-friendly. For example, the ethnic minorities in Southwest China maintained landscapes through traditional land use and cultural practices, placing a high value on protecting forests, landscapes and water catchments while preserving biodiversity. These practices were maintained through religious beliefs, hunting taboos and the protection of sacred sites. From the 1950s, however, decisions about major land use and conservation in the regions became the result of centrally planned policy.

Frequent oscillations in government forestry policy and land tenure insecurity since the 1950s have led to the erosion of many local institutions and the loss of indigenous knowledge (US Congressional-Executive Commission on China 2005b, p. 6; Xu et al. 2006).

Likewise, ethnic minorities do not always have a say in grasslands management in Inner Mongolia and Tibet. As a result, their nomadic lifestyle is increasingly endangered. In Inner Mongolia, official policies were directly responsible for over-reclamation of marginal lands for farming that damaged Inner Mongolian pastures during the Cultural Revolution. Since 1978, the government has inadequately addressed the overstocking of sheep and goats, which is further driving pasture degradation in Inner Mongolia. Due to inadequate efforts by the government, there is desertification in Qinghai and Xinjiang (US Congressional-Executive Commission on China 2005b, pp. 18, 21; Xu et al. 2006, p. 6; see also Hays 2012).

Similar ecological crises/damage have occurred in other minority regions. The forests of south-east Tibet, western Sichuan, northern Yunnan, south-west Gansu and south-east Qinghai have been the homes of many ethnic minority groups for generations. Beijing designated the forests as China's 'second timber production base' in 1950. The forests were then subject to indiscriminate felling by state timber production firms and were not managed on a sustainable basis, as most of the firms did not have a long-term management plan. In some areas, annual felling was four times more than the sustainable yield. As a result, forest cover fell in Tibet from 9 per cent in 1950 to 5 per cent in 1985, in Yunnan from 55 per cent in the 1950s to 30 per cent in 1975, and in Sichuan from 30 per cent in 1950 to 6.5 per cent in 1998 (Studley 1999, pp. 9–10; Trac et al. 2007, pp. 276–7).

Horrific mudslides and floods in 1998 killed nearly 4,000 people and displaced some 18 million people in China. This wake-up call compelled the people and leaders in China to think in a new way about the value of natural ecosystems. The CCP has made some efforts including financial incentives to encourage sustainable farming and restore eroded forestland. One of the most ambitious plans was a ten-year, over $40 billion reforestation programme known as the Sloping Land Conversion Programme that aims to turn 37 million acres back into forest or grasslands in the Yangtze and Yellow River basins where some ethnic minorities have lived (Bennett 2008; Hance 2011; Hesterman, 2011; Trac et al. 2007, pp. 277–9). It is important to point out that while news about government initiatives is released from time to time, their effects on environmental protection are unknown.

EVALUATIONS OF STATE SUPPORT TO MINORITY AREAS

Despite Beijing's efforts, there has been an enduring gap in economic development between Han regions and minority regions in China. Han coastal regions benefited from modernization drives from the late nineteenth century partly because they had access to foreign capital, technology, markets, etc., whereas minority regions (and Han interior regions as well) remained economically impoverished partly because they did not have good infrastructure and access to foreign technology and investments. The Matthew effect, which refers to the fact that the rich get richer and the poor become poorer, has meant a growing disparity between Han coastal regions and minority regions since 1949, as Beijing has, as outlined above, supported minority regions mainly in the form of promotion of basic education and financial subsidies to local budgets. Beijing has not focused its efforts to raise a skilled labour force, develop markets for minority manufacturers, or build strong infrastructure in minority regions, and despite its efforts, minority literacy rates and levels of educational attainment have remained below those of Han Chinese (US Congressional-Executive Commission on China 2005a, p. 13; Yang and Wu 2009, pp. 117–18; Wang 2007,

p. 154). As a result, options for economic development in minority regions are limited. Mining and ethnic tourism have become two main sources of growth for many minority regions, but as discussed above, they have benefited the central government and Han Chinese more than the minority regions or minority nationality groups. The CCP should compensate minorities for the natural resources extracted from their territories, but state policies have often ignored these provisions. It is alleged that the oil and gas reserves of Xinjiang are exploited largely for processing and consumption in China's interior, and that these resources are not paid for locally. Neither are those in Qinghai and Inner Mongolia (US Congressional-Executive Commission on China 2005a, pp. 18, 21).

In addition, Beijing's control over resource allocation has disadvantaged the basic-level governments of a minority area. For example, the Hulunbuir Municipality (formerly the Hulunbuir League) government in Inner Mongolia took away 60 per cent of the tax benefits owed to the Oroqen Autonomous Banner (OAB) over which it had jurisdiction, although 'Such a claim can hardly be accepted by the authorities of OAB, particularly in view of their financial difficulties' (US Congressional-Executive Commission on China 2005a, p. 13; Lundberg and Zhou 2009, pp. 289–90). Even if the local government of a minority region receives a grant directly from the central government, it does not necessarily mean that all ethnic minority groups in the region will benefit, because the central grant is awarded to the minority region where Han Chinese are often the largest ethnic group. 'Indeed, minorities are not allowed to ask for special treatment for themselves, but must instead call for benefits for nationalities in general, or for all those living within an autonomous area' (Kaup 2002, p. 882). For example, the Zhuang people do not receive special tax breaks, the Guangxi Zhuang Autonomous Region does, and Han Chinese are the majority group in Guangxi. Generally, Han residents in minority regions have benefited more from state support to minority areas than minority residents given the inter-group differences in education, political connections, etc.

Finally, Han regions have developed at a faster rate than minority regions since 1949. As noted above, over 45 per cent of the poor counties listed by the central government in 2001 were located in minority regions, and more than 80 per cent of the people who suffered from shortage of basic necessities such as food and clothing lived in the minority regions (Clothey 2001, p. 3; Guo et al. 2010, p. 201; Zheng 2009, pp. 41–2). Mackerras (2011a, p. 117) writes that 'China's official Xinhua News Agency reported a vice-director of the government's State Ethnic Affairs Commission as stating that about 7 per cent of China's minority people were living in absolute poverty, as opposed to about 2.6 per cent of the total population.'

These statistics are alarming since the ethnic minorities represent less than 9 per cent of China's total population, i.e., they have disproportionately suffered from deficiencies in basic necessities and schooling. This situation has in fact become increasingly problematic since the 1990s, as 'The gap in GDP per capita between ethnic regions and the nation steadily increased from 1,773 yuan in 1995 to 5,488 yuan in 2006 while the ratio of the gap to ethnic GDP per capita has been declining from the peak of 76% in 2000 down to 52% in 2006.' The weak capacity for local revenue generation in minority regions, reflected in lower local fiscal expenditure per capita than nationwide, has hindered the provision of public services for the ethnic minorities (Lai 2009a, p. 10; Tapp 2010, p. 104; Yang and Wall 2009, p. 77).

AFFIRMATIVE ACTION

In addition to its policies to promote socioeconomic development in minority regions, Beijing has implemented affirmative action policies to reduce inter-group inequality in China. Unlike the development policies that have affected both ethnic minorities and Han Chinese in the minority areas, the affirmative action policies have been designed for individuals from ethnic minority groups in both minority areas and Han areas. The Soviet preferential policy in the promotion of minority language, education, financial aid and employment (Martin 2001) has shaped the PRC's affirmative action programmes (Ma 2007a, p. 10; Yang and Wu 2009, p. 118). Beijing has regarded preferential policy as an effective way to reduce ethnic tensions through redistributive justice, thereby maintaining social stability and the political legitimacy of the CCP's leadership in the minority regions (Clothey 2001, pp. 3–4; Wang 2007, pp. 157–8). Today, preferential treatment policies provide individuals from ethnic minorities with easier access to education, employment and political office and certain exceptions from family planning and special tax breaks (Shan and Chen 2009, p. 16; Yang and Wu 2009, p. 118).

Marriage and Family Planning

Beijing has offered ethnic minority groups preferential treatment in marriage and family planning. For example, minority people can marry two years earlier than the minimum marriage age requested for Han Chinese (Sautman 1997, p. 5). Despite this favourable policy, the average age at first marriage of young minority people in urban areas is rising and exceeds the legal marriage age by a large margin. One example is Uyghurs in Ürümqi (Zang 2008b). Young minority people in urban areas are worried about employment, income and costs related to childrearing, child education, etc., and have to delay marriage and childbirth until they achieve some degree of financial security. In rural areas, however, some minority people customarily get married before they are 20 years old, and do not apply for a marriage certificate from the local Civil Affairs Bureau until they reach the legal marriage age. Government officials have turned a blind eye to this practice.

Regarding family planning, after the PRC promulgated their one-child birth control policy in 1979, each urban Han couple is allowed to have one child (it was not until November 2013 that the CCP changed its one-child birth control policy), whereas each urban minority couple can have two children and a rural minority couple can have up to four children. Furthermore, Article 44 of the Law of the People's Republic of China on Regional National Autonomy permits the local governments of an autonomous region to adopt family planning measures in light of local conditions (Sautman 1997, pp. 5–10; also http://www.novexcn.com/regional_nation_autonomy.html). In other words, there is flexibility in implementing birth control in minority regions. For example, the Xinjiang government did not implement the one-child birth control policy among minority nationalities until 1989, ten years after the official promulgation of the policy by the central government. As another example, Beijing issued a statement in 1999 that Tibetan farmers and herdsmen in the Tibet Autonomous Region could have as many children as they liked (Mackerras 2003, pp. 134–41). Beijing has also allowed each ethnic minority group with a population of less than 50,000 members to have three births per urban couple and four births per rural couple (Chang 2003, p. 30). Unsurprisingly, the fertility rates of ethnic minorities have been higher than those of Han Chinese partly because of the differences in family planning between the two groups (Mackerras 2011a, p. 113). Using the 2000 census as the baseline, the population of ethnic minorities increased by 15.88 per cent between 2000 and 2005, as compared with 2.03 per cent reported by Han Chinese during the same period of time (Xinhua 2008).

Education

In addition to promoting education in minority regions in general, Beijing has carried out affirmative action in school admissions for minority students. Some elite universities in China are required to establish special classes for ethnic minority students, and quotas for minority applicants in university admissions are mandatorily maintained (Clothey 2001, pp. 14, 17; Sautman 1997, pp. 11–17; Wang 2007, pp. 157–8; Yang and Wu 2009, p. 119; Zhou and Hill 2009). Thirteen national minority universities were set up and are run specifically for the education of minority students, who can choose to take a college entrance examination in their native language or in Mandarin (Clothey 2001, pp. 16–17). Moreover, minority students have since the 1950s received extra points on the national university entrance examination, tuition fee waivers and living expense stipends once enrolled at university (US Congressional-Executive Commission on China 2005a, p. 18; Leibold 2010, p. 6; Yang and Wu 2009, p. 118). The requirements for university admissions in autonomous regions are generally lower than those in Han regions, and are lower for minority applicants than Han applicants in both minority regions and Han regions. For example, in 2004, the minimum admission score in Shandong province was 600 points, while it was 490 for Han Chinese students and 350 for ethnic minority students in Tibet. The preferential policy has been extended from the higher education sector 'to cover secondary education, adult education and graduate education as well' (Lai 2009a, p. 9; Wang 2007, p. 153).

Minority students are treated differently under the affirmative action programme. For example, minority students from minority regions and remote areas receive more bonus points than their co-ethnics who reside in Han regions (because the latter are presumably more acculturated than the former), and less acculturated minority groups receive more bonus points than more acculturated minority groups in the same minority region. In Xinjiang, for example, 'the minimum admission score is 10 points lower for students of Hui nationality, and 50 points lower for students whose parents are Uyghur, Kazak, Mongolian, Kirgiz, Tajik, Xibe, Uzbek, Tatar, Daur, Tibetan, or Russian, and 10 points lower for students with only one parent belonging to one of the above-mentioned ethnic groups' (Wu 1998, p. 203; Wang 2007, pp. 149–50). The assumption is that Hui students and those with only one minority parent are culturally more accultur-ated into Han society and hence are less disadvantaged than other minority students. The affirmative action programme has received some bad publicity in recent years as some Han students assumed false ethnic identities in order to take advantage of the preferential policies when they applied for admission into university (Wang 2007, p. 160). While Han Chinese have condemned the students who have acted unethically, they have also questioned or challenged the fairness of the programme.

Employment

In theory, Chinese law prohibits ethnic discrimination in the labour market. Article 12 of the Labour Law of the PRC stipulates that 'Laborers, regardless of their ethnic group, race, sex or religious belief, shall not be discriminated against in employment' (Zeng 2007, pp. 993, 1006). Article 22 of the Law on Regional National Autonomy stipulates that the government of a national autonomous area may adopt special measures to provide preferential treatment to job seekers with minority status. Articles 23 and 62 stipulate that when recruiting personnel, firms and institutions in an autonomous area shall give priority to applicants from minority nationalities (http://www .novexcn.com/regional_nation_autonomy.html; Sautman 1997, p. 295). In the Tibetan areas, for example, Tibetans enjoy preference in becom-ing legal workers (Mackerras 2005b, p. 24). Hui workers in Lanzhou were heavily recruited to work in the leather industry before 1978 partly because it was historically regarded as a Hui trade in the city. Minority status may be required for a post, or a minority quota may apply, if a business is catering to the needs of an ethnic minority group. Minority applicants receive some bonus points when they take examinations for certain posts. There have been proposals to set up minority quotas in the private sector in some minority regions (Lai 2009a, p. 10; Sautman 1997, pp. 23–4).

Legal Protection

Article 134 of the 1982 Constitution stipulates that

> Citizens of all nationalities have the right to use the spoken and written languages of their own nationalities in court proceedings. The people's courts and people's procuratorates should provide translation for any party to the court proceedings who is not familiar with the spoken or written languages in common use in the locality. In an area where people of a minority nationality live in a compact community or where a number of nationalities live together, hearings should be conducted in the language or languages in common use in the locality; indictments, judgments, notices and other documents should be written, according to actual needs, in the language or languages in common use in the locality. (http://english.peopledaily.com.cn/constitution/constitution.html; see also Mackerras 2005b, p. 24)

Equally important, some minority suspects get more benefits than Chinese law provides for. Hu Yaobang, former CCP General Secretary, formulated a three restraints and one leniency policy as part of his ethnic policy in 1980. In 1984, the government officially required judges to exercise constraint in prosecuting crimes committed by individuals with minority status and to treat them leniently in sentencing (Hao 2009; Woeser 2009). It is alleged that 'in legal and civil disputes, authorities throughout the nation tend to side with ethnic minorities for the sake of preserving ethnic unity, even to the dissatisfaction of the Han' (Lai 2009b, p. 3; 2010, p. 77) Minority suspects also enjoy favourable treatment in judicial and civil disputes involving Han

Chinese (Lai 2009a, p. 8). It is necessary to point out that this policy is used only in minority areas and not for minority persons who are CCP members and state cadres, or have a good education, or have lived for a long time in Han areas or among Han Chinese (Sautman 2012), probably because they are presumed to be more acculturated into Han society and therefore should be treated like Han Chinese rather than like members of ethnic minority groups.

Political Careers

The PRC Constitution stipulates that 'all the minority nationalities are entitled to appropriate representation' in the National People's Congress (NPC). Sautman (1999, p. 297) observed that the proportion of minority deputies to the NPC in the total number of NPC deputies has always exceeded the proportion of minority peoples in China's total population. This practice has persisted into today's NPC: for the Seventh NPC (1988–93), for example, 455 deputies (i.e., 15 per cent of the total number of deputies) came from minority nationalities. The corresponding figure for the Eighth NPC (1993–7) was 439 (14.8 per cent), for the Ninth NPC (1998–2001) 428 (14.4 per cent), for the Tenth NPC (2002–7) 428 (14.4 per cent), and for the Eleventh NPC (2008–13) 411 (13.76 per cent) (Sautman 1997, pp. 25–7; Xinhua 2011b; see also http://en.wikipedia.org/wiki/National_People%27s _Congress). Twenty-five of the 161 members of the Standing Committee of the 11th National People's Congress held in March 2009 were from ethnic minorities, accounting for 15.5 per cent of the total (Information Office of the State Council 2010a, p. 228). At present, all 55 ethnic minority groups have deputies to the NPC and members of the Chinese People's Political Consultative Conference (which is China's political advisory body or 'upper house' without the power of the upper house in the UK). Minority deputies are the majority or a major bloc in local people's congresses in minority regions

(Sautman 1999, p. 294). It is, however, necessary to point out that people's congresses are not a powerful political machine in the PRC. The presence of minority deputies mainly serves the CCP's need to demonstrate its political legitimacy and portray China as a multi-ethnic country.

For similar reasons, the CCP has actively recruited cadres from ethnic minority groups to govern minority areas and employed nearly 3 million non-Han party members in 2007, up from merely 10,000 in 1950. The share of ethnic minorities in the PRC cadre corps was 73.9 per cent in Tibet, 47 per cent in Xinjiang, 34 per cent in Guangxi, 23.4 per cent in Inner Mongolia and 17.5 per cent in Ningxia (Lai 2009a, p.7). Nationwide, in 1992, 2.3 million minority cadres accounted for 7.1 per cent of the cadres in China (Sautman 1999, p. 298). The corresponding figures for 1998 were 2.7 million and 6.9 per cent, and for 2010 2.9 million and 7.4 per cent (Xinhua 2009b; 2010b; 2011b). The CCP has run annual training programmes for officials from ethnic minorities since 1978. Minority cadres in less developed areas have since 1990 been offered temporary posts in central government departments and more developed coastal provinces for about six months as part of their training in management (Lai 2009a, p. 7; Xinhua 2009b).

CCP Membership

CCP membership is often an essential requirement for an official position in the CCP and the government and therefore a treasured public good in China. Beijing has never hidden its interest in recruiting CCP members from minority groups and has treated some minority groups such as Uyghurs and Tibetans favourably in recruitment. Its interest is politically motivated, although it benefits minority people who have ambitions to climb up in the PRC political system. The government has relied on CCP minority members to divide and rule in minority regions. In addition, its effort to recruit minority people into the CCP can also reduce the possibility that minority people consider the CCP an outside political organization, thereby strengthening its influence and political legitimacy in minority regions. Beijing is more interested in recruitment from some non-Han groups than others, and is more successful in recruitment from some minority groups than others, as will be discussed in chapter 5.

Nationwide, there were 2.8 million CCP members who were from ethnic minority groups in 1990, representing 5.7 per cent of the CCP members in China. This figure was 0.2 per cent higher than in 1957 (Mackerras 1994, p. 157), and increased to 6.1 per cent in 1999 (Sautman 1999, p. 297). By 2002, there were 4.1 million CCP members from ethnic minority groups, equivalent to 6.2 per cent of the total CCP membership of 66.4 million (Lai 2009a, p. 7). Nevertheless, the 2002 figure is still lower than the minority population share in China (i.e., 8.4 per cent), despite its affirmative action in CCP recruitment.

EVALUATIONS OF THE AFFIRMATIVE ACTION PROGRAMMES

Some scholars in the West have held positive views on the PRC's affirmative action, arguing that 'China's ethnic policies include a growing network of laws to improve relations among Chinese of diverse ethnicity by advancing the interests of historically subaltern peoples', and that the minority rights schemes in the PRC generally provide both legal entitlements to persons of minority origin and group rights to preserve minority ethnic identity and culture and compensate for prejudice and discrimination (Mackerras 2011a, pp. 116–17, 124; Sautman 1999, pp. 284, 300–2). Lai (2009a, p. 8) claims that 'Ethnic minorities in China enjoy favourable social treatment comparable to affirmative action enjoyed by minorities in the US.'

However, other scholars have maintained that requirements for ethnic origin have operated in China as a potential discriminatory mechanism by which employers might screen applicants in the labour market (Zeng 2007, p. 997). The minimum hiring quotas for ethnic minorities have faded into oblivion because the state sector has declined since 1978 and the rising private sector is not legally obliged to recruit workers from ethnic minority groups and is largely responsible for rising ethnic discrimination in the labour market (Human Rights in China 2007, pp. 2, 20–1; Shan and Chen 2009, pp. 16, 20; Zang 2010, p. 344; 2011a, p. 141). Chinese law is thus accused of paying lip service to stamping out ethnic prejudices, and does not provide for regularized state intervention to protect the interests and dignity of ethnic minorities from affronts by 'Great Han chauvinism' (US Congressional-Executive Commission on China 2005a, p. 17; Sautman 1999, p. 285; Smith 2004, p. 14).

Opinions about the affirmative action programmes also vary among PRC citizens and are emotionally charged. Some Han Chinese have bitterly complained about the lenient treatment and sentences that minority criminals have received from the Chinese courts, charging that the policy violated the PRC Constitution as all the citizens of the PRC ought to be equal before the law. Other Han Chinese have called Hu Yaobang, the father of the two restraints and one leniency policy, Hu Luanbang, meaning that he made a big mess (Shan and Chen 2009, pp. 17–18, 20; see also Hao 2009; Kaltman 2007). Some of them have developed resentment towards minority entitlements in family planning, university admissions and employment (Leibold 2010, p. 15; Rossett 1991, pp. 1525–6; Sautman 1997, pp. 29–31), and have demanded 'the scrapping of preferential university admissions on grounds of quality control and equity' (Sautman 1997, p. 30). Ma Rong (2009), an influential scholar of ethnicity in China, recommended that the policies in favour of minorities could continue, but the target of these policies should be gradually shifted from 'all members of minority groups' to all residents of 'poor areas', and then to 'all individual citizens who need the help.'

Nor are ethnic minorities happy about the equal opportunities programmes because they do not agree that the government has done enough to reduce inter-group inequality. Some minority intellectuals have regarded existing affirmative action programmes as weak and inadequate and as failing to offer ethnic minorities adequate protection from discrimination and offer an effective solution to the erosion of indigenous ethnic cultures in China (Sautman 1997, pp. 33–4). It has also been pointed out that although the government has provided minority students with preferential treatment for access to secondary schools and universities, it has not addressed the issue of the cultural exclusion that minority students have encountered on campus (Yi 2008; Zhao 2010). There are also negative social and psychological implications associated with equal opportunity programmes for ethnic minority groups. To some minority people, affirmative action is an insult to their dignity and pride: the unspoken assumption among Han Chinese is that minority ethnicity is linked to equal opportunities because it symbolizes backwardness and incompetence. They assert that they are as intelligent as Han Chinese and are poor only because of the socioeconomic system and ethnic discrimination.

There are other issues related to the government affirmative action programmes. As noted above, minority access to equal opportunities (e.g., university admissions) decreases as one becomes increasingly acculturated into Han society. Ironically, this negative association is detrimental to Beijing's *ronghe* policy because it actively encourages minority students who want to make use of equal opportunities to strengthen their ethnic identity as much as possible and to be as little acculturated as possible. But if minority students choose to act this way, they are subject to discrimination and prejudice and would be treated as incompetent persons in society. As a result, they suffer either way.

EMPIRICAL EVIDENCE OF ETHNIC INEQUALITY

An exciting development in research on ethnic minorities in China is a growing literature on inter-group inequality in the post-1978 era. Using Chinese census data, Hasmath (2007; 2008) shows that ethnic minority groups in Beijing have achieved greater educational attainment than Han Chinese, but when it comes to their occupational outcomes in 'high-status' and high-wage posts, ethnic minority groups are disproportionately under-represented. Using the 1988 Chinese Household Income Project (CHIP) data, Johnson and Chow (1997) showed that in all specifications across urban and rural areas, minority ethnicity was negatively related to income. Ethnic minorities received wages that were approximately 19 per cent less than Han Chinese in rural areas and approximately 4.5 per cent less than Han Chinese in urban areas. H. Li (2003) finds that ethnic minorities made 9 per cent less than Han Chinese in 1995. Using 2001 survey data conducted in Lanzhou, Zang (2008a) shows that during market reforms, the government has not been able to protect Hui workers as promised by its equal opportunity policy. Hui workers have faced barriers in finding a job in both state firms and government agencies: 54.3 per cent of the Han respondents work in state firms, as compared with 45.2 per cent of the Hui respondents; 25.5 per cent of Han Chinese are employed in government agencies, whereas only 11 per cent of Hui Muslims report the same institutional affiliation. Using survey data gathered in Ürümchi in 2005, Zang (2010) shows that 52.3 per cent of the Han respondents work in state firms, as compared with 28.5 per cent of the Uyghur respondents. A job in the state sector is a treasured achievement in Ürümchi. In fact, any job in urban areas is hard to come by today given cut-throat competition in the labour market in China. Zang (2011a) also finds that Uyghur workers earn 52 per cent less than Han workers in non-state sectors.

More alarmingly, the gap in socioeconomic status between ethnic minorities and Han Chinese is actually becoming wider during the post-1978 market reforms. 'Overall growth, however, masks a large and increasing income disparity' between ethnic minorities and Han Chinese (Barabantseva 2008, p. 244; US Congressional-Executive Commission on China 2005a, pp. 16–17; Dreyer 2005, p. 82; Hansen 2005, p. 117; Sautman 1999, p. 285). Using census data from 1982 and 1990, Hannum and Xie (1998) find a major gap in occupational attainment between Han Chinese and ethnic minorities in Xinjiang, which widened further between 1982 and 1990. Gustafsson and Li (2003) examine survey data from 19 provinces in China and identify a per capita income gap between Han Chinese and minority people of 19.2 per cent in 1988 and 35.9 per cent in 1995.

DISCUSSION

Overall, the CCP has made efforts to reduce ethnic inequality in the PRC by promoting economic development in minority areas and affirmative action programmes. Minority areas are more developed and ethnic minority groups are better off today than in 1949. There is little doubt that ethnic minority groups are better educated, have more access to public services, and are less marginalized politically and economically. However, ethnic inequality has intensified in the post-1978 market reforms, as Han areas are developing at a faster rate than minority areas, and Han Chinese are doing better than minority nationalities. Beijing supports minority regions rather than minority groups. Han Chinese in minority areas have benefited disproportionately from government policies due to inter-group differences in education, access to loans and government offices. Moreover, the effect of affirmative action programmes has decreased due to the decline of state enterprises, and the private sector is not subject to affirmative action. Although an increasing number of minority students graduate from university each year, the rapid expansion of higher education in China has devalued the credentials they receive. More importantly, a minority applicant's university education does not necessarily translate into a job after graduation. Furthermore, some government policies have been implemented at the expense of minority interests. For example, ecological migration has been promoted in the name of protecting the ecological system in minority areas, but this policy has involved ending nomadic economies and lifestyles and has been hugely controversial.

Finally, a major development in ethnic relations is a recent proposal by the CCP to limit or significantly reduce minority entitlements in the PRC. Zhu Weiqun stated in February 2012 that state support for the reduction of poverty should focus on impoverished areas supporting all ethnic groups in the areas. In his opinion, the Great Western Development and the Border Region Development do not mean an exclusive emphasis on the improvement of life chances among ethnic minorities. The government should strive to make sure that everyone is equal before the law, and should not emphasize the importance of minority ethnicity in such a way that ethnic minorities become more equal than Han Chinese (Zhu 2012).

RECOMMENDED READING

Ajit S. Bhalla and Shufang Qiu, *Poverty and Inequality among Chinese Minorities* (London: Routledge, 2006).

Colin Mackerras (ed.), *Ethnic Minorities in Modern China*, Vol. II (London: Routledge, 2011).

3 | Minority Cultures ─────────────

A people's culture comprises its language, literature, religions, performing arts, crafts, amongst other things. This chapter asks: What has the CCP done to protect minority cultures in the PRC? Has the CCP treated all aspects of minority cultures equally? Has the PRC nationality policy promoted diversity and multiculturalism? In comparative perspective, has the CCP done a better job of protecting minority cultures than it has of reducing ethnic inequality? Has the post-1978 economic development affected minority cultures in China positively or negatively? Are minority cultures in China thriving or endangered?

These questions are important: ethnic minority groups are a major concern in research on China, partly because of their religious beliefs and ways of life (Zang 2011b, p. 1). Most non-Han peoples, with but a few exceptions, are not distinguishable from one another solely on the basis of phenotypic characteristics, and their identification mostly depends on cultural and linguistic differences that over time have been relatively persistent (Dreyer 1976; Fei 1980; Gladney 1994; Poston and Shu 1987). Inter-group differences are reflected mainly in folkways, religions and lifestyles in terms of customs, dress, diet, etiquette, funerals, etc. In theory, Beijing has taken the protection of minority cultures seriously and promulgated a series of laws, regulations and policies to serve this purpose. Article 4 of the PRC Constitution (1982) states that all nationality groups have the freedom to use and develop their own spoken and written languages and to preserve or reform their own ways and customs, and that the state helps minority nationalities speed up their economic and cultural development in accordance with their peculiarities and needs. Article 121 stipulates that local governments of national autonomous areas must employ the spoken and written language or languages in common use in the locality (Lundberg 2009, pp. 404–5; Sautman 1999, p. 293). Some scholars have claimed that the CCP prohibits 'language discrimination and prejudice in any form' in China (X. Huang 2003, p. 2; Zuo 2007, p. 90).

However, the CCP's promise to protect minority cultures in the PRC should not be taken at face value, especially with regard to Western criticisms of Beijing's minority culture policy. Baranovitch (2001, p. 359) points out that 'among some minorities, people commonly express discontent with their status and how their group is represented in mainstream culture.' Bulag (2002, p. 202) highlights 'minority resistance' within the context of Han hegemony that has promoted a national 'One China' identity at the expense of minority languages and cultures (see also Zhou 2000, p. 146; Nelson 2005). The US Congressional-Executive Commission on China (2005a, p. 15) has claimed that Beijing has 'tightened controls over minority cultural representation and launched an extensive propaganda campaign on the role of China's minorities in building a united, multi-ethnic nation. The same campaign stresses that future prospects for minorities depend on cooperating with the Han majority.'

It is unclear how valid these criticisms are due to inadequate research on the preservation of minority cultures in the PRC. Baranovitch (2001, p. 395) claims that minority paintings, literature and academic and general discourse in China have not been studied 'extensively'. This chapter is an attempt to narrow this knowledge gap. It first outlines the CCP's policy towards minority cultures since the 1930s. Next, it discusses minority customs, arts and crafts in the PRC. It then reviews the general state of minority languages and examines the state control of religions among ethnic minority groups. Finally, it examines the controversy over Beijing's minority culture policy.

STATE POLICY ON MINORITY CULTURES IN THE POST-1949 ERA

In the First National Congress of the Chinese Soviet held in November 1931, the CCP proclaimed that it would make efforts to develop minority cultures and promised to establish schools, compile printing presses for minority peoples to use their own languages and scripts, and allow the use of minority languages and scripts in all government organs (see Chinese Soviet Republic 1931). Subsequent CCP documents and resolutions comprised stipulations concerning the protection of minority languages and scripts (Liu and Alatan 1988, p. 149), at least in theory. For example, respect for minority cultures was a key component in the *Declaration of the Chinese Soviet Republic to the Mongolian Nationality* (Government of the Chinese Soviet Republic 1935) proclaimed in December 1935, and the *Declaration of the Chinese Soviet Republic of the Hui Nationality* (Government of the Chinese Soviet Republic 1936) proclaimed in May 1936. The 1941 Administrative Guidance of the Shanganning Border Region reiterated the CCP's commitment to Mongolian and Hui autonomous regions (Li 2009; CCP Politburo 1941). Mao Zedong (1953, p. 1085) called for help for minority nationalities in all aspects of their lives including minority cultures in his report to the CCP Seventh National Congress held on 24 April 1945. Following his call, the CCP published the *Yanbian Daily* in the Korean language in Jilin province in 1948 (http://www.hybrb.com/), the *Xinjiang Daily* in Chinese, Uyghur, Kazak and Mongolian languages in 1949, and the first Tibetan newspaper, *Qinghai Tibetan Journal*, in 1951 (State Ethnic Affairs Commission 2006).

More importantly, the right of ethnic minority groups to use and develop their native languages and writing systems was written into the provisional constitution of the PRC in 1949 (*The Common Program of the Chinese People's Political Consultative Conference* 1949; Zuo 2007, p. 85). The 1952 Program for the Implementation of Regional Ethnic Autonomy stipulated that the language most commonly used in a minority area should be used as an official language there. The 1954 Constitution permitted autonomous governments to develop their own regulations on languages (Kaup 2000, p. 78; Lai 2009a, pp. 5–6). In 1956, Beijing reaffirmed that minority groups had the right to use their native languages, and that Mandarin should be mandated for Han Chinese only (Wang and Phillion 2009, p. 3; see also Schwarz 1962). Although the CCP carried out socialist transformations to wipe out the old ruling classes in minority areas in the pre-1957 era, it was cautious in enforcing assimilation policy on the minority nationalities before the Cultural Revolution of 1966–76.

In fact, Beijing devoted considerable resources to documenting and rescuing the culture heritage of non-Han peoples during the period 1949–65. In the 1950s, it sent seven work teams of more than 700 employees to conduct linguistic surveys of 42 minority nationality groups in 15 provinces. These surveys were instrumental for Beijing to create ten new minority scripts and improve seven existing minority scripts (Lai 2009a, p. 8; Liu and Alatan 1988, p. 149; Zhou 2000, pp. 131–2; Zuo 2007, pp. 85–6; see also Ma Xiaoyi 2009; Zhou 2003). The government required Han cadres to be trained in minority languages before they were sent to minority areas to work, or to undertake on-the-job training in minority languages (Bruhn 2008, p. 6; Casas 2011, p. 2; Zhou 2000, p. 132).

At the same time, the CCP attempted to transform minority performing arts to serve its political purposes. Several years before 1949, the CCP 'sent Han musicians to minority areas to familiarize themselves with local musical idioms, compose new songs that combined those idioms with socialist messages, and train local artists in the new revolutionary artistic practices' (Baranovitch 2001, p. 364; Mackerras

1984, p. 194; 1992, p. 30). Moreover, the CCP tried to instil 'a consciousness of being Chinese in minority peoples and of helping them to feel a sense of participation in a multinational Chinese state', and promoted Mandarin among citizens as an essential step in the development of China as a unified nation (Barabantseva 2008, p. 578). It marked the inventories of cultural traits and customs as a key object of ideological struggle in non-Han areas and alleged that non-Han modes of social organization, family and marriage, and ritual practice were contaminated by slave, feudal or capitalist class interests (Litzinger 1998, p. 226). During the 1957 Hundred Flowers campaign, some members of non-Han groups asked for more ethnic autonomy and more freedom of expression of ethnic identity. In response, Beijing replaced the moderate ethnic policies with political radicalism to carry out forced and rapid integration of minority groups into Han society (Dreyer 1976, pp. 160–1; Lai 2009b, pp. 6–7).

This radical policy approach was intensified during the Cultural Revolution when the expressions of time-honoured minority culture, including folk songs and dances, were condemned as 'feudal, capitalist, revisionist, poisonous weeds' (Baranovitch 2001, p. 365; Heberer 1989, pp. 27, 107–10; Lai 2009b, p. 7; Tapp 2010, p. 101). Non-Han performing arts such as Tibetan drama survived the Cultural Revolution by adopting revolutionary tones, all of which treated Han themes, not minority themes (Mackerras 1984, p. 198; 1992, pp. 13–14, 30–1). In many minority areas, places of worship were dismantled. Of 6,259 monasteries and nunneries in existence in Tibet prior to 1950, only 13 survived the destruction of the Cultural Revolution. Traditional ethnic holidays were forbidden, and those who celebrated them were labelled 'counterrevolutionary' and punished accordingly. The traditional health care that non-Han peoples had practised was labelled 'superstitious', and forbidden (Clothey 2001, p. 10; Hess 2009, pp. 79–80). Ethnic minority scripts and customs were condemned as 'backward'. 'Presses that printed nationality languages were shut down, and newspapers and radio broadcasts in minority languages were discontinued. Almost all schools for minorities were closed, and those that continued provided instruction only in Mandarin' (Clothey 2001, pp. 9–10; see also Zhou 2000, pp. 132–3; 2003, pp. 72–98). Wang and Phillion (2009, p. 3; see also Lin 1997) claim that 'Requests for bilingual education and minority curriculum were regarded as challenges to ideological correctness and as opposition to socialism.' Accelerated assimilation became the goal of Beijing's minority culture policy.

This forced assimilation policy was abandoned after 1978. Beijing partly restored the moderate ethnic polices it had pursued from 1949 to 1957 (Lai 2009b, pp. 7–8), increasing the institutional promotion of minority cultures and publicly stating that minority groups have the right to use their languages and practise their religions and cultures (Baranovitch 2001, p. 365; Bruhn 2008, p. 7; Litzinger 1998, pp. 225–6, 235; Mackerras 1992, p. 30; 2005b, p. 8; Wang and Phillion 2009, p. 2; Zuo 2007, p. 85). Ethnic minority groups were given permission to worship and practise their religions (often including practices such as shamanism that are still officially banned among Han Chinese) and express their cultural differences through arts and popular culture (Cultural Survival 1997). The 1982 PRC Constitution restores and expands the privileges for regional ethnic autonomy stipulated in the 1954 PRC Constitution. Articles 37 and 47 of the 1984 Law for Regional Autonomy allow for the use of local languages in schools and courts. Article 49 provides incentives to promote bilingualism among officials in the PRC. Article 65 requires the expansion of minority-language mass media (http://www.novexcn.com/regional _nation_autonomy.html).

What is not clear so far is what Beijing has actually done to protect minority cultures and languages in the post-1978 era. Wang and Phillion write (2009, p. 1) that 'it is urgent to examine China's minority language policy and practice to discover the discrepancies between its minority policy and practice and to take measures to protect minority groups' language rights.' Accordingly, the rest of this chapter gives some detailed information about the efforts Beijing has made for the pro-tection of minority cultures and evaluates the effects of these efforts on the protection of minority customs, arts, crafts, languages and religions.

MINORITY CUSTOMS, MEDICINES AND SPORTS

Some of the official portrayals of non-Han peoples in China highlight their unique customs and festivals (White 2008). Indeed, due to dif-ferences in historical processes and natural environment, ethnic groups differ from one another in their material and cultural lives, including clothing, food, housing, marriage, funerals, festivals and etiquette. Sautman (1997, p. 5) writes that 'the 156 ethnic minority autonomous areas can proclaim holidays for traditional festivities. Even in cities outside the autonomies, minorities are entitled to leave at full pay to attend their festivities. Special meals must be provided at work to Muslims and articles needed by minorities were, until recently, pro-duced by state enterprises for sale at subsidized prices.' The government set up Muslim canteens or supplied Muslim food in state organs, schools and enterprises and allotted land for cemeteries for minority peoples with the tradition of inhumation (Information Office of the State Council 1999b). The burial custom of Tibetans has been main-tained as they can choose the forms of burial they prefer, including 'sky burial', inhumation or 'water burial' (TibetTrip n.d.; also Li and Jiang 2003, pp. 115–24).

Some minority medicines in China such as Tibetan traditional medicine and Uyghur traditional medicine are among the world's oldest known medical treatments (di Sarsina et al. 2011; Fan and Holliday 2006). Beijing has reportedly valued minority medicines, trained specialists in minority medicines, and established medical research institutes of Tibetan, Mongolian and Uyghur medicine in

Tibet, Inner Mongolia and Xinjiang. There were 157 ethnic hospitals in China in 2003. Of these, 55 were hospitals of Tibetan medicine, 41 hospitals of Mongolian medicine, 35 hospitals of Uyghur medicine, one hospital of Dai medicine, and 25 hospitals of other types of ethnic medicine. Several centres for the making of Mongolian, Tibetan and Uyghur pharmaceutical preparations were established in 1992, which have to date manufactured more than 100 different kinds of minority medicines (Fan and Holiday 2006; Janes 1995; Hofer 2008; Information Office of the State Council 1999b), responding to the increasing popularity of minority medicines among Han Chinese in recent years.

The Chinese government has trained minority people in ethnic sports. In 1953, the first traditional ethnic sports show and competition, known as the First National Traditional Ethnic Minority Sports Meet, was held in Tianjin. Since 1982, such meets have been held once every four years, and the Ninth National Traditional Ethnic Minority Sports Meet was held in September 2011 in Guiyang. The National Traditional Ethnic Minority Sports Meet is only for minority athletes. 'The games are said to be the only nationwide traditional, multi-ethnic sports event in the world' (Gerin 2011; Miao 2011). Nevertheless, the games are in large part a political show and have little impact on the daily lives of non-Han peoples.

While some aspects of minority customs, such as minority medicines, have fared relatively well in the post-1978 era, rapid social and economic development has generated a challenge to the preservation of other aspects of non-Han customs and traditions in China. Historically, many non-Han peoples passed on their customs and rituals visually, as young men and women learned their traditions by watching performances by the elders (Mackerras 1984). In the post-1978 era, many young minority people have moved to cities to work, where they have accepted the Han lifestyle and have lost interest in their time-honoured rituals, and for this reason it is believed that many non-Han customs could disappear in one generation (Feng 2007). At

the same time, Beijing has educated non-Han peoples to create awareness among them 'about how outmoded institutions and customs can
harm their physical and mental well-being'. Non-Han peoples have
been officially 'encouraged to adopt new, scientific, civilized and healthy
customs in daily life, as well as in marriages and funerals' (Liu and
Alatan 1988, p. 154; see also Information Office of the State Council
2005). There is little doubt that the 'new, scientific, civilized and healthy
customs' are invariably part of Han culture, and that the official encour-
agement would lead to assimilation into Han society.

MINORITY LITERATURES, ARTS AND CRAFTS

The minority literature in China includes, among other forms, myths,
epics, novels and poems (Dayton 2006; Zhao 1991). After 1949, the
CCP organized writers, artists and experts in anthropology, sociology
and ethnology to collect and preserve some non-Han folk cultures and
arts. The compilation of ten collections of literature, music and dance
of non-Han peoples aimed to comprise 450 volumes in 450 million
words. Among them, the Collection of Chinese Folk Songs, the
Collection of Folk Instrument Tunes of China's Ethnic Minorities, the
Collection of Chinese Folk Tales, and the Collection of Chinese Folk
Proverbs have been completed and 310 volumes have already been
published. The government also mobilized 566 libraries and 163
museums to collect, translate and study Gesar, an oral Tibetan epic,
Jangar, a Mongolian epic, and Manas, an epic of the Kirgiz people
(Information Office of the State Council 2005; Mackerras 1984,
pp. 193–4, 198–9).

Beijing has fostered literary talents among non-Han peoples. Many
non-Han writers have written and published literary works. Nearly
600 writers belonging to ethnic minorities are members of the Chinese
Writers' Association, representing more than 10 per cent (Information
Office of the State Council 1999b). Well-known minority authors

include Zhang Xianliang, a male Hui writer, Huo Da, a female Hui writer, and Jing Yi, a female writer from the Bai people. However, given the censorship system in China, these minority writers cannot publish their works unless they are politically correct and support ethnic unity in the PRC, and now they are given a new task: Li Changchun, a former senior CCP leader, urged minority writers to 'write for the people and the times' and help increase the influence of China's culture in the world (Xinhua 2012).

Ethnic minorities in China are often portrayed in the official media as having special talent in singing and dancing. Large folk song and dance gatherings have for centuries been the custom among non-Han groups (Mackerras 1984, pp. 202, 209; Rees 1995–6; White 2008). This portrayal has been reinforced by minority films such as *Wuduo jinhua* (Five Golden Flowers, 1959) and *Liu sanjie* (Third Sister Liu, 1960) (Zhang 1997, pp. 79–80). Minority performing arts were central to courtship and marriage as well as religious ceremony, and served as a medium for transmitting historical, philosophical and eco-logical knowledge among non-Han groups (Mackerras 1984). Ethnic folk songs included shamans' songs, labour chants, love songs and drinking songs. Folk songs and ethnic dances were important before 1949 because many non-Han peoples were illiterate (Ingram 2011, p. 439; Mackerras 1988, pp. 52, 61–2; 1992, pp. 25–6; see also Jun and Stuart 1992). Mackerras (1984, pp. 187, 197–8) regards ethnic folk songs and dances as 'the most important of the cultural forms of the minorities because of their mass appeal and particularly close relations with society'. Non-Han children learn traditional folk songs and dances as part of their cultural heritage from adults in the family or community, especially during holidays.

Minority performing artists had low social status before 1949. Mackerras (1984, p. 212) points out that 'professional troupes were notable for their rarity among the minority nationalities. Artists also tilled the fields in agricultural nationalities or were herdsmen among pastoral peoples. The Mongolian, Uygur, or Tibetan bards who wandered round with their instruments on their backs chanting the long narrative songs received very little money for their art and had to take on other work.' This situation has changed since 1949, especially with regard to the professionalization of minority performing artists. The government formed the Central Ethnic Song and Dance Ensemble in the early 1950s, with performers from various non-Han groups performing ethnic songs and dances both in China and abroad. Later, the government set up the Bai Cultural Work Team in 1958 and founded the Tibetan Drama Troupe of Tibet in 1960. The government also helped some minorities produce dramas in their own languages, including Mongolians, Tibetans, Uyghurs, Koreans, Miao and Yi, before 1966. 'Although the Cultural Revolution caused the composition of such works to be suspended, this effect resumed and even increased after the fall of the Gang of Four in 1976' (Mackerras 1984, pp. 188, 191, 213–17, 219; 1992, pp. 12–13, 15). It is estimated that 534 art troupes, 194 sites for art performances, 82 mass art centres, 679 cultural centres, and 7,318 culture dissemination stations operated in minority areas by 2006. The government has set up 24 arts colleges and a number of art schools in minority areas to train performing artists from non-Han groups (Mackerras 1992, pp. 27–8; Sautman 2006, p. 246; Ingram 2011; State Ethnic Affairs Commission 2006).

Beijing has sponsored the Dong's Kam big song, the Mongolian *Long Tones*, and the Uyghur *Twelve Mukamu* to be enlisted into the world non-material cultural heritages recognized by UNESCO's Representative List of the Intangible Cultural Heritage of Humanity for better preservation. Before 1950, only two or three elderly Uyghur musicians could sing the *Twelve Mukams* completely. Now many can and an Art Troupe and a research office in Xinjiang are devoted to the revival of Mukam (Information Office of the State Council 1999b). Other examples of minority performing arts that have been revitalized include the Mongolian operas *Haolaibao*, *Xiaokeyare* and *Wuliger* in the Mongolian language and Zhuang operas in the Zhuang language (State Ethnic Affairs Commission 2006). It is necessary to recognize that these efforts are politically motivated as their expected outcome is to showcase China to the outside world as a harmonious multicultural society (Mackerras 1984, pp. 193–5; 1992, pp. 4–7, 9, 16–17, 20–4; Zhang 1997, p. 80).

Because of the CCP's management of minority performing arts, the songs and dramas of non-Han groups have become more integrated with Han performing arts since 1949 (Mackerras 1992, p. 30). In addition, the government has had no particular interest in supporting grass-roots non-Han performing arts and has done little to preserve these non-Han cultural heritages. It is possible that Beijing does not see any value in them for its political purposes because they are grass-roots and thus insignificant. As a result, some of them have become endangered. In 1984 Mackerras (1984, p. 188) already witnessed the decline of traditional folk song and dance among non-Han peoples in China. This trend has accelerated since then. For example, zuochang, literally translated as sitting and singing, is a stage performance popular among Hui Muslims in north-western Ningxia dating back hundreds of years. Today, zuochang is on the verge of becoming an art form only seen in museums, as there are only a few professional zuochang performers in China. This is not an exception, as the problem of having no successors plagues many grass-roots arts and crafts practised by China's non-Han peoples (Feng 2007; Ingram 2011).

MINORITY LANGUAGES

Language is a key dimension of a culture, and language rights are part of minority rights that are used to evaluate the chances of survival of ethnic minorities and their identity. Typical linguistic demands include the use of minority languages in the public media, the public education system and communications with public authorities and courts. International norms require a national government to protect minority languages under its jurisdiction, and not to exert any assimilationist pressure (Henrard 2001, pp. 45–6; Lundberg 2009, pp. 400–1).

The official language of the PRC is Mandarin or *Putonghua*, also known as the Beijing dialect. As noted, in China most Hui Muslims and Manchus speak Mandarin. The other 53 minorities speak their own languages. There are altogether about 120 minority mother tongues that belong to four different language families: Altaic, Sino-Tibetan, South Asian and Indo-European language families. Many of these languages do not have writing systems and are further divided into mutually unintelligible dialects (Moukala 2003, p. 2; Ramsey 1987, pp. 157–292; Wang and Phillion 2009, p. 1; Zuo 2007, p. 84). Chinese laws prescribe that minority people have the right to use their spoken and written languages in civil proceedings. Autonomous regions such as Inner Mongolia, Xinjiang and Tibet have rules and regulations on the use and development of the spoken and written languages of the ethnic groups under their jurisdiction (Liu and Alatan 1988, p. 150; see also Information Office of the State Council 1999a).

Some non-Han languages are apparently respected by the Chinese government. For example, inscriptions in Mongolian, Tibetan, Uyghur and Zhuang are on China's currency notes (in addition to Chinese). The spoken and written languages of some minorities are used in the fields of administration, education, political life and the like in the PRC. The official documents for the sessions of the CCP National Congress, the NPS, and the Chinese People's Political Consultative Conference are available in Mongolian, Tibetan, Uyghur, Kazak, Korean, Yi and Zhuang. Simultaneous translation in these minority languages is provided during the sessions (Information Office of the State Council 2005; Zuo 2007, p. 87). At the sub-national level, Inner Mongolia uses both Mongolian and Han languages and scripts;

Xinjiang uses Uyghur, Kazak, Mongolian and Han languages and scripts; and Tibet uses both Tibetan and Han languages and scripts.

In the late 1950s, Beijing created 14 writing systems using Latin scripts for the languages spoken by ten minorities: Zhuang, Buyei, Yi, Miao, Hani, Lisu, Naxi, Dong, Wa and Li. Plans for language writing systems of Tu, Jingpo, Bai, Dulong, Qiang and Tujia were proposed in the early 1980s (Zuo 2007, p. 86). It is estimated that in 2003, 22 non-Han groups in China used 28 written languages (Mofcom 2009; see also Liu and Alatan 1988, p. 137). Mongolians, Uyghurs, Tibetans and Koreans have permission to produce textbooks in their own languages, and some subjects are taught in their languages (Liu and Alatan 1988, p. 151; X. Huang 2003, pp. 1–2). A recent development is the use of computer technology to promote minority languages in China. The Mongolian, Tibetan, Uyghur, Korean and Yi languages have coded character sets and national standards for fonts and keyboard. Software in the Mongolian, Tibetan, Uyghur and Korean languages can be run in the Windows system. Applied software in the languages of non-Han peoples has been successfully developed and marketed, and some achievements have been made in research into the optical character recognition of minority languages and machine-aided translation in China (Sautman 2006, p. 246; Zuo 2007, p. 86; see also The China. biz 2011).

Beijing has supported the development of school-based minority language education (Postiglione 1999; Tsung 2009), trained researchers and teachers of minority languages, and published minority language textbooks (Liu and Alatan 1988, p. 151; X. Huang 2003, pp. 1–2; see also Bradley 2005; 2009). For example, some Yao students were recruited from their home villages in the 1950s to be trained as ethnologists, historians or linguists of the Yao language (Litzinger 1998, p. 225). The government has also financed various projects to compile books about the linguistics of minority languages and collected traditional masterpieces written in minority languages. By 2003,

4,787 books in minority languages totalling 50.34 million copies, 205 magazines in minority languages totalling 7.81 million copies, and 88 newspapers in minority languages totalling 131.30 million copies had been published (Liu and Alatan 1988, p. 150; Zuo 2007, p. 86; see also Information Office of the State Council 2005; The China.biz 2011; Zhao and Li 2009). It is claimed that each and every minority nationality group in China could find at least one publishing house producing publications in its language. In addition, 73 radio broadcasting stations offer 441 broadcasting programmes in minority areas, of which 105 programmes are in ethnic minority languages. The TV stations managed by local governments in minority areas use more than ten non-Han languages or dialects in the locally produced broadcasting programmes, including, but not limited to, Dai, Kazak, Kirghiz, Korean, Mongolian, Tibetan, Uyghur and Zhuang languages (State Ethnic Affairs Commission 2006; Zuo 2007, pp. 88–9). In 2002, the UNESCO Office Beijing, the Chinese Academy of Social Sciences and the State Commission of Minorities Affairs joined forces to rescue the endangered minority languages in China (X. Huang 2003, p. 5; Zuo 2007, p. 86). Casas (2011, p. 2) asserts that Beijing has striven to preserve and develop non-Han written and spoken languages in China.

Nevertheless, the outcomes of these efforts by the Chinese government are dubious at best, and it seems that Beijing is more interested in sponsoring linguistic research on minority languages than in promoting the public use of minority languages in the PRC. Mackerras (1988, p. 54) finds that 'A Bai writing system based on Latin letters was devised in the late 1950s, but even now virtually all Bai writers use Chinese.' Zuo (2007, p. 90) argues that 'there is little empirical evidence to indicate their effectiveness in preserving minority languages or cultures.' Others have gone further, asserting that Beijing's minority language policy is 'equality in theory and inequality in practice' (Zhou 2004, p. 71) because it does not promote the public use of minority languages in the PRC. There is no evidence that Beijing's minority language policy has strengthened non-Han languages. On the contrary, Zhou (2000, p. 134) finds that in Inner Mongolia, 'in primary and secondary schools, about 180,000 students took subject courses in Mongolian in 1962, but only 163,286 students took them in Mongolian in 1989, even though the Mongolian population has more than doubled.'

More seriously, 60 out of the 120 minority languages in China are believed to be on the verge of extinction (Moukala 2003, p. 2; Zuo 2007, p. 84; see also Bradley 2005; Zhao and Li 2009). Only 35 of them have more than 50,000 speakers each, 51 languages have between 10,000 and 50,000 speakers each, and 20 minority languages have less than 1,000 speakers each (Ramsey 1987, pp. 157–292; Wang and Phillion 2009, p. 1; X. Huang 2003, pp. 2, 5). Bruhn (2008, p. 11) asserts that in 2002, only 1,200 out of more than 7.1 million She people spoke the She language. He (2003, p. 227) claims that the Manchu language influenced Mandarin's vocabulary and pronunciation, but only about 2,000 out of more than 10 million Manchus could speak it. In many non-Han villages, the number of people who can talk in their mother tongue has been steadily declining. For example, the Gelao people in Guizhou used to speak the Gelao language, but only a handful of elderly Gelao villagers understand it nowadays (Feng 2007).

The decline of the non-Han languages is partly due to market forces. Non-Han groups with moribund languages have often chosen 'not to make an issue of language maintenance', seeing no economic incentive to resist the adoption of Mandarin (Bradley 2005, p. 9), because 'Mastering the Chinese language seems to be the most viable option. Many ethnic parents want their children to speak Mandarin to fare well in the job market' (Lai 2009a, p. 10; Wang and Phillion 2009, p. 1). As a result, 'Chinese has tended to become increasingly dominant in the public sphere, resulting in the decline of ethnic languages. Among several ethnic minorities, especially Tibetans and Uygurs, this has been a matter of enormous concern and resentment' (Mackerras 2011a, p. 118). Increasing contact with Han Chinese is another factor in the endangerment of minority languages: young minority people leave their villages to work in urban Han areas, and rural minority people are influenced by increasing contact with Han tourists (Bruhn 2008, p. 9).

State policies are also partly responsible for the decline of non-Han languages. These languages have faced a real threat from the Chinese education system and its nationally standardized curriculum. Firstly, although they are used in instruction at lower levels of schooling in some minority areas, almost all higher education is in Mandarin (Bruhn 2008, pp. 1, 8–9). Secondly, government bilingual education policy has promoted Mandarin at the expense of non-Han languages. In Xinjiang, for example, the bilingual policy began in the 1990s with the elimination of Uyghur as a medium of instruction at the university level. In 2004, the Xinjiang authorities initiated policy measures man-dating Chinese as the primary medium of instruction at the pre-school level. Uyghurs are acutely aware of the dramatic impact this policy has had on the ability of Uyghur youth to speak their own language and the consequent impact on their cultural and ethnic identity (Amnesty International 2009).

However, Beijing has insisted that ethnic minorities want to learn Mandarin and that it will facilitate this language trend and make sure that there is no going back (Zhu 2012; see also Lai 2009b, p. 8). Zhou (2000, pp. 129–30) summarizes that 'China's language policy as a whole appears to have had more negative impacts' on many minor-ity languages including those of Dai, Jingpo, Lisu, Lahu, Miao, Naxi, Va and Yi. Bruhn (2008, p. 9) argues that 'the future of endangered minority languages in China, therefore, can best be described as grim. Both governmental policies and economic factors favour the adoption of Chinese, and many minority communities seem unwilling to resist.'

RELIGION

Religion is a very strong social institution among many minority nationalities as it is often interwoven with customs and habits, and in many cases interwoven with the national question. Hui, Uyghur, Kazaks, Kyrgizs, Tatars, Uzbeks, Tajiks, Dongxiang, Salas and Baonan embrace Islam; northern Buddhism is prevalent among Tibetans, Mongol, Tu, etc.; Theravāda Buddhism has its followers among Dais, Blang and some of the Wa; part of Yi, Miao and some minority nationalities in Yunnan province are Christians; Naxis have their own religion called 'Dongba'; Russians and some Ewenkis follow the Eastern Orthodox Church; and a variety of religious beliefs and practices are found among Drung, Nu, Wa, Jingpo, Oroqen, etc. (Liu and Alatan 1988, p. 137; Ching 1993, pp. 170–85; Wickeri and Tam 2011); and the Bai people 'place no emphasis on categorizing religions by name. They are quite happy to accept deities from the local pantheon, or from the Buddhist or Daoist. Shamanistic rites coexist with Buddhist' (Mackerras 1988, p. 54).

As noted in chapter 1, non-Han peoples were persecuted for having religious beliefs and practices during the Cultural Revolution. Religious practices have been revived in non-Han areas (and Han areas as well) in the post-1978 era due to the relatively relaxed political environment in China. Since the 1990s, the Chinese government has been suspicious of and suppressed Islam in Xinjiang and Buddhism in Tibet, yet it is estimated that in 2003 there were over 24,300 mosques and 28,000 Muslim clergymen in Xinjiang and over 1,700 venues for Tibetan-Buddhist activities, with 46,000 monks and nuns living in temples in Tibet (Information Office of the State Council 2010a, p. 229). Tibetan Buddhism is 'seen to possess a spirituality that many Han Chinese, especially young urbanites, are now looking for . . . Tibet has come to symbolize the ultimate in spirituality' (Baranovitch 2001, p. 385; Sautman 2006, p. 256).

In theory, Beijing protects the freedom of religion (Article 36 of the PRC Constitution). Indeed, ethnic minorities outside of Xinjiang and Tibetan areas are allowed to practise their religions in registered religious venues managed by state-licensed clergy. Mackerras (2011a, p. 118) observes that 'on the whole religions and faiths of various kinds flourish openly among the ethnic minorities.' In multi-ethnic Yunnan province, non-Han peoples 'enjoy a relatively high level of religious freedom, not in opposition to the party-state but with its full blessing.' Despite its hostile attitude towards Islam in Xinjiang (see chapter 6), the CCP neither promotes nor discourages the religious life of Hui Muslims in both Xinjiang and other parts of China as long as their religious practice does not affect government policy or ideology. Interestingly, some ethnic minorities practise religions unique to their ethnic groups, which Beijing tacitly allows as a 'minority custom' rather than as a religion (US Congressional-Executive Commission on China 2005a, p. 19).

Beijing has helped religious groups build seminaries, trained clergymen of ethnic minorities, subsidized the repair of religious venues in some minority areas, and earmarked a good amount of funding for the maintenance of religious sites in many minority areas, such as the Potala Palace of Tibet and the Kizil Thousand Buddha Grottoes of Xinjiang. The repair of the Potala Palace in Tibet alone cost Beijing 53 million yuan and 1,000 kilograms of gold (Information Office of the State Council 2005; State Ethnic Affairs Commission 2006; The China.biz 2011; Zuo 2007, p. 87).

However, according to the US Congressional-Executive Commission on China (2005b, pp. 4–5), Beijing requires places of religious activity to be registered with the religious bureau of the local government and managed by 'patriotic religious groups', whose members must be patriotic and law-abiding and safeguard the state ethnic policy. Any attempt to edit, publish or distribute religious materials, including video and audio recording, is not allowed without prior government approval.

The activities of self-proclaimed preachers are strictly prohibited. No foreign donations for proselytizing activities may be accepted by any party. Major donations from foreign organizations or individuals cannot be accepted without central government approval. Foreigners may not, without government approval, 'broadcast' audio- or video-tapes of sermons by foreign religious persons or distribute religious tracts in China.

Some people and organizations in the West maintain that Beijing has restricted and controlled religious practice and institutions in Tibet and Xinjiang (US Congressional-Executive Commission on China 2005a, p. 19; Human Rights in China 2007, pp. 2, 29–30; Mackerras 2011a, pp. 118–19; Sautman 2012, p. 17). For example, Beijing sets a quota and an application system for monks and nuns in Tibet. Applicants who wish to become a monk or nun must be certified by the local government to be patriotic (i.e., politically correct) and law-abiding. CCP members are not allowed to practise Buddhism in Tibet (Mackerras 2005b, p. 16). Rudelson and Jankowiak (2004) write that the CCP maintains tight control over mosques and religious clergy in Xinjiang, intervening in the appointment of local imams, stationing police within and outside mosques, and monitoring all religious activities. Government employees including teachers, police officers, state workers and civil servants risk losing their jobs if they engage in religious activity. Children under the age of 18 are not allowed to receive any sort of Islamic education. Local governments are required to teach 'scientific thinking', a catchphrase for atheism, in the public school system and must prevent religion from 'infiltrating' the school system (US Congressional-Executive Commission on China 2005a, p. 19). Despite government suppression, Mackerras (2011a, p. 119) doubts 'a more general death of religious faith and practice among the ethnic minorities'. Nor does he 'foresee the day when Buddhism is no longer a social force among the Tibetans or Islam among the Uyghurs, Hui or a range of other ethnic groups in China'.

DISCUSSION

As noted, Beijing has made some efforts to promote minority cultures. Scholars have claimed that the Han attitude towards non-Han cultures had mixed derogation, even detestation and fear, with desire and fascination before 1949 (Baranovitch 2001, p. 374; Khan 1996, pp. 127–8). Beijing has since enhanced cultural infrastructure construction to preserve the cultural heritage of ethnic minorities such as arts and folklores, and has enacted laws to safeguard the rights of national minorities to use their native languages and to organize cultural activities for ethnic minorities (State Ethnic Affairs Commission 2006; Sautman 2006, p. 246). Mackerras (2011a, p. 112) claims that, on the whole, 'China has managed this cultural diversity quite well'. Dondrub Wangben, Vice Minister of the PRC State Ethnic Affairs Commission, said in 2007 that Chinese society had since 1978 attached unprecedented importance to the preservation of ethnic minority culture (Feng 2007; X. Huang 2003, pp. 5–6). Zhu Weiqun, the executive deputy minister of the State Ethnic Commission, claimed (2011, p. 15) that the PRC had made great efforts to preserve and promote Tibetan culture in recent years.

Nevertheless, this chapter shows that Beijing's minority culture policy is apparently less than satisfactory. For example, research on minority linguistics has enjoyed admirable growth in China, and there has been professionalization of some minority performing arts since 1949. However, Beijing supports these aspects of minority cultures because it has turned them into part of the propaganda machine with which it has bolstered an image of China as a tolerant and 'harmonious', multicultural society (Baranovitch 2001, pp. 363–4, 374–5; Williams 2008, p. 1). Baranovitch (2001, p. 364) observes that 'orthodox minority songs have always aimed primarily at fostering national unity and legitimizing state and party control and ideology.' Beijing does not support other aspects of minority cultures such as grass-roots performing arts because they cannot serve its political agendas. Nor does it tolerate outlets for ethnic identity expression that may challenge its policy towards minority affairs. The general view has been that minority representation in the nationally distributed media is monopolized by the Chinese state and the Han majority, and that ethnic minorities themselves are passive, powerless and voiceless (Baranovitch 2001, p. 361; Gladney 1995, p. 170; Zhang 1997). Han cultural nationalists do not respect Tibetan or Mongolian cultures and see minority self-rule as returning to either an undesirable federal system or despotism (He 2004, pp. 119–20).

In addition, Beijing has held negative attitudes towards some traditional life patterns and ways of thinking among ethnic minorities that it deems 'backward' or 'uncivilized' (Harrell 1995a), has restrained the freedom of religion among Tibetans and Uyghurs, and has not done enough to reduce the negative impact of market reforms on minority languages and cultures. Its education policy has inadvertently stifled some minority languages and undermined the ethnic identities of the speakers of these endangered languages, and from time to time Beijing restricts the use of some minority languages if they are used to enhance ethnic identity and collective action. Johnson and Chhetri (2002, p. 150) argue that 'Tibetan language instruction beyond the elementary level is unlikely because the Chinese government recognizes that Tibetan language is linked with Tibetan nationalism and is therefore a threat to national unity.'

In comparative perspective, is Beijing more successful in the reduction of ethnic inequality than in the promotion of minority cultures? This question cannot be satisfactorily answered because the outcomes of these two programmes cannot be compared. Nevertheless, it is clear that Beijing has been very selective in promoting certain elements of minority cultures. An element of minority culture is officially promoted if it serves the political agendas of the PRC, and vice versa. In comparison, there is no such prerequisite in Beijing's campaign to narrow Han–minority disparities. In addition, Beijing has promulgated many laws and policies for the reduction of ethnic inequality and preservation of minority cultures. However, it seems to be more likely to implement policies and laws to reduce ethnic inequality than to preserve minority cultures. Moreover, when any ethnic unrest takes place, Beijing's first response has always been a call for more government efforts to reduce Han–minority disparities in education, employment and income, and the Chinese government has never attempted to reduce ethnic tensions through a better cultural policy. These contrasts are understandable given Beijing's *ronghe* policy. As noted in chapter 1, *ronghe* (i.e., fusion or amalgamation) refers to the supposedly historical process of cultural exchange between Han Chinese and non-Han groups, which will cause the eventual decline and disappearance of non-Han languages, cultures and knowledge (Wang and Phillion 2009, p. 2). As noted in chapter 2, Beijing has maintained that reduction of ethnic inequality is central to solving the nationality issue in China, which explains why Beijing is evidently more willing to address ethnic inequality than to promote minority cultures. Promotion of minority cultures defers acculturation and assimilation. Indeed, it may be difficult for readers to image how the promotion of *ronghe* ideology can coexist with the preservation of minority cultures.

Despite Beijing's *ronghe* ideology, many scholars are confident that assimilation is not on the immediate horizon anywhere (Mackerras 1992, p. 31). It is claimed that 'To a large degree, many minority groups can still be identified clearly and have not been subject to any major assimilation with the Han' (Wong 2000, p. 54). Mackerras (2011a, p. 115) points out the rise of consciousness among some minorities since the 1980s: 'Scholarly works have noted this rise of identity feelings among such peoples as the Hui (Gladney 1991), and the Zhuang and Yao of the south-western region of Guangxi and elsewhere (Kaup 2000, Litzinger 2000). Observers have given more attention to ethnic minorities like the Tibetans and Uygurs, but that does not mean they are the only ones to have experienced a growing ethnic identity.' This is partly because minority cultures are resilient and resist assimilative pressures from Beijing (Bulag 2002, p. 202; Zhou 2000, p. 146; see also Nelson 2005). Equally important, non-Han intellectuals have actively participated in discourse to reclaim minority cultures, 'to wrestle it back from its previous symbolic impoverishment as nothing more than a signifier of "backwardness" (luohou) and "feudal superstition" (fengjian mixin)' (Litzinger 1998, p. 226). In some minority areas such as Tibet and Xinjiang there have been religious revivals and rising ethnic consciousness, accompanied by renewed interest among minority people in their languages and arts (Baranovitch 2007; Smith Finley 2007a; Zang 2013), which will be discussed in some detail in chapter 6.

RECOMMENDED READING

Colin Mackerras, *China's Minority Cultures* (New York: St. Martin's Press, 1995).

Colin Mackerras (ed.), *Ethnic Minorities in Modern China*, Vol. III (London: Routledge, 2011).

Gerard A. Postiglione, *China's National Minority Education: Culture, Schooling, and Development* (London: Routledge, 1999).

4 | Regional Autonomy ————————————

Chapters 2 and 3 examined ethnic inequality and the preservation of minority cultures in China, respectively. This chapter focuses on the politics of autonomy arrangements for minority nationalities in China. It first outlines how the CCP's policy on minority autonomy has evolved historically, and then asks what minority autonomy means in the PRC today, i.e., how real is regional autonomy in China? Next, this chapter shows how Beijing gives different amounts of power to the government of an autonomous region in its handling of regional economic development, education, language, religion, legislation and government, and discusses possible reasons why Beijing should make this differential arrangement. Finally, this chapter examines how Han migration into minority regions has affected regional autonomy.

HISTORICAL CONTEXT

Autonomy arrangements for minority nationalities are seen globally as a way of helping them realize their right of self-determination, which is 'a right of cultural groupings to the political institutions necessary to allow them to exist and develop according to their distinctive characteristics' (Anaya 1995, p. 326; Claude and Weston 1992, pp. 184–5; Smith 2004, p. 1). Paragraph 35 of the 1990 Copenhagen Document (CSCE Conference on the Human Dimension 1990) states:

> The participating States will respect the right of persons belonging to national minorities to effective participation in public affairs, including

participation in the affairs relating to the protection and promotion of the identity of such minorities. The participating States note the efforts undertaken to protect and create conditions for the promotion of the ethnic, cultural, linguistic and religious identity of certain national minorities by establishing, as one of the possible means to achieve these aims, appropriate local or autonomous administrations corresponding to the specific historical and territorial circumstances of such minorities and in accordance with the policies of the State concerned.

(See also Henrard 2000, pp. 275–6.)

In theory, Beijing has upheld that regional autonomy for ethnic minorities 'enables them to bring into full play their regional advantages and promote exchanges and cooperation between minority areas and other areas, and consequently quickens the pace of modernization both in the minority areas and the country as a whole and helps achieve common development of all regions and prosperity for all ethnic groups' (Information Office of the State Council 2005). Shan and Chen (2009, p. 17) claim that the 'pillar of China's current ethnic policies is regional autonomy for ethnic minorities'. Indeed, Mr Jiang Zemin, the PRC president from 1993 to 2003, proclaimed that regional ethnic autonomy was one of the three fundamental political institutions of the Chinese state (Lai 2009a, p. 12). How has the PRC's policy on national autonomy evolved historically?

In pre-modern times, autonomy was practised as a means for the Chinese state to colonize and assimilate a conquered frontier tribal state, or to build an alliance with a frontier state against other 'barbarian' states. The Chinese imperial state exercised control over non-Han peoples in its border regions through hereditary native chieftaincies (*tusi*) in the Yuan, Ming and Qing dynasties for some 700 years (Took 2005). When a Chinese empire was powerful, it might appoint local rulers of its choice. Most of the time, a Chinese emperor offered a seal of office and title(s) to a local chieftain, who regarded these as confirmation of his legitimacy and power over his own people. The chieftain enjoyed a number of autonomous powers, such as the right to tax and the right to exercise custom laws. In return, he was responsible for the taking of censuses, peace-keeping, etc., which were interpreted by the Chinese state as evidence of its sovereignty over the area. The title would be inherited by his son after the confirmation of central authority. Generally speaking, the Chinese state did not interfere with local affairs unless 'developments directly threatened imperial control of the area' (He 2004, pp. 111–12; Smith 2004, p. 2; Thierry 1989).

An example was Tibet, which enjoyed a great degree of autonomy during the Yuan dynasty (1271–1386), independence during the Ming dynasty (1368–1644), substantial autonomy during the Qing dynasty (1644–1911), and de facto independence during the Republic of China (1911–1949). In Xinjiang, the Qing government relied on a *Beg* (a generic term for chiefs of Turkic groups in various oases appointed by the central government) system to govern the region (see chapter 6). Similarly, Mongol princes were granted some autonomy during the Qing dynasty and maintained certain privileges in local governance after the demise of the Qing dynasty in 1911 (Howland 2011, pp. 11–12). Other examples include the hereditary headmanship of various forms that 'was prevalent among minority peoples in Sichuan, Yunnan, Guizhou, Guangxi and Qinghai provinces', which existed before the CCP came to power in 1949 (Liu and Alatan 1988, p. 139; see also Lai 2010, pp. 64–5).

The CCP was apparently enlightened by the native chieftaincy system when it chose the form of regional autonomy for non-Han groups in non-Han regions, and drew heuristics from Dr Sun Yat-sen's idea about self-determination when it developed the substance of regional autonomy after 1949. Dr Sun and his comrades interpreted self-determination as both China's right to freedom from foreign interference and the right to equality among ethnic groups in China, but not as a right of any of China's nationalities to independence (Smith 2004, p. 7). Like Dr Sun, Chiang Kai-shek and his Nationalist Party embraced the notion of the Chinese people and supported the assimilation of 'all the regional peoples and Sino-Linguistic speech communities' into one national group in China (Barabantseva 2008, pp. 569–70; Gladney 1996, pp. 83–95). 'Chiang, like Sun before him, interpreted self-determination as equal access of all nationalities in China to the benefits of Chinese civilization.' In 1945 Chiang promised Tibet and other minority groups self-determination ranging from 'a very high degree of autonomy' to independence, probably due to the anti-colonialist spirit of the time (Smith 2004, p. 8). He did not deliver his promise though.

The CCP considered itself the heir to Sun Yat-sen's nationalist doctrines (Smith 2004, p. 8). Yet in its early years it followed Lenin's theory of the right of self-determination for ethnic minorities. This was partly because it was established with the help of, and directed by, the Communist International (i.e., *Comintern*) and the USSR, where the right of self-determination of ethnic minorities was written into its constitution (Lenin 1972; see also Howland 2011, pp. 2, 8–9; Lai 2010, p. 65; Smith 2004, p. 2; Zhou 2009, pp. 332–3). In its Second National Congress held in 1922, the CCP proposed that ethnic minorities should enjoy the right of self-determination and the right of creating independent national republics, and that a federal state would be founded on the basis of the autonomy being practised in Mongolia, Tibet and Huijiang (Zhu and Yu 2000, p. 48; Li 2009).

When the Chinese Soviet Republic (1931) proclaimed its constitution, it stipulated in Article 14 of the Constitution that

> The Soviet government of China recognizes the right of self-determination of the national minorities in China, their right to complete separation from China, and to the formation of an independent state for each national minority. All Mongolians, Tibetans, Miao, Yao, and others

: they may
either join the Union of Chinese Soviets or secede from it and form
their own state. The Soviet régime will do its utmost to assist the
national minorities in liberating themselves from the yoke of imperial-
ists, the KMT militarists, *t'u-ssu* [tribal headmen], the princes, lamas,
and others, and in achieving complete freedom and autonomy. The
Soviet régime must encourage the development of the national cultures
and of the respective national languages of these peoples.

(See also He 2004, p. 116; Howland 2011, p. 9; Hyer 2009, pp. 263–4;
Liu and Alatan 1988, pp. 141–2; Moneyhon 2002, pp. 129–30;
Sautman 1999, p. 287; Zhou 2009, pp. 332–3.) The CCP proposed
to turn Mongolia, Tibet and Huijiang into democratic autonomous
states, and then unify them with China proper to form a Federal
Republic of China (Liu and Alatan 1988, p. 142; Moneyhon 2002,
p. 129; Smith 2004, p. 8).

According to Gladney (1996), this official position was reaffirmed
when the CCP and its Red Army walked through the areas inhabited
by non-Han groups such as Tibetans and Muslims during the Long
March of 1935. The reaffirmation was motivated partly by the fact that
the CCP could not afford to fight Chiang Kai-shek's army and the
non-Han groups at the same time, and partly by better understanding
of the strong ethnic identity of Hui Muslims and other non-Han
groups which the CCP encountered during the Long March. The Red
Army helped the Tibetan and Yi people establish their own governments in some areas of their residences. After the CCP moved its
headquarters to Yanan in Northwest China, populated by Muslims
and other non-Han groups, it promised equal status to all non-Han
peoples and expressed its support for the right to national self-determination, offering non-Han groups not only privileges but also the
right to secede from China after the CCP came to power. The CCP
proclaimed the *Declaration of the Chinese Soviet Republic to the*

Mongolian Nationality (Government of the Chinese Soviet Republic 1935) in December 1935 and the *Declaration of the Chinese Soviet Republic to the Hui Nationality* (Government of the Chinese Soviet Republic 1936) in May 1936 (Gladney 1996, pp. 87–9; Li 2009). A Hui autonomous government in Tongxin, Ningxia was established in October 1936 and a Mongolian autonomous committee of Chenchuan in the south of Yikezhaomen was also established (Zhu and Yu 2000, p. 48; see also Gladney 1996, p. 87; Liu and Alatan 1988, p. 143). Item 17 of the 1941 Administrative Guidance of the Shanganning Border Region reiterated the CCP's commitment to Mongolian and Hui autonomous regions (CCP Politburo 1941).

Like other CCP leaders, Mao Zedong supported the right of self-determination by non-Han peoples in the 1920s and early 1930s. However, he withdrew his support after 1937, sensing that the right had been used by Japan to promote the independence of Mongolia. Mao and his comrades decided that the right to self-determination could be exercised only in the case of oppressed nationality groups casting off the rule of imperialism and colonialism. Like Sun Yat-sen and Chiang Kai-shek, Mao regarded the Chinese people as the 'whole country' comprising 'all nationalities' in China. Tibetans, Mongolians, Uyghurs and other minorities were among the broad masses of the Chinese people (He 2004, pp. 115–16; Howland 2011, pp. 7–8; Zhou 2009, pp. 333–4; Zhu and Yu 2000, p. 49). Mao asserted that all that non-Han peoples wanted was equal treatment within the Chinese state (Smith 2004, p. 8). In 1940, Mao offered non-Han groups limited regional autonomy rather than self-determination. He argued that self-determination (and secession) was not practicable since ethnic groups in China were interdependent, and the exercise of regional autonomy should facilitate 'national unity' and had nothing to do with separatism (Barabantseva 2008, pp. 574; He 2004, p. 116; Gladney 1996, p. 88; Howland 2011, pp. 9, 14; Sautman 1999, pp. 287–8). Mao claimed that Tibetans and Mongolians would not ask for self-determination because of their inclusion within the country of China (Howland 2011, p. 11).

Consistent with Mao's view on the ethnic unity of the Chinese nation, the CCP departed from the idea of self-determination and federalism in a directive issued by the Secretariat of the CCP Central Committee in 1945. According to the CCP, while non-Han groups would have the right to administer their internal affairs, they would voluntarily choose to unite with China 'because they would realize that their cultural and economic interest lay in union with the more advanced state. The fate of China's minority nationalities was said to be historically determined – to be assimilated within the Chinese multinational state' (Smith 2004, p. 9; see also Zhu and Yu 2000, p. 49).

In 1949, the CCP made it clear that it would not talk any further about the right to self-determination for non-Han peoples, and regarded its ascent to political power in China as the beginning of 'the lengthy process of assimilation via the dialectical route of territorial autonomy for all compact national groups' (Gladney 1996, pp. 89–90; Moneyhon 2002, pp. 130–1). Thus, although the CCP learned almost everything from the Soviet Union at that time, it did not copy the Soviet style of federalism, which granted 'republic' status to larger national groups in the USSR (Hyer 2006, p. 77; Leibold 2010, p. 5). It adopted a regional autonomy system for ethnic minorities instead. The legitimacy of this system was initially based on various pacts including the 'seventeen-point agreement' and directives the CCP signed with non-Han collaborators in minority areas such as Tibet and Xinjiang around 1949. When the CCP's army approached these areas, the major non-Han people of the minority regions joined the PRC in 1949 *as groups* – with their elites acting as their political representatives in the new PRC state system (Hao 2009).

Since 1949, regional autonomy has been portrayed as an important means of helping ethnic minorities develop their economies and cultures. According to the CCP, the promotion of regional autonomy is not the end itself; rather, its purpose is to bring about eventual *ronghe*:

assimilation is impossible until socioeconomic and cultural gaps between Han Chinese and ethnic minorities disappear. Regional autonomy would help close these gaps and lead to the disappearance of non-Han languages, cultures and knowledge because Han society represents higher stages of human development and Han Chinese (i.e., the big brother) have the responsibility and obligation to bring non-Han peoples (i.e., younger brothers) into line with progress and civilization (Chung 2006, p. 86; Gladney 1996, pp. 72–3; Mackerras 1984, p. 190; Sautman 1999, pp. 284, 291–2).

Scholars have suggested other reasons for the CCP to establish autonomous regions after 1949. One possible reason was the need for the CCP to deliver its promise made before it came to power. In relation to the establishment of the Inner Mongolian Autonomous Region, it is suggested that it 'was a product of the Chinese Communists need for Mongol support in the Civil War' (Bulag 2004, p. 90; Lundberg and Zhou 2009, p. 277). In relation to the establishment of the Guangxi Zhuang Autonomous Region, it is claimed that it was part of the efforts by the CCP to suppress local Han opposition to central authorities and break up the strong regional identity of the inhabitants of Guangdong and Guangxi provinces (Moseley 1973, p. 85; also Lary 1996). Lundberg and Zhou (2009, p. 295) argue that in addition to geopolitical and historical issues, state security and concerns for territorial integrity significantly motivated the implementation of regional autonomy. Howland (2011, p. 16) regards regional autonomy as a policy of 'divide and conquer' – the creation of a mosaic of autonomous zones in order to prevent any collective action against the PRC.

THE DEVELOPMENT OF REGIONAL AUTONOMY SINCE 1949

The CCP included regional autonomy in the Common Program, issued on 29 September 1949, as the legal framework for the establishment of the PRC on 1 October 1949. Article 51 of the Common

Program (http://www.fordham.edu/halsall/mod/1949-ccp-program .html) stipulates that regional autonomy must be exercised in areas where ethnic minorities are concentrated, and various kinds of autonomous organizations for the different nationalities must be set up according to the size of the respective peoples and regions. In places where different nationalities live together and in the autonomous areas of the national minorities, the different nationalities shall each have an appropriate number of representatives in the local organs of state power. Article 53 stipulates that all ethnic minorities shall have the freedom to develop their spoken and written languages and preserve or reform their traditions, customs and religious beliefs (also Lai 2010, p. 66; Zhu and Yu 2000, p. 50). In 1952, the PRC State Council issued the Program for the Implementation of Regional Ethnic Autonomy of the People's Republic of China, which included clear provisions on the establishment of ethnic autonomous areas and the composition of organs of self-government, as well as the right of self-government for such organs (Howland 2011, p. 15; Lai 2010, pp. 66–7; Smith 2004, p. 10; Zhou 2009, p. 335; Lundberg and Zhou 2009, 303–4; see also Information Office of the State Council 2005).

In the 1950s and 1960s, top Chinese leaders emphasized that they were creating not a federation but a people's republic, and that minority nationalities could exercise a right not to self-determination but to self-government. The right to self-determination could only be exercised by the majority and minority nationalities together against foreign imperialism but not by non-Han groups against Han Chinese (Howland 2011, p. 13; Zhou 2009, p. 331; Zhu and Yu 2000, pp. 50–1). Similar provisions were reiterated in the first PRC Constitution (1954) and the following three Constitutions (1975, 1978 and 1982). They were developed and expressed in detail in the Law on Regional Autonomy for Minority Nationalities of the PRC, adopted on 31 May 1984 (http://www.novexcn.com/regional_nation _autonomy.html). The Standing Committee of the National People's

Congress made further revisions to the Law on Regional Ethnic Autonomy in 2001, and it was reissued on 28 February 2003 (US Congressional-Executive Commission on China 2005a, p. 4; Moneyhon 2002, pp. 135–6; Sautman 1999, p. 288; Smith 2004, pp. 10–11, 13–14).

The PRC system of regional autonomy has included autonomous regions, prefectures, counties and ethnic townships. The first provincial-level autonomous region for ethnic minorities in China, the Inner Mongolia Autonomous Region, was established in 1947 (Lai 2010, p. 65). The Xinjiang Uyghur Autonomous Region was established in 1955, the Guangxi Zhuang Autonomous Region in 1958, the Ningxia Hui Autonomous Region in 1958, and the Tibet Autonomous Region in 1965. The Xinjiang Uyghur Autonomous Region makes up more than one-sixth of China's territory (1,660,001 square kilometres); the Tibet Autonomous Region has a total area of 1,228,400 square kilometres; the Inner Mongolia Autonomous Region occupies a total area of 1,183,000 square kilometres; the Guangxi Zhuang Autonomous Region covers a total area of 236,700 square kilometres; and the Ningxia Hui Autonomous Region is the smallest autonomous region in China with an area of 66,000 square kilometres (Briney n.d.).

In addition to the autonomous regions, the CCP created an autonomous prefecture or an autonomous county if a significant number of members of an ethnic minority group resided in an area. For example, besides the Inner Mongolian Autonomous Region, Mongol autonomous prefectures and autonomous counties were founded in Qinghai, Xinjiang, Gansu, Heilongjiang and Jilin provinces. There are the Ningxia Hui Autonomous Region, the Linxia Hui Autonomous Prefecture in Gansu province, and the Mengcun Hui Autonomous County in Hebei province. For the Tujia people, there are the Xiangxi Tujia and Miao Autonomous Prefecture in Hunan province, the Enshi Tujia and Miao Autonomous Prefecture, the Changyang Tujia Autonomous County, and the Wufeng Tujia Autonomous County in

Hubei province, and the Yanhe Tujia Autonomous County and Yinjiang Tujia and Miao Autonomous County in Guizhou province. There are also four Tujia autonomous counties and a Tujia autonomous district in Chongqing. Apart from the Tibetan Autonomous Region, Tibetan autonomous prefectures are found in Qinghai, Gansu and Sichuan provinces. It is important to note that about 97 per cent of the Qinghai province is composed of Tibetan autonomous prefectures. It was part of Gansu until 1928 when it became a province. The Chinese government has not explained why it has maintained Qinghai as a province rather than as an autonomous region.

Hui Muslims, Mongolians, Tibetans and Tujias have sub-provincial autonomous units partly because they each have a large population. Some small ethnic minority groups also have their own autonomous prefectures or counties (Howland 2011, pp. 15–16; Harrell 2001, pp. 37–47; Schein 2000, pp. 70–88; Zhou 2009, pp. 337–8). Examples include Chuxiong Yi Autonomous Prefecture in Yunnan, Kizilsu Kirghiz Autonomous Prefecture in Xinjiang, Sunan Yugur Autonomous County in Gansu, and Huanjiang Maonan Autonomous County in Guangxi. There has been an increase in the number of sub-provincial autonomous units, perhaps due to minority population growth. In 1965, there were 29 autonomous prefectures and 64 autonomous counties/leagues with 35 of the 55 ethnic minorities having their own autonomous areas (Lai 2009a, pp. 6–7; 2009b, p. 6). In 2005, there were 30 autonomous prefectures, 117 autonomous counties and three autonomous banners had been set up. Among the 55 ethnic minorities, 44 have autonomous areas containing 75 per cent of the total ethnic minority population and accounting for 64 per cent of China's total land area (Information Office of the State Council 2005; see also Chang 2003, p. 21; Lai 2010, pp. 67–9; Leibold 2010, p. 6; Lundberg and Zhou 2009, pp. 295, 299–300; Sautman 1999, p. 296).

There is great variation in ethnic population composition among autonomous units. An autonomous unit can be heavily populated by one ethnic minority group, as in the Tibet Autonomous Region. Or it can be dominated by two ethnic minority groups, as in the Taxkorgan Tajik Autonomous Prefecture in Xinjiang, where a Tajik group (the majority group) coexisted with a Kirghiz group (a minority group). Still, an autonomous unit can consist of several minority groups such as the Longsheng Gezu Autonomous County in Guangxi, which is the hub for ten ethnic minority groups including Zhuang, Yao, Miao and Dong. This kind of autonomous area is also called a joint autonomous area. Among the 155 autonomous areas in 2008, 43 are joint autonomous areas. The status of national autonomy is bestowed by the central government. How does it decide that a county or a prefecture is 'ethnic' enough to be converted into an autonomous unit? Can a county or a prefecture where several small minority groups co-reside with a Han majority become an autonomous unit if each of the small minority group consists of less than 5 per cent of the total population? In theory, Beijing practises regional autonomy in an area where 20 per cent or more of the population belong to ethnic minorities (Lai 2009a, p. 2; Zhou 2009, p. 340), regardless of whether there is one ethnic minority group or several ethnic minority groups in the area.

THE POWER OF AUTONOMOUS REGIONS

It is understood internationally that autonomy refers to a system in which a sub-state entity, often an ethnic minority group, has de facto control over its own cultural, economic and even domestic political affairs in the area in which it resides in recognition of some ethnic, national or historical distinctions (Smith 2004, p. 1). In theory, in the PRC, the local government in an autonomous area is given powers by the central government to govern a wide spectrum of affairs including legislation, government, trade and economic growth, education, cultural development, etc., in the areas under its jurisdiction (Howland 2011, p. 16; Lai 2009b, p. 7). Below is an outline of the

PRC autonomous system, to be followed by an assessment so that readers can decide whether it is different from the international norms and understandings of national autonomy.

Legislation and Government

Article 8 of the PRC Law of Regional National Autonomy stipulates that higher government authorities shall guarantee the exercise of the power of autonomy by the local governments of national autonomous areas, and shall help them speed up their socialist construction. The government of an autonomous region handles the internal affairs of the minority nationalities and exercises the rights of self-government in accordance with Chinese law. Legislatively, the local government and people's congress of the autonomous region have in theory the right to adopt special policies and flexible measures on financial, economic, cultural and educational affairs according to local political, economic and cultural characteristics. They can apply for permission to make alterations to or desist from implementing resolutions, decisions, orders and instructions made by higher-level state authorities if these policies are not in accordance with the situation in the autonomous region. Thus, the governments of the national autonomous regions such as Xinjiang and Guangxi presumably can make a decision on tax exemptions or reductions. However, a decision by an autonomous prefecture or county on tax exemption or reduction must be reported to its provincial or autonomous regional government for approval (Ghai and Woodman 2009, pp. 31–6; Lundberg and Zhou 2009, pp. 313–16).

Article 17 of the PRC Law of Regional National Autonomy stipulates that the chairman of an autonomous region, the prefect of an autonomous prefecture, or the head of an autonomous county must be a citizen of the minority nationality exercising regional autonomy in the area concerned. Han Chinese are legally not eligible for these posts. Other posts in the government of an autonomous region, an autonomous prefecture or an autonomous county should, whenever possible, be assumed by people from the minority nationality exercising regional autonomy and from other minority nationalities in the area concerned (Information Office of the State Council 2010a; Xinhua 2011b). Article 18 of the PRC Law of Regional National Autonomy stipulates that the officials working for the government of a national autonomous area should, whenever possible, be chosen from among citizens of the minority nationality exercising regional autonomy and of other minority nationalities in the area. It has been stated that 'the proportion of nationality cadres in the total number of cadres [should] match the ratio of the population of minority nationalities to the total population of the autonomous locality' (Sautman 1997, p. 4; see also US Congressional-Executive Commission on China 2005a). In theory, Beijing has called on autonomous regions to employ a sizable number of minority officials. Understandably, minority cares are often under-represented in Han regions but over-represented in autonomous regions (Sautman 1997, pp. 17–24).

Article 22 of the PRC Law of Regional National Autonomy stipulates that the government of an autonomous region must take various measures to train large numbers of officials at different levels and various kinds of specialized personnel, including scientists, technicians and managerial executives, as well as skilled workers from among the local nationalities, and pay attention to the training of cadres at various levels and of specialized and technical personnel of various kinds from among the women of minority nationalities.

Economic Development and Environmental Protection

Beijing stipulates that under the guidance of state plans, the government of a national autonomous area must steadily increase labour productivity and raise the living standards of minority people under its jurisdiction (Information Office of the State Council 2005). On the principle of not contravening the Constitution and the laws, Beijing allows the local government of the national autonomous area to adopt special policies and flexible measures in the light of local conditions to speed up the economic and cultural development of the area. For example, local governments in autonomous areas in Guanxi negotiated their tax and profit contracts with the administrative authorities immediately above them (Kaup 2002, p. 881; Shan and Chen 2009, p. 17).

In addition, under the guidance of state planning, the government of the autonomous area can independently arrange local capital construction projects and grant preferential treatments including tax reduction and exemption to local projects. It is given power to manage local enterprises and institutions, engage in foreign trade in accordance with the central provisions, and open ports for direct foreign trade after obtaining approval from the State Council. In short, autonomous areas enjoy state preferential policy treatment in foreign trade and have the right to manage local financial matters. All financial revenues belonging to ethnic autonomous areas under the state financial system can be used for local affairs without any restrictions (Information Office of the State Council 2005).

Articles 27 and 28 of the PRC Law of Regional National Autonomy prohibit any 'damage' to grasslands, whether by individuals or collectives, and call on the autonomous authorities to give 'priority to the rational exploitation and utilization of the natural resources that the local authorities are entitled to develop' (US Congressional-Executive Commission on China 2005b, p. 8; Law of the People's Republic of China on Regional National Autonomy 1984). From time to time, Beijing has issued directives or red-head documents requiring the local governments of autonomous areas to prevent and deal with pollution and other public hazards, uphold firmly the right to use pastures and forests, manage and protect local natural resources carefully, and determine the priority in developing and using the natural resources that are available to them (Information Office of the State Council 2005).

Despite these legal and administrative provisions, environmental deg-radation has occurred in many autonomous regions including Inner Mongolia and Xinjiang (US Congressional-Executive Commission on China 2005a, p. 22), as noted in chapter 2.

Education, Language and Religion

The government of an autonomous area can in theory determine the educational plan, the establishment of schools, choices of school systems, curricula, languages used for teaching and methods of enrol-ment. Public ethnic primary and middle schools that provide boarding and allowances to minority students are set up in some pastureland and mountainous regions. According to the Chinese government, schools and other educational institutions whose students are pre-dominantly from ethnic minority families should, if possible, use text-books printed in their own languages, and lessons should be taught in those languages. Article 6 of the PRC Law of Regional National Autonomy stipulates that the local government of a national autono-mous area shall inherit and carry forward the fine traditions of national cultures and steadily raise socialist consciousness and scientific and cultural levels of minority people. A certain degree of flexibility is given in the application of educational and cultural policies as appropriate (Information Office of the State Council 2005; Sautman 1999, p. 293). Finally, religious freedom for all ethnic groups is guaranteed. No state agency, social group or individual can force any one to adopt a belief or disavow a religious belief, or discriminate between citizens who are religious and those who are not.

EVALUATIONS OF REGIONAL AUTONOMY IN CHINA

Despite the impressive powers given by the PRC central authorities to local governments of the autonomous areas, opinions about regional autonomy in China vary greatly. Barabantseva (2008, p. 586) claims that the parameters of regional autonomy give ethnic minorities the right to some political control over their own areas and make provisions for equal treatment of ethnic groups, and promote policies to develop various aspects of ethnic minorities and their regions. Zhou (2009, pp. 330–1) agrees that regional autonomy 'has a group rights orientation', and 'is an institutional arrangement for safeguarding the specific rights of certain minority nationalities living concentrated in their inhabited areas'. Other scholars assert that, despite deficiencies, minority regions are accorded 'true autonomy' with regard to some sensitive policies on areas such as family planning and some 'soft issues' such as economic development, education, culture, language, the environment, health care, etc. (Ghai and Woodman 2009, pp. 43–4; Mackerras 2011a, p. 115; Phan 1996, p. 99).

In contrast, some scholars have regarded the regional autonomy system as deficient or as symbolic rather than representing real autonomy rules and mechanisms (Lundberg and Zhou 2009, p. 319; Moneyhon 2002, pp. 10–11; Sautman 2000, p. 73). Some have dismissed the autonomous system as 'a sham' or 'paper autonomy' (Becquelin 1997, p. 19; US Congressional-Executive Commission on China 2005b, pp. 8–9; Lundberg and Zhou 2009, p. 275; Phan 1996, pp. 84–5; Sautman 1999, p. 293; Shan and Chen 2009, p. 17). Human Rights in China (2007, pp. 2, 7) contends that the Chinese government grants different degrees of autonomy to minority regions according to subject matter, e.g., higher degrees of autonomy for economic growth than for security matters, and that 'the very autonomy system that should empower self-governance in autonomous regions works as a mechanism for minority exclusion and state control.'

Others have argued that the rights enumerated in the PRC Regional Autonomy Law are 'non-actionable': the enforcement of the law 'rests entirely on the conscience and awareness of the departments concerned. If a state organ fails to implement such a law, there is no legal basis to hold such an organ responsible and hence no remedy can be sought ... Past experience has shown that the Regional Autonomy Law has rarely been cited to decide court cases.' And the law does not specify legal consequences if a right is abridged, nor does it indicate where redress may be pursued (US Congressional-Executive Commission on China 2005b, pp. 12, 16; Lundberg and Zhou 2009, pp. 275–6; Mackerras 1994, pp. 153–66, 264–5; Smith 2004, pp. 14–15). It is alleged that few if any government agencies have monitored the implementation of the law of regional autonomy. If deficiencies are found and reported to a local People's Congress, for example, they are rarely addressed. It is asserted that 'the Regional Autonomy Law, as amended in 2001, does little to protect minority rights' (US Congressional-Executive Commission on China 2005b, p. 13; Lundberg and Zhou 2009, pp. 275–6).

Still others have claimed that Beijing gives autonomous areas rights and powers and then, by tying the exercise of these rights and powers to central government approval, effectively takes back most of them. The legislative and administrative power of an autonomous area is limited (US Congressional-Executive Commission on China 2005b, p. 10; Ghai and Woodman 2009, p. 38; Moneyhon 2002, p. 137; Zhou 2009, pp. 345–6). It is said that some minority leaders have grumbled about the 'half-legislative power' accorded autonomous areas (Ghai and Woodman 2009, p. 30; Sautman 1999, pp. 296–7). Although the government in an autonomous region is theoretically to be determined in accordance with the wishes of the minority nationality or nationalities, in fact it performs the same functions and maintains the same relations to central authorities as a local government in a Han area (Smith 2004, p. 11). Ghai and Woodman (2009, p. 44) claim that the five autonomous regions in fact 'enjoy less legislative autonomy than ordinary provinces'. This claim makes sense if one thinks that the central government is motivated to have more control over the autonomous regions such as Xinjiang and Tibet than over ordinary provinces because of increasing challenges from restless minority groups demanding more rights or even secession from the PRC.

Ironically, the minority challenges are partly the outcomes of the regional autonomy system set up by the PRC state. Some scholars have argued that regional autonomy has produced unintended consequences, reconfiguring or reinforcing ethnic consciousness and identity in minority areas (Barabantseva 2008, p. 586; US Congressional-Executive Commission on China 2005b, pp. 8–9; Becquelin 1997, p. 19; Moneyhon 2002, p. 135; Phan 1996, pp. 84–5; Sautman 1999, p. 293). For example, the official category of Uyghurs and the Xinjiang Uyghur Autonomous Region, maintained by the Chinese government, has broken down pre-1949 oasis boundaries among oasis inhabitants and promoted a pan-Uyghur identity among oasis communities in the region. As another example, residents of Zhuang communities did not have a word for 'Zhuang' in their native language and perceived themselves as members of separate communities before 1949. The official recognition of the Zhuang altered the group identity of the diverse peoples living in western Guangxi and eastern Yunnan. The formation of the Zhuang Autonomous Region in 1958 has since created a coherent Zhuang identity (Kaup 2002, pp. 869, 876–9, 883).

So far, Beijing has maintained effective control over autonomous areas despite the minority challenges including rising ethnic consciousness and demands for greater autonomy or even self-determination. This is partly because regional autonomy applies only to the people's congress and government of a minority area, but not to the local CCP organizations, the military, the public security bureau, and the court in that area. Although top administrative posts in an autonomous area are open to native candidates from the local minority group(s), the secretary of the CCP committee of the autonomous area, which is where the real authority lies, is always a Han Chinese (Hess 2009, p. 77; Ghai and Woodman 2009, pp. 30, 45; Lai 2009b, p. 9; Smith 2004, p. 15; Lundberg and Zhou 2009, pp. 306–7; Shan and Chen

2009, p. 17). 'In 2000, each of the 125 regional, prefectural, municipal, and county-level Party first secretaries in Xinjiang was Han' (US Congressional-Executive Commission on China 2005a, p. 17; Hansen 2005, p. 48). The Han secretaries hold real power, whereas minority officials are often figureheads. As a result, ethnic minority groups have the worst of both worlds: they are represented in local governments and people's congresses through 'affirmative action' that generates resentment from Han Chinese, but do not actually control decision making to protect minority interests because local CCP leaders are Han Chinese (US Congressional-Executive Commission on China 2005b, p. 8). It is claimed that 'Uighurs and other non-Han have never enjoyed representation in government organs commensurate with their proportions in the population, and have been even less well-repre-sented in the Party.' Moreover, Uyghur officials have been selected not for their responsiveness to minority concerns, but for their political loyalty to the CCP. This is also the case with regard to the officials recruited from minority groups in Tibet and other autonomous areas in the PRC. When these minority officials are appointed, local minor-ity communities have little say in their appointments, and these minor-ity officials do not always promote policies to benefit their communities (US Congressional-Executive Commission on China 2005b, p. 12; Kaup 2002, p. 883; Lai 2009a, p. 9).

There are other issues associated with regional autonomy. Central authorities have determined development strategies with little input from minority residents. Ethnic minority groups have little or no control over resource exploitation and profit sharing in autonomous areas; the local government does, but the local government is just part of the PRC state. There is the lack of recourse by an affected popula-tion if there is a gap between the legislative intent and implementation (US Congressional-Executive Commission on China 2005b, p. 13). Also, Beijing makes it clear that regional autonomy has nothing to do with independence. Article 4 of the Chinese Constitution specifies that

'All the national autonomous areas are inalienable parts of the People's Republic of China.' The CCP maintains that the PRC is a 'unitary multiethnic state', separation of any territorial units from China is strictly prohibited, ethnic unity must be preserved, and separatist activities must be severely punished (Lai 2009a, p. 9). The CCP has argued that since the Chinese nation was created 'through blood relationship of multiple ethnic groups in Chinese history,' no ethnic groups within the PRC should be entitled to special territorial rights' (Hansen 2005, p. 169). In other words, none of China's national minorities are in exclusive possession of contiguous territories free of other minorities or Han Chinese (Chang 2003, p. 13; Smith 2004, p. 9).

Some scholars in the PRC have also had serious reservations about regional autonomy but for entirely different reasons. Ma Rong, the influential scholar on minority ethnicity in China, claims (2009) that the ethnic quota system for official appointments in the local governments of minority areas has helped some minority candidates achieve positions they are not really qualified for, resulting in a reduction in the efficiency of administration. Ma argues that 'autonomy is history: it is a policy that served its purpose of incorporating peripheral areas into the new state and now has little meaning.' Ma points out that some scholars in China have advocated that 'collective rule' (*gongzhi*, between the state and autonomous areas, and between different ethnic groups, including Han Chinese) 'is now a better model for ethnic policies than autonomy.'

Ma (2007a, 2009) also claims that when a group has been officially recognized by the central government and has its own 'territory' in the form of an autonomous region, its desire to become an independent nation through the 'right of self-determination' may emerge, which is detrimental to the PRC. Autonomy is a key ideological-political source of separatism among some minority groups. Regional autonomy may turn traditional 'tribal states' into modern 'nations/nationalities' and turn the PRC into a 'union of many nations/nationalities'. The problem and danger of nationalist separation is created, at least in part, by regional autonomy. 'Politicizing' ethnicity through measures such as autonomy serves only to inflame ethnic tensions. Ma argues that China should return to pre-modern policies of 'culturalization' of minority groups, and the sense of a 'nationality's territory' should be reduced gradually.

HAN MIGRATION INTO MINORITY AREAS

Han migration into minority areas has become a major issue in the study of regional autonomy in China. Hansen (2005, pp. 2, 13, 45, 243) highlights the 'strong negative' images outside China towards large-scale resettlement of Han Chinese in minority areas and internationally sensitive or politicized discussions on 'minorities' rights to self-determination versus Han 'rights' to move freely within the PRC (especially to Tibet and Xinjiang). Notions of internal colonialism have been applied to the study of Han migration into minority areas in China, as Han settlers have been regarded as the agents of the PRC state to subjugate, control, educate and transform local residents into willing subjects in minority regions (Hansen 2005, pp. 5–7; Gladney 1994; Harrell 1995a; Schein 2000).

According to Hansen (2005), Han migration into minority areas is not a new development. Historically, Han migrants moved to minority areas following successful military campaigns by the Chinese state against border 'barbarians'. Other Han migrants settled in minority villages during the periods of peace and stability. In some cases, Han men married minority women while retaining their sense of Han identity, and yet eventually became a kind of minority themselves. In other cases, a population of non-Han descent became acculturated and almost indistinguishable from Han Chinese while retaining peculiarities of speech and custom, as was the case with the Bai people (Hsu 1971). Overall, pre-1950 Han migrants and their descendants were a small percentage of the local population in non-Han areas. In Xinjiang, for example, only six per cent of the population was Han Chinese in 1949 (Zang 2011b, p. 28).

Han Chinese have quickly outnumbered the minorities in many minority areas since 1949. From the 1950s to the 1970s, Beijing promoted Han migration through state-organized projects. Many early Han settlers 'worked together, and shared social positions and living quarters' with minorities, and respected local customs and learned minority languages. Some of them even joined the local religious services of the minority groups (Hansen 2005, p. 86; Pasternak and Salaff 1993). The number of Han migrants was relatively small. Ethnic minority groups welcomed and viewed them as a positive force, there was little conflict between local residents and Han migrants, and there were no negative reports on Han migration into minority areas.

Since 1978, Beijing has encouraged Han migration into minority areas in order to 'promote national solidarity and in consideration of the needs of economic and cultural development' (Banister 1992, p. 554). New Han migrants have been driven in search of economic opportunities. Unlike early Han settlers, they have migrated with no connection to government projects (Hansen 2005, pp. 2, 7, 229). They watch the same television programmes in their new homes as they did in home villages, do not have regular social contacts with members of local minorities, and are uninterested in minority customs and languages. Unlike their predecessors in 1949–76, Han cadres and educated Han have maintained 'paternalistic judgements' in their relationships with the minorities, which 'allowed the Han to feel superior in terms of technological and cultural development' (Hansen 2005, pp. 201–2).

Han migration into minority areas has often resulted in the previous majority becoming a minority group within their own terrain (Tapp 2010, pp. 101–2). In the past, an autonomous region was often a minority entity with a high population of a particular minority group and some legislative rights (Ghai and Woodman, 2009). Sautman (1999, p. 286) points out that, today, minorities make up only 45 per cent of the 160 million people in China's autonomous areas, and minority populations consist of less than 15 per cent of the total population in many autonomous counties in China. Han Chinese are a significant part of the population in the Xinjiang Uyghur Autonomous Region (40.6 per cent or even more) and the majority group in the Ningxia Hui Autonomous Region (65.4 per cent), the Guangxi Zhuang Autonomous Region (61.6 per cent), and the Inner Mongolia Autonomous Region (79.2 per cent) (US Congressional-Executive Commission on China 2005a, p. 8; Zhou 2009, pp. 341–2). When the Oroqen Autonomous Banner of Inner Mongolia's Hulunbuir League was established in 1951, the proportion of Oroqens in the area was 99.5 per cent. Now only 0.7 per cent of the population are Oroqens (Lundberg and Zhou 2009, p. 283), and nearly 88.3 per cent of the residents are Han Chinese. Similarly, until 1949, the Sipsong Panna area in Yunnan was almost exclusively occupied by the Dai and other minority peoples. Han Chinese accounted for 2.3 per cent of the population in 1950, but now at least one-third of the population is Han Chinese, with the Dai people accounting for only another one-third and other peoples for the remainder. It seems that the continuing Han migration to, and domination of, local economies in non-Han areas have threatened minority cultures and ways of living in autonomous regions and exacerbated ethnic tensions in Tibet, Xinjiang, Inner Mongolia and other parts of China (US Congressional-Executive Commission on China 2005b, p. 13; Lundberg and Zhou 2009, pp. 282–3; see also Fischer 2013; Yeh 2013).

DISCUSSION

This chapter has examined the historical development of regional autonomy in the PRC and outlined the major scope of regional autonomy in minority areas as specified by the PRC Constitution and the 1984 Law of the PRC on Regional National Autonomy. This outline described what regional autonomy in China should be rather than what it actually is. The chapter then went on to critically assess the system of regional autonomy, including a discussion of Han migration into minority areas. The regional autonomy system was set up to instil a sense of ethnic unity with the PRC regime and as a tool to remove both Han and non-Han peoples from their former attachments and unite them around the mission formulated and promoted by the CCP (Barabantseva 2008, p. 577; see also Ghai and Woodman, 2009). However, regional autonomy has not shown its full utility to protect minority rights and cultures and promote economic growth in minority areas, and has not offered satisfactory solutions to ethnic tensions and conflicts in China.

The performance of regional autonomy is disappointing as it is a major issue in the governance of minority ethnicity in China and it should be doing better. According to the CCP, Han–minority parity could be gradually achieved through socialist transformation among ethnic groups that included economic and cultural policies and a system of autonomous regions in the PRC. There are currently no signs that this system will be modified to improve its performance or give more power and rights to ethnic minorities. In 1987, Deng Xiaoping remarked that Mao Zedong was right in not copying Soviet federalism of allowing for secession of minority areas, thus maintaining China's unity. Post-Deng Chinese leaders have maintained this stance (Lai 2009a, p. 12), asserting that regional autonomy is an 'immensely successful' system which has proved a wise choice to promote harmonious relations among ethnic groups. They would like to stick to this important component of China's political mechanism, which has brought peace and prosperity for all Chinese citizens (Information Office of the State Council 2005; Lundberg and Zhou 2009, p. 269; Xinhua 2008; Zhou 2009, p. 346).

Despite the rhetoric, the system of regional autonomy would seem to be facing an uncertain future. Some people in China have regarded the system of nationality-based regional autonomy as a proven failure and have called for its cancellation, pointing out that the US respects ethnic diversity but does not have 'autonomous' areas that would give hope to separatist movements (Hao 2009; Ma 2009). More importantly, there has appeared to be a major change in Beijing's policy towards regional autonomy. In February 2012, Zhu Weiqun openly attributed the collapse of the former Soviet Union and Yugoslavia to regional autonomy. Zhu (2012) asserted that instead of improving ethnic relations in these two countries, regional autonomy strengthened ethnic boundaries and resulted in ethnic conflicts. Therefore, the CCP should learn this lesson. Zhu argued that instead of further enhancing regional autonomy, the CCP should educate nationality groups, improve ethnic relations and deal with separatism resolutely. It should also promote the exchange of goods, capital, information and officials between autonomous areas and Han areas as a means of maintaining the unity of the PRC and the authority of the PRC central government.

This policy approach is consistent with *ronghe* ideology, serving the pressure for ethnic minorities to acculturate and assimilate into Han society. This is partly why the CCP has made sure that regional autonomy is a 'unique combination' of two aspects, being neither a regional autonomy nor 'an ethnic autonomy' (Lundberg and Zhou 2009, p. 320). Thus, the degree of regional autonomy varies according to the nature of the subject matters (higher as regards cultural and economic matters than political and security ones) and the degree of political sensibility (less subject to central intervention where the PRC sovereignty is not disputed). To maintain this policy approach, Beijing will increase its support for economic development in minority areas but will not promote minority cultures unless they can be used to enhance the political legitimacy of the CCP to govern China and its minority regions. This policy approach shows the pecking order of its nationality policy: its first priority in managing ethnic relations in China is given to economic development and the reduction of ethnic inequality, followed by the preservation of some elements of minority cultures that are beneficial to the CCP's legitimacy and governance, and its lowest priority is regional autonomy because a great degree of regional autonomy would enhance minority identity and consciousness and would be detrimental to *ronghe*. In comparative perspective, the CCP is most interested in economic development because it considers the reduction of ethnic inequality an essential step to the success of *ronghe*; it is selective in preserving minority cultures because some elements of minority cultures may inhibit *ronghe*; and it is least interested in regional autonomy because this system poses the greatest threat to *ronghe*.

RECOMMENDED READING

Gardner Bovingdon, *Autonomy in Xinjiang: Han Nationalist Imperatives and Uyghur Discontent* (Washington, DC: East-West Center in Washington, Policy Studies 11, 2004).

Yash Ghai (ed.), *Autonomy and Ethnicity* (Cambridge: Cambridge University Press, 2000).

Warren Smith, *China's Policy on Tibetan Autonomy* (Washington, DC: East-West Center in Washington, Working Papers, No. 2, 2004).

Intra- and Inter-Group Differences

This chapter provides an analysis of the intra- and inter-group differences among minority peoples and how and why the minority nationality groups are treated differently in the PRC. It examines whether there are inter-group differences among ethnic minorities in family behaviour, levels of acculturation and status attainment (education, employment, income, etc.). It also outlines how intra- and inter-group differences in the levels of acculturation and status attainment among minority people affect the political orientations of minority elites in the PRC. Next, it investigates how inter-group differences affect Beijing's policy towards minority nationalities. In particular, it asks whether Beijing treats them equally. If not, what are the plausible reasons for its bias towards some minority nationalities and against others? Do Beijing's perceptions of different minority groups affect the distribution of public goods among ethnic minority groups in China?

These questions are asked here partly because in chapters 2–4, minority nationalities are compared with Han Chinese as if there were no differentiation among the former in terms of demographics, socio-economic status, etc. This is not an unusual practice, as China scholars often use terms such as 'non-Han groups', 'minority peoples', 'minority men/boys' or 'minority women/girls' in their studies of ethnic relations in the PRC (Hannum 2002, pp. 102, 104–5; Poston and Shu 1987, p. 703; Shih 2002, p. 235; Shan 2010, p. 13; Shan and Chen 2009, p. 18–19). Yet in fact the differences among the non-Han peoples in demographics, cultures, schooling, labour market outcomes, etc., are no smaller than or as large as the aggregate Han–minority differences. There is also variation in socioeconomic status, political orientation, etc., among the members of each minority nationality group. Moreover, chapters 2–4 discuss the relationship between the PRC state and minority nationality groups as if the former did not treat the latter differently. Again, this is not an unusual practice in the study of ethnic minorities in China (Gustafsson and Li 2003, p. 805; Harrell 2007, pp. 222–3). This chapter shows that the reality is more complex.

There is no intention here to criticize the ordinary citizens in the West for holding these misconceptions about ethnic minorities in China. They are partly the victims of the infatuated efforts by the CCP to promote the image of national cohesion and the idea of an all-inclusive Chinese nation by notions such as the 'Zhonghua nation' (中华民族) and the 'people of the dragon' (龙的传人). The 56 nationality groups in China have been described as Chinese citizens (中国人), members of the Chinese family (中华民族大家庭的成员) and the 'descendants of Yan and Huang' (炎黄子孙) (Barabantseva 2008, p. 570; Hyer 2009, pp. 76–7; Qarluq and McMillen 2011, p. 1; see also Huang 2002; Zhu 2011). Representatives from the 55 ethnic minority groups dressed in their unique costumes, or more conveniently Han people dressed in minority costumes, have been a compulsory part of major state occasions, such as the launch of China's fifth manned space mission on 13 June 2013, to showcase ethnic unity in the PRC. The CCP is obsessed with and is willing to do almost anything to carry out this practice. During the Beijing Olympics opening ceremony in 2008, 56 children dressed in different ethnic costumes to represent the 56 ethnic groups carried the PRC national flag into the Bird's Nest National Stadium to be hoisted at the most solemn moment of the ceremony. They were later exposed to be Han Chinese (Hutcheon 2008).

The CCP has gone so far to maintain the multicultural image of China because it is politically correct from the perspective of the international minority rights regime (chapter 7), and is helpful in fending off international criticisms of China's minority policies and generating revenues from international tourism. The CCP's efforts have been partly responsible for strengthening the perceived dichotomy between Han Chinese and the ethnic minorities, thereby giving rise to the tendency to overlook inter- and intra-group variation among non-Han peoples in China. This chapter addresses the above misconceptions about non-Han groups in the PRC.

INTRA-GROUP DIFFERENCES

Generally speaking, there are two major types of intra-group differences within each minority group in China. Firstly, members of each ethnic minority group may be differentiated from one another culturally and linguistically. More often than not, each official minority nationality group includes internally diverse populations as a result of the ethnic classification project of 1953. One example is Uyghur Muslims in Xinjiang. Exactly when a unified Uyghur nation was formed is a subject of debate. Rudelson (1997, p. 39) maintains that most Uyghurs were oriented towards their oases before 1949. Shichor (2005, p. 127) insists that Uyghur nationalism did not begin to take shape until the 1920s and 1930s. Gladney (2004a, p. 103) argues that 'the people of the (Xinjiang) oases lacked any coherent sense of identity.' In the early 1930s, Sheng Shicai, the Han warlord who ruled Xinjiang at that time, used 'Uyghur' to categorize Turkic residents in all oases following the recommendation of his Soviet advisors. According to Rudelson (1997), the immensity and harshness of the Tarim Basin continued to separate the oasis centres in Xinjiang from each other. The practice of oasis endogamy (marriage within the community) further perpetuated a strong local identity. He argues that oasis identities undermined hopes to develop a coherent Uyghur national identity (Rudelson 1997, pp. 116, 144; see also Schluessel

2007, p. 270). After 1949, 'the CCP maintained the pre-existing KMT policy of labeling the disparate oasis-based Turkic Muslims as "Uyghurs"' (Hess 2009, pp. 76, 83–4; Gladney 2004a, pp. 104–6, 108).

Another example is the Dai people, who are culturally and linguistically similar to the Thais of Thailand and the Shan of Myanmar. One aspect of this similarity is religious practice: they practise Theravāda Buddhism almost alone among China's peoples. However, they form several distinct cultural and linguistic groups. The two main languages of the Dai are Dai Lü and Dai Nüa; two other written languages used by the Dai are Tày Pong and Tai Dam (Mackerras 2005a). The Yao people similarly consist of several subgroups who speak different dialects and practise different religions including Buddhism, Taoism and Christianity. The Miao people include many distinct subgroups such as Hmong, Hmu and A Hmao, which differ from each other in architecture, costume, ritual and dialect. There are also internal differences in dialects and styles of farming among each Miao subgroup. For example, there are Black Hmong, White Hmong and Red Hmong among Hmong, who speak different dialects and engage in different cultural practices (Tapp 2002a, pp. 71–3, 75–6, 81; see also Deal and Hostetler 2006; Schein 2000; Tapp 2002b; 2002c). Before 1949, the subgroups of the so-called Zhuang people lived in different geographic areas, spoke different dialects, wore different costumes, and practised different rituals. They did not necessarily define their ethnic affiliation in terms of the broad Zhuang category (Kaup 2002, pp. 867, 869, 873). This vast intra-group difference takes place mainly because of the ethnic classification project discussed in chapter 1, as the broad nationality categories such as Hui, Yi or Miao were conveniently invented or used to cover internally diverse or unrelated populations. There are different accounts of why the CCP adopted this wide coverage (Alberts 2007; Jonsson 2000; Litzinger 1998; 2000). One possible reason was administrative convenience (Hess 2009, p. 83; Tapp 2002a, p. 70). The other possibility, as noted in chapter 1, is that it is in Beijing's interest to limit the number of minority nationalities with regard to the selection of minority deputies to the NPC, which compelled it to use the limited categories of minority nationality to cover vastly different populations.

Secondly, many people associate non-Han groups in China with adjectives such as 'impoverished', 'poorly educated', 'deprived' and 'underprivileged'. Yet in fact the members of each ethnic minority group are differentiated greatly in terms of status attainment. This is self-evident as there is stratification in most human societies. While some individuals of minority nationalities have suffered from poverty (chapter 2), a growing number of people of minority status have become part of the middle class or even the new rich in the post-1978 era. Some Hui and Uyghur business people have made good money from their entrepreneurial activities including transnational trade and the restaurant business (Gladney 1996; Mackerras 2005a). Better-educated members of the minority nationalities have also done well. For example, Mishra and Smyth (2010) find that among Korean Chinese, 'A senior middle school or polytechnic education provides the highest rate of return. Possessing a senior middle school, or polytechnic education, would earn 40.7 per cent more than just completing junior middle school. Finally, possessing a university degree would earn 31 per cent more than just completing senior middle school or having a polytechnic education.'

Thirdly, stratification in socioeconomic status leads to different political orientations among status groups within each minority nationality group. During his fieldwork in Xinjiang, Rudelson found strong class distinctions between intellectuals, merchants and peasants due to their differences in education, occupational attainment and political interests. Before the 1980s, Islam could not define the identity of all Uyghurs, as the majority of Uyghur intellectuals strongly rejected the Islamic conservatism found among rural Uyghur peasants. There were political differences between urban secular activists and rural Islamic movements in Xinjiang. Uyghur 'identity is formed according to social class and occupation rather than family types, descent, or pan-oases solidarity' (Rudelson 1997, pp. 117, 119).

Other scholars have focused on the distinction between *minkaomin* and *minkaohan* in Xinjiang. Uyghurs who have chosen to study in Uyghur language schools are called *minkaomin*. Uyghurs who have enrolled in Mandarin schools are called *minkaohan* (Benson 2004, pp. 198–9, 213–14; Smith Finley 2007a, p. 641; Fuller and Lipman 2004, pp. 334–5; Schluessel 2007, p. 259; Rudelson and Jankowiak 2004, pp. 310–11). It is claimed that *minkaohan* are taught in the Chinese language, learn about the Chinese cultural heritage, and absorb the Chinese version of history. They tend to speak, dress and act like Han Chinese (Smith Finley 2007a, p. 641; Dwyer 2005, p. 38). Taynen (2006, p. 45) concludes that *minkaohan* take on many Chinese characteristics culturally and linguistically. Schluessel (2007, p. 260) asserts that *minkaohan* education is preferable to some Uyghurs who are 'willing to sacrifice or risk their cultural identity'. *Minkaohan* are accused of advancing their careers by entering the structure of the Chinese state. They find difficulty functioning in Uyghur environments (Steiner 2010, p. 44; Schluessel 2007, p. 259; see also Smith Finley 2007b), but are favoured for admission into Chinese society and receive political and employment advantages over *minkaomin*, who remain linguistically and culturally Uyghur. Some *minkaohan* are integrated into the PRC state, serve as its functionaries, and are described by *minkaomin* as the fourteenth minority in Xinjiang – neither Han Chinese nor Uyghur but an entirely different group altogether (Fuller and Lipman 2004, pp. 334–5; Rudelson 1997, pp. 127–8; Rudelson and Jankowiak 2004, p. 313; Schluessel 2007, p. 259).

Fourthly, status attainment (education, employment, income, etc.) among members of a non-Han group is often related to acculturation in Han society. Baranovitch (2001, p. 364) argues that 'minority artists and intellectuals were trained in Han-dominated official institutions, acquiring politically correct knowledge about their ethnic identity and learning how to represent it artistically in politically accepted venues – a practice still prevalent today.' For example, most Uyghur elites, who are *minkaohan*, are the product of the government affirmative action policy and work for the Chinese government as officials, teachers, performers, etc. Beijing expects their role to focus on advancing the processes of integration of minority nationalities into Han society (Qarluq and McMillen 2011, pp. 5, 8–11, 14–15; Hess 2009, pp. 76–7, 85; see also Rudelson 1997). It is not surprising that, in general, non-Han elites are a 'small coterie of urban intellectuals who are much more part of the general Chinese culture than are the people they are representing' (Chung 2006, p. 86; Gladney 2004b, p. 378; Hess 2009, p. 88). In Inner Mongolia, the identity and attitudes of the Mongolian elite are asserted to be oriented towards the Chinese state and the Han majority (Khan 1996). The intra-group difference has been used by the CCP to divide and rule ethnic minority groups in the PRC.

INTER-GROUP DIFFERENCES AMONG ETHNIC MINORITIES

Mackerras (2011a, p. 112) points out that although there are many commonalities among ethnic minority groups, 'they illustrate great diversity in terms of language, religion, the arts, architecture, diet and family practices'. Inter-group differences are apparent for reasons of history, geography, different levels of development and acculturation, etc. In this section, inter-group differences among non-Han peoples are examined with regard to family behaviour, levels of acculturation and status attainment. Like intra-group differences, inter-group differences have had impacts on state–minority relations, which have been exploited by Beijing for the governance of the non-Han groups and minority areas in the PRC.

Family Behaviour

The PRC government has allowed an earlier marriage age for the ethnic minority groups than for Han Chinese. But each of the minority groups has responded to this policy differently for a variety of reasons including customs and living environments. Using data from the 1987 One Percent National Survey, Chang (2003, p. 25) finds that Uyghurs have the highest percentage of women (82.6 per cent) and the Bouyei people have the lowest percentage of women (26.3 per cent) married between the ages of 15 and 19. In Chang's estimates, Uyghurs, the Hui and Yi have between 50 and 80 per cent of women who married before the legal marriage age of 20. Compared with other ethnic groups, Tibetan and Dong women have higher proportions of women getting married between the ages of 30 and 34.

Similarly, although Beijing has carried out a preferential policy with regard to family planning among the minority nationalities, each of them has exhibited different patterns of reproductive behaviour due to their different socioeconomic profiles. Tibetan women have maintained a high fertility rate. Goldstein et al. (2003, pp. 771–2; see also Goldstein et al. 2002; Childs 2008, pp. 114, 202) report that the currently married Tibetan women aged between 50–54 and 55–59 they studied had, on average, 6.9 and 7.1 live births, respectively; the currently married women aged 35–39 had 4.1 live births, and those aged 40–44 had 5.7 live births:

> The proportion of births that were third, fourth, or a higher birth order also indicates high fertility and is evidence for the absence of any program of systematic forced birth limits in Tibet's rural areas. Of the 131 births that occurred in 1997 to the women in our study, 45.4% were third or higher birth order, 31.5% were fourth birth order or higher, and 20.8% were fifth or higher. Similarly, 70.1% of the 1,110 women who have ever given birth . . . had three or more live births,

55.9% had four or more, and 41.4% had five or more. (Goldstein et al. 2003, pp. 771–2)

Other non-Han groups have reported lower fertility rates. Using the micro-data from the One Percent 1990 Census of China, Chang (2003, pp. 25–6, 111, 115) estimates that women from the Mongolian, Tujia and She nationalities reportedly had 0 to 3 children, whereas women from the Tibetan and Dongxiang nationality groups reportedly had 0 to 10 children. The fertility rates for Koreans, Hui and Manchus were close to 2 or even lower, whereas other ethnic minorities, especially Muslim groups, still had high levels of fertility, e.g., Tajik 6.21; Kirgiz, 6.2; Kazak, 4.74; Uyghur, 4.76; Jingpo, 4.21; Bulang, 4.23; Salar, 4.12; Deang, 4.98; Dulong, 5.43; and Menba,4.23.

Using the same data set, Poston et al. (2006, pp. 77, 81–2, 88) find that, contrary to the common perception that Han Chinese had lower fertility rates than the ethnic minority groups, both Koreans and Manchus had mean fertility scores of less than two children ever born, which were less than the fertility score of 2.1 for the Han majority. Korean and Manchu women had about one-third fewer children ever born than Han women. Mongolians, the Hui, Zhuang and Miao had fertility values from 2.3 to 2.8 children. Yi had 3.0 children ever born and Uyghur 3.2. Poston et al. (2006) find that education has a negative effect on fertility rates: the higher the educational level a minority nationality group attains, the lower its fertility rates.

Status Attainment

The above discussion on different fertility rates leads to attention to variation in status attainment as they are related to each other (Murphy et al. 2011; Wang 2012). Different levels of status attainment among minority nationality groups can be attributed, in part, to compositional differences in history, geographic location of residence and family background (Hannum 2002, pp. 95–6). For example, Manchus ruled China from 1644 to 1911 and had centuries of close contact with Han Chinese. Compared to many other minority nationalities in China, the Manchu people are advanced in terms of socioeconomic status and similar to Han Chinese with respect to their population distributions in education, occupation and industry (Chang 2003, pp. 32–3).

Likewise, Koreans have had close interaction with Han Chinese for hundreds of years. They have been portrayed as a model minority with a higher level of social accomplishments than other minority groups (Poston et al. 2006, pp. 71–2; Park and Han 1990, pp. 161, 164; see also Gao 2010). Gao (2009) finds that the Korean minority has the highest level of college attendance and lowest illiteracy rate among the minority nationalities in China. Hannum (2002) shows that the enrolment rate for Korean boys (98.5 per cent) and girls (98.7 per cent) aged 7–14 is the highest among the ethnic minorities and outpaces the corresponding percentages for the Han majority, which are 94.2 per cent and 88.9 per cent, respectively. Kim (2010) reports that compared with other ethnic minorities, Koreans have high occupational status. Relative to the size of their population, ethnic Koreans are over-represented in the CCP as cadres and in professional occupations such as the judiciary, police force and management, partly because of their educational attainment.

The inter-group difference in schooling can also be seen in terms of literacy rates. The percentage of illiterate minority people ranges from a low of 4.95 for Xibe to a high of 76.56 for Dongxiang. Five ethnic minority groups have fewer than 10 per cent illiterate, namely, Koreans, Manchus, Kazaks, Daur and Xibe. Five ethnic minority groups have over 50 per cent illiterates, namely, Lisu, Lahu, Tibetans, Hani and Dongxiang. The level of educational segregation (from Han Chinese) for the Mongolians is 4.6; Li, 8.8; Manchus, 8.8; and Tujia, 9.8. The corresponding figure for Dongxiang is 58.4; Lahu, 45.0; Tibetans, 44.5; Lisu, 35.6; Hani, 32.3; and Wa, 31.2 (Chang 2003, pp. 115–16).

The higher the level of educational segregation, the lower the level of educational achievement.

Using census data from China, Hannum (2002, pp. 100–1) shows that the ethnic minority groups residing in the more developed north and north-east regions of China typically exhibit strong indicators of socioeconomic development and educational attainment comparable to those of Han Chinese. In contrast, the majority of the ethnic minority groups residing in the western interior of China exhibit weak indicators of status attainment. Enrolment rates close to or exceeding those of Han Chinese are found for boys among Mongols, Zhuang, Bouyei, Koreans, Manchus, Dong, Bai, Tujia and Kazaks. For girls, enrolment rates close to those of Han Chinese are found among Mongols, Koreans, Manchus and Bai. Mongols, Uyghurs, Zhuang, Koreans, Manchus, Yao and Dai have considerably more equitable enrolment rates by gender, whereas the Hui, Tibetans, Yi, Bouyei and Dong have a much less equitable distribution of basic education by gender.

Poston and Shu (1987, pp. 711–12, 714–16, 718–19) show that the ethnic minority groups that are geographically less differentiated from Han Chinese tend to be better off socioeconomically than those that are more differentiated. They are also more similar to Han Chinese demographically than those that are more differentiated. Hui, Manchus and Mongolians appear more similar to Han Chinese in social, demographic and economic characteristics, and may be more integrated into Han society than many of the other ethnic minorities – namely, Uyghurs, Yi, Miao, Tibetans, Bai and Hani. These ethnic minorities are much less integrated into Han society and have poorer socioeconomic status attainment.

Poston et al. (2006, p. 77) show that the more the ethnic minority groups are like Han Chinese in terms of socioeconomic and residential characteristics, the greater their structural assimilation with Han Chinese. Although religion is regarded as an influential factor in deciding residence choices in the sociological literature on ethnic relations in the West, it does not appear to cause or be related to different levels of integration into Han society among the ethnic minority groups in China. Chang (2003, p. 115) reports that the level of residential segregation from Han Chinese varies greatly among the ethnic minority groups, from the highest of 99.4 per cent for Kazaks, to the lowest of 68.7 per cent for the Hui, although both ethnic groups are Muslims.

Acculturation

Some ethnic minorities are very close culturally to Han Chinese, and some of them are so close as to be almost assimilated. They 'were already well acculturated with the Han before 1949 and in that respect sharply different from many of China's nationalities' (Mackerras 1988, p. 53). One example is Manchus, mentioned above. Nowadays they speak Mandarin and dress and act like Han Chinese. Few Manchus can speak their traditional language, and the Manchu written language has almost disappeared (Mackerras 2005a, p. 815; see also Rhoads 2000). Another example is the Hui people, who adopt Han customs and do not have their own language. Lipman (2004, pp. 22, 28, 47, 49) argues that some Hui take pride in the government's affirmation of their 'national' existence, 'while others find it false, condescending, or downright silly'. Lipman also points out that 'After all, the vast majority of Hui, even some of those who have traveled extensively in the Middle East, are clearly Chinese in their language, material culture, and textual lives outside the mosque . . . Despite the Hui being defined as an "ethnic minority", we must nonetheless regard them as unequivocally Chinese, though sometimes marginal or even despised Chinese' (see also Zang 2007).

Mackerras (1988, p. 53) points out that there is a whole range of the ethnic minorities in China's south-west who have become quite well integrated into the Han majority, even though they retain their own cultures and languages a bit more extensively than peoples like Manchus and the Hui. The Bai people did not have 'strong national feeling' before

1949. Many travellers regarded them 'as an absorbed people hardly to be distinguished' from Han Chinese. They 'would be seriously offended' if their Chinese identity were questioned or denied (also Fitzgerald 1941, pp. 14–15). Although they spoke the Bai language as their mother tongue, they were like Han Chinese even to the extent of binding their women's feet (Hsu 1971). After 1949, some Bai people passed as Han Chinese before the government policy of positive discrimination towards ethnic minorities was enacted (Tapp 2002a, p. 73).

There are other acculturated minority groups in China. Despite the major intra-group differences among the Zhuang mentioned above, they have had a close affiliation with Han Chinese for centuries and are one of the most acculturated ethnic minority groups in China. Many Zhuang in urban Guanxi speak Mandarin and take the Han cuisine (Kaup 2002, p. 868), and it is an impossible challenge for anyone to separate them from Han Chinese. The evolution of the Yao culture similarly shared many elements with mainstream Chinese culture. Other ethnic minority groups (such as Tujia and Miao), especially those who have long lived near or amongst the majority society, have used Mandarin and been educated in the Han-style system (Qarluq and McMillen 2011, pp. 8–9).

In contrast to south-western minorities, Tibetans in the Tibet Autonomous Region and Uyghurs in southern Xinjiang live in cohesive communities largely separated from Han Chinese and have supporters outside China (including Tibetans and Uyghurs in exile) for their demand for independence from the PRC. Mackerras (2005a, p. 816) writes that Tibetans are believers in a form of Tantric Buddhism special to Tibetans (i.e., Tibetan Buddhism). Tibetan is a different language from Han Chinese, and Tibetan diet, architecture and dress are also different from those of Han Chinese. But even more distinct from Han Chinese are the Turkic peoples of north-western China, such as the Kazaks, Kirgiz and Uzbeks, and most noticeably Uyghurs. Some people think that Tibetan belongs to the same language family as Han Chinese. In comparison, Uyghur and other Turkic languages belong to the Altaic language family, which is totally different from the Sino-Tibetan language family. These Turkic peoples are Muslims and, at least among Uyghurs, Islam is gaining in strength, both culturally and socially. Uyghur arts, architecture and diet are distinctively Turkic, not Sinic. Following Muslim proscriptions, Uyghurs abstain from pork, which forms a major part of the Han Chinese diet. Uyghur music and musical instruments are quite similar to those found in Turkey, but do not have much in common with those of Han Chinese.

According to Mackerras (1992, p. 29), the different acculturation levels of the minority nationality groups by Han culture can be observed in the contents of minority dramas and other forms of performing arts. At one end of the acculturation scale, influence from Han Chinese is very slight. In this category could be put the folk Tibetan dramas, Uyghur operas, Mongolian epics and Kirgiz epics. In the middle of the scale one would put Dai drama, which is quite strongly influenced by Han culture. At the other end of the scale is the traditional Dong theatre, which owes its evolution to Han theatrical styles and uses mainly Han instruments for accompaniment while retaining its basis in Dong poetry, Dong epic songs and its Dong style. The relationship of Bai and Zhuang dramas with Han culture goes down the spectrum towards amalgamation.

Political Ramifications

In general, more acculturated ethnic minority groups are more likely than others to be oriented towards Beijing. For example, there have been movements for independence in Tibet and Xinjiang, and Han–Tibetan and Han–Uyghur conflicts have drawn international attention. In comparison, the Hui, Manchus, Zhuang, Bai and Miao have maintained positive or neutral relations with the Chinese state, and they happen to be the more acculturated minority groups in China. Mackerras (1988, p. 78) claims that

> [i]t seems that the Bai are quite happy with the strengthened accultura-
> tion of the 1980s. One reason for this is the immeasurably greater
> economic development and higher standard of living that have accom-
> panied it. In addition, their history, and, in particular, long experience
> of dealing with the Han, have given them great skills in coping with the
> process of acculturation.

Mackerras (2011a, p. 112) also writes that 'the great majority of the members of the ethnic minorities appear willing, even happy, to remain within the PRC'.

Unsurprisingly, the CCP has pursued different policies towards different minority nationality groups. The CCP has allegedly violated minority rights in Tibet and Xinjiang, but elsewhere it has taken certain steps to improve the life chances of minority nationality groups as outlined in chapter 2 (US Congressional-Executive Commission on China 2005b, p. 15); at least it has done so in theory. Also, as mentioned in chapter 3, the CCP has tightened control over religious activities among Uyghur Muslims but has been far less restrictive with regard to religious activities among Hui Muslims. The determining factor in Beijing's attitude towards an ethnic minority group is its political inclination: the minority nationalities that are willing to accept state control and the official depiction of their ethnic groups and histories have been treated favourably. Beijing is more willing to grant them some freedom to exercise their lawful rights, practise their cultures and religions, and join CCP and government ranks. The minority nationality groups such as Tibetans and Uyghurs that have demanded more control over their identities, more autonomy, or even independence, have regularly been confronted with government repression (Hansen 2005, p. 243; US Congressional-Executive Commission on

China 2005a). However, it is interesting to find out whether Beijing has similarly punished individual members of the 'unruly' minority nationality groups because of the collective behaviour of their ethnic groups. I examine this question below.

THE STATE'S PERCEPTIONS OF MINORITY THREAT

Historically, the central governments throughout all the Chinese dynasties have viewed ethnic tribes as external threats (Chang 2003, p. 10). Nevertheless, the degree of threat from each ethnic minority group is different, dependent on, among other things, the levels of acculturation and integration. Today, the inter-group differences among the ethnic minorities mentioned above have shaped Beijing's perceptions of minority threat to the Chinese state, which in turn has affected how it treats individual members of different minority groups in the PRC.

In the West, the dominant group similarly ranks ethnic minority groups differently with regard to perceived minority threat. The ranking is based on a variety of factors such as group size and demographic distribution. A large ethnic minority group is perceived by the dominant group to be a bigger threat than a small ethnic minority group, probably because group size is related to numerical strength, which is regarded as an indicator of the ability to mount a genuine challenge against the dominant group. Similarly, a geographically concentrated ethnic minority group is more likely than other ethnic minority groups to be seen as a big threat by the dominant group. This is probably because minority residential concentration is thought to be conducive to mobilization for collective action against the dominant group (Jacobs and Tope 2008; Quillian 1995; Semyonov et al. 2006).

There is also a cultural dimension to minority threat: stereotypical perceptions define each ethnic minority group as either 'backward' or 'advanced'. 'Backward' minority groups are less acculturated and are viewed as unintelligent, lazy and the like, whereas 'advanced' minority groups are more acculturated and are viewed as enterprising, civilized and the like (i.e., it is more like the dominant group culturally). These stereotypes define the distribution of group worth and affect inter-group relations and the strategies of ethnic competition. A less accul-turated ethnic minority group is perceived by the dominant group to be a bigger threat than a more acculturated ethnic minority group – a dialogue may be carried out and a compromise may be reached between a more acculturated ethnic minority group and the dominant group due to their cultural similarity (Horowitz 2000, pp. 21–41, 148, 169, 233; see also Blanton et al. 2001; Mason 2003; Riek et al. 2006).

Perceived minority threat is related to prejudice and discrimination and thus has an impact on ethnic inequalities, because perceived group threat invites sanctions against minority groups by members of the dominant group. The greater the perceived threat from a minority group, the more likely it is to be subject to ethnic discrimination by members of the dominant group (King and Wheelock 2007; Kunovich 2004; Semyonov et al. 2002; 2004). In comparison, less threatened minority groups are likely to be given more room to manoeuvre in mainstream society by the majority group.

Interaction between majority and minority groups affects state per-ceptions of minority threat and thus state policy towards different ethnic minority groups. State action is more important than majority responses with regard to the well-being of a minority group because the state controls more resources and coercive power and is more organized than individual members of a dominant group. This is par-ticularly the case in countries such as China that have a strong and centralized state. It is possible that, like the individual members of the majority group, the state also relies on factors such as levels of assimilation into mainstream society to assess threat from different ethnic minority groups. Like the individual members of the majority group, the state also finds a variation in perceived threat to it from different minority groups. It is thus possible that all ethnic minorities in the PRC are regarded as a threat to the Chinese state as it is essentially a Han regime. But some minority groups (such as Tibetans and Uyghurs) are viewed by the CCP as more threatening than other minority groups (such as Hui Muslims): these 'more threatening' groups differ from other minority groups greatly in terms of numerical strength, geographic concentration and nationalistic aspirations.

In addition, as noted above, there is a positive link between perceived group threat from an ethnic minority group and the rise of prejudice among, and sanctions against, the ethnic minority group by members of the ethnic majority. This is true both in and outside China. However, the PRC state may not treat minority groups in the same way as individual Han Chinese do. On the contrary, the PRC state may give more concessions to a more 'threatening' group than to a less 'threatening' group. The state and the individual Han Chinese act differently because the state must take a broad view on ethnic relations and guard national interests such as territorial integrity and social order, whereas individual Han Chinese are concerned about private issues such as labour market competition, neighbourhood safety, etc.

Of course, the CCP may discriminate against or even suppress the more 'threatening' minority group in China. But at the same time it is cost-effective for the Chinese state to accommodate the individual members of the minority group, especially if the minority group has a large population and the potential to become a secessionist force. It is possible that the more a minority group is perceived to be a 'threatening' people, the more the CCP uses incentives to integrate its members into mainstream society and to divide and rule. A comparative study of CCP membership attainment by Hui Muslims and Uyghur Muslims in the next section shows this is indeed the case. CCP membership is a valued public good and a key indicator of upward mobility in China. Beijing has favoured some population segments from which CCP members have been disproportionately recruited. For example, state workers were a key target of membership recruitment during the Cultural Revolution (Walder 1986). Similarly, the PRC state may for political purposes prefer to recruit members from one minority group than from another minority group. Ethnic variation in CCP membership attainment thus may reflect Beijing's policies towards different minority nationality groups (Zang 2012).

A COMPARATIVE STUDY OF THE HUI AND UYGHURS

Most Hui are Sunni Muslims. Gladney (1996) writes that Hui are the descendants of foreign Muslim merchants, militia and officials, who came to China from Arabian and Central Asian countries from the seventh to fourteenth centuries and later intermarried with Han Chinese (see also Mackerras 1995; 2003). The 2010 census recorded nearly 10.6 million Hui, establishing them as the second largest minority group in China. The Hui celebrate many Han festivals, read, speak and write Chinese, and wear Chinese costumes. They maintain their ethnic identity by upholding Islamic beliefs, practising endogamy and observing pork avoidance. But young Hui are increasingly moving away from these practices (Gillette 2000). Some scholars claim that the Hui have been essentially assimilated to Han society (Dreyer 1976, pp. 264–5; Heberer 1989, p. 73; Naquin and Rawski 1987, p. 128).

As noted in chapter 1, Uyghurs are a major Sunni Muslim group in China. The 2010 census recorded nearly 10.1 million Uyghurs in Xinjiang. Unlike Hui Muslims, Uyghurs are a Turkic group, wear their costumes and have their own language. Many Uyghurs do not read, speak or write Chinese. They celebrate their own festivals. Horowitz (2000, pp. 28, 135) argues that cultural divergence reduces the levels of inter-group communication and 'generalized collaboration'. Relations between two ethnic groups are less tense when they are close to each other than when they are far apart on the 'backward'–'advanced' scale (see also Riek et al. 2006). Accordingly, the Hui should be less likely than Uyghurs to be viewed as a threat by the Chinese state because of their different levels of acculturation as noted above. The more integrated an ethnic minority group into mainstream society, the more likely it is to invest its future in the existing socioeconomic system, and to advance its interests through bargaining, negotiations and reforms within the overall framework of the status quo. Thus, Han Chinese, who are also the 'advanced' group, and the Chinese state, may consider a 'backward' group such as Uyghurs as a greater threat than a less 'backward' minority group such as the Hui due to their different levels of assimilation into mainstream society.

The Hui and Uyghurs also differ from each other in geographic concentration. The Hui outnumber Uyghurs, but they are spread all over China and are a minority group in virtually all the places they live. In comparison, over 95 per cent of Uyghurs live, and are the majority group, in Xinjiang (Mackerras 1995; 2003; Rudelson 1997; Rudelson and Jankowiak 2004; Toops 2004). Beijing may consider Uyghurs a greater threat than the Hui as the probability of collective action is greater for Uyghurs than for the Hui, and geographic concentration facilitates Uyghur mobilization. More importantly, Uyghurs have regarded Xinjiang as their homeland and Han migrants in the territory as uninvited guests. Some Uyghurs have resented Han migration into Xinjiang, as Han migrants have allegedly taken jobs and resources away from them (Becquelin 2000; Bovingdon 2002; Smith 2002; Yee 2003). The Hui cannot make a similar territorial claim since they are a 'guest' people in China. Many Hui seek to climb the socioeconomic hierarchy in Han society (Gillette 2000; Lipman 2004) and are more likely than Uyghurs to be interested in CCP membership. In contrast, it is found that some Uyghurs reportedly prefer to stay away from the official channels of upward mobility, and a Uyghur may be regarded as a traitor by other Uyghurs if he or she becomes a government official or a CCP member (Mackerras 2011a, pp. 115–16; see also Becquelin 2000; Bovingdon 2002; Smith 2002; Yee 2003). In 1987, only 38.4 per cent of CCP members in Xinjiang were non-Han, although ethnic minorities comprised more than 60 per cent of the population. By 1994, the percentage of non-Han Party members in the region had decreased to 36.7 per cent (US Congressional-Executive Commission on China 2005a, p. 12).

Finally, some Uyghurs have sought by all means to form an independent nation state in Xinjiang. In comparison, the Hui are happy to be a member of the PRC (Lipman 2004). Of course, only a few Uyghurs in Xinjiang have joined the separatist movement. But they are influential due to their efforts to split China through violence. Beijing requested that the UN Security Council list a major Uyghur separatist organization, the East Turkistan Islamic Movement based in Istanbul, Turkey, as a terrorist group. This request was granted in a motion passed by the UN Security Council on 12 September 2002.

Thus, it is clear that the CCP considers Uyghurs as a more 'threatening' group than the Hui, especially with regard to the Uyghur demand for an independent nation state in Xinjiang. Xinjiang occupies one-sixth of China's territory with natural resources such as petroleum and natural gas, iron ore, etc. Much greater state interests are at stake in the interaction between the CCP and Uyghurs than between the CCP and the Hui. The CCP has suppressed Uyghur separatism with an iron fist. At the same time, it is motivated to make efforts to integrate as many individual Uyghurs into the PRC regime as possible to counter-balance Uyghur separatists in Xinjiang. It does not have such a need for the Hui. Hence, it should be easier for Uyghurs to join the CCP than the Hui: Hui applicants have to compete with Han Chinese on an equal (or lower) footing for CCP membership, whereas Uyghur applicants are actively sought by the CCP.

Survey data on the Hui in Lanzhou and Uyghurs in Ürümchi collected in 2001 show that the percentage of CCP members among the Hui (7.1 per cent) is lower than that among Han Chinese (26.4 per cent) in Lanzhou, and that the percentage of Uyghurs with CCP membership is lower than that of Han Chinese (13.6 per cent vs. 24.7 per cent) in Ürümchi. In Lanzhou, the Hui are 79 per cent less likely than Han Chinese to join the CCP. In Ürümchi, the Uyghurs are 52 per cent less likely than Han Chinese to become CCP members. These findings are not surprising given that the CCP is, and is regarded as, the political party of Han Chinese, as Han Chinese dominate both the membership composition and leadership positions of the CCP (Smith 2000). When control variables such as age, sex and educational attainment are introduced into the data analysis, the Hui are 53 per cent less likely than Han Chinese to become CCP members. In contrast, Uyghurs and Han Chinese do not differ from each other in CCP membership attainment when background variables such as age, sex and educational attainment are controlled for. In other words, the difference in CCP membership between Uyghurs and Han Chinese is the outcome of the inter-group gaps in background factors such as age and education; whereas the difference in CCP membership between the Hui and Han Chinese is not. When applying to join the CCP, Uyghurs are treated equally by the CCP as Han Chinese, whereas the Hui are not. Apparently, Beijing favours Han Chinese over the Hui in CCP recruitment, although many Hui are interested in CCP membership, as noted above. In comparison, Beijing does not discriminate against Uyghurs, although many Uyghurs are not interested in CCP membership, as noted above.

These findings are interesting because Beijing is required by the PRC Constitution to implement affirmative action for all minority nationality groups. All of them are officially entitled to equal opportunity programmes in many tangible areas such as university admission and employment in the state sector in China (chapter 2). Nevertheless, the above findings show that there is a different ballgame in political recruitment. This is because the Chinese state is mandated to safeguard national interests such as territorial integrity and social order. It is motivated to treat a minority group preferentially if it is powerful and has the potential to pose a threat to national interests. Beijing has used force to suppress separatist attempts. It has also tried to accommodate some members of the 'threatening' minority in order to divide and rule. It is less likely to do the same for a minority group that does not pose a serious threat to the status quo because there is no need to divide and rule. Since the Hui and Uyghurs pose different levels of threat to the Chinese state, Beijing treats Uyghurs and Hui differently, which explains why Uyghurs have a better chance of joining the CCP than the Hui do. Beijing needs to actively recruit Uyghur members to counterbalance Uyghur separatists. Hui applicants do not provide this sort of political service and thus have to compete with Han Chinese for CCP membership.

Reflecting on his fieldwork in Inner Mongolia, an American anthropologist told me that the above analysis of the difference in CCP membership attainment between Uyghurs and the Hui also held for Mongols. Mongols have based their demand for ethnic perks on their insistence on greater affirmative action and regional autonomy. Their verbal positioning and insistence that Inner Mongolia is Mongolian land combined with Beijing's concern about ethnic loyalty have enabled them to receive concessions from the Chinese state. Many Mongols who were critical of the government policies admitted they wanted to join the CCP as it would help with career advancement, and many of them were invited to join.

DISCUSSION

The chapter has examined intra- and inter-group variations among the minority nationalities in the PRC. Tapp (2010, pp. 102–3) points out that, after the burgeoning of minority studies in China over the past 30 years, 'there is more and more interest in the hybridities and complexities of ethnic identification'. He identifies the efforts by some scholars 'to move away from an exclusive focus on state–society opposi-tions, as indeed from "Han/other" dichotomies, towards a more nuanced understanding of the complexities of identifications in locali-ties and the interrelations formed between local people without neces-sary regard for state intervention'. Several scholars have argued that minority populations should not be viewed as if they were homogene-ous (Baranovitch 2001, p. 360; Hansen 2005, pp. 16, 204; see also Khan 1995; 1996; Upton 1996).

Nevertheless, there are still problems inherent in past and existing approaches to focusing on officially demarcated 'ethnic minorities' in an isolating way, and they have significantly influenced how people under-stand the minority nationalities in China. This chapter shows major intra-group variations among minority people. Equally important, levels of status attainment are related to variation in political orienta-tions among minority people. The minority elite that Beijing has raised have generally supported the government nationality policy. Willingly or reluctantly, they have played a strategically important role in the policy of divide and rule by Beijing in its governance of the minority nationalities and minority regions in the PRC.

This chapter also shows major inter-group differences in family behaviour, status attainment and acculturation among China's ethnic minorities. The inter-group differences have significant political rami-fications for the relationships between the Chinese state and the ethnic minorities. Generally speaking, the more acculturated a minority nationality group is, the less likely it is to challenge the status quo because its interests are likely to be embedded in the status quo. Yet partly because of its political allegiance, Beijing is less likely to reward the individual members of the ethnic minority group. Beijing is more motivated to use divide and rule to deal with a more threaten-ing minority group. Part of Beijing's rationale is that the more the CCP recruits and rewards the individual members of this threatening minority group, the less likely the ethnic minority group is to be able to engage in successful separatist activity. In particular, Beijing has a great need for divide and rule in Tibet and Xinjiang.

It is important to note that Beijing has exploited divide and rule only as a short-term, transient strategy to govern ethnic minorities. In the long run, Beijing's hope is to gradually remove variations among non-Han peoples as a necessary step for minority acculturation and assimilation into Han society. Its ultimate goal is not simply to control non-Han peoples and minority areas but to achieve *ronghe* in the PRC, as documented in the previous chapters. However, Beijing's efforts have not always been especially fruitful, partly because of the shortcomings in its nationality policy, and the variations (especially inter-group differences) among non-Han peoples have become a major barrier in Beijing's march towards *ronghe*. In particular, Beijing has not worked out why it has been able to solicit cooperation from some minority groups but not from others. Nor has it figured out how to curb 'recalcitrant' and 'unruly' non-Han peoples such as Tibetans and Uyghurs from developing nationalistic aspirations. As Mackerras (2011a, p. 124) points out,

> in some ways, China's handling of ethnic problems has been successful, in other ways not. The country is probably better integrated than it used to be, with less likelihood of splitting up or separatist movement succeeding . . . In most places, ethnicity is not a marker when it comes to relations among people . . .
>
> On the other hand, there are respects in which success is much less obvious. In the Tibetan areas and Xinjiang, ethnic relations are still tense and have probably worsened over the decades since the Cultural Revolution.

Thus, the next chapter studies why the escalation of ethnic tensions rather than the celebration of *ronghe* has dominated the social and political landscape in Tibet and Xinjiang. Rising ethnic tensions in these two regions are a lens for us to observe the shortcomings of Beijing's nationality policy in promoting *ronghe*.

RECOMMENDED READING

Xiaowei Zang, *Ethnicity and Urban Life in China: A Comparative Study of Hui Muslims and Han Chinese* (London: Routledge, 2007).

Xiaowei Zang, *Islam, Family Life, and Gender Inequality in Urban China* (London: Routledge, 2011).

6 | Tibet and Xinjiang ————————

The central question this chapter examines is why the CCP has fallen short in its attempts to promote ethnic unity (let alone minority acculturation and assimilation) in Tibet and Xinjiang despite rapid economic development in these two regions since 1978. To answer this question, this chapter first outlines the historical contexts of Tibet and Xinjiang. It then discusses what the CCP did to implement the social transformation of Tibet and Xinjiang between 1949 and 1965, why Beijing regarded the nationality question in Tibet and Xinjiang as an issue of class struggle during this period, and how the CCP raised new elite groups that supported socialist construction in Tibet and Xinjiang. Next, this chapter examines how the Cultural Revolution of 1966–76 created inter-group antagonism between Han Chinese and Tibetans and between Han Chinese and Uyghurs. This chapter also shows that since the Cultural Revolution the Chinese leadership has made efforts to develop local economies in Tibet and Xinjiang as a means of promoting ethnic unity and *ronghe*. However, post-1978 economic development in Tibet and Xinjiang has been accompanied by rising ethnic tensions rather than minority acculturation. Finally, this chapter explains why the current nationality policy is ill-equipped to promote inter-group harmony in these two regions.

HISTORICAL BACKGROUND

This chapter is devoted to ethnic issues in Tibet and Xinjiang because they symbolize ethnic conflict, draw international attention to minority rights in China, and test the CCP's capacity to pursue its *ronghe* policy more than any other minority region. Many people in the West have become interested in non-Han groups in the PRC partly because of alleged ethnic conflicts, religious suppression and human rights violations in Tibet and Xinjiang. Many NGOs and governments in the West have used Tibet and Xinjiang as a lens to observe minority rights and religious freedom in China. This chapter is devoted to ethnic issues in Tibet and Xinjiang also because they are of strategic significance to the PRC. Their geographical positions serve as the buffers between China, India and Central Asia (Elmer 2011, pp. 6, 10), and they represent 42 per cent of the PRC's territory and are rich in natural resources. Since 1949 the CCP has invested a significant amount of resources in governing these two regions and obviously invested a lot more in these two regions than in other minority areas. Ma (1996, p. 218) reported that in 1988, cash from central budgets made up a large part of local government budgets in Tibet (99.8 per cent) and Xinjiang (60.1 per cent). From 1959 to 2008, fiscal assistance from the central budget to Tibet reached 201.9 billion yuan, with an annual increase of nearly 12 per cent. Beijing also spent more than 1.8 billion yuan in the past 30 years on health care in Tibet (Lai 2009a, p. 13; Sautman 2006, p. 254; Information Office of the State Council 2005; 2009). Similarly, from 1955 to 2008, fiscal assistance from the central budget to Xinjiang reached 375.202 billion yuan, with an annual increase of 11 per cent (Information Office of the State Council 2009). No other minority areas are treated in a similar way by the central government. Clearly, the CCP cares a lot about Tibet and Xinjiang and has been anxious to see if its nationality policy would achieve success in these two regions.

To Beijing's disappointment, Tibet and Xinjiang are known to the outside world for their independence movements. The CCP has associated terrorism in China with Uyghur separatists and radical members of the Tibetan Buddhist clergy because they have allegedly agitated for violence and independence and thus posed a challenge 'to the idea of Chinese national unity through ethnic minority regionalism' (Chung 2006, p. 76). Why has the CCP faced this challenge from Tibet and Xinjiang? To understand this question, it is necessary for readers to examine some background information about these two regions.

Tibet

Tibet has drawn international attention partly because of the debates over the accusation by Tibetan activists within and outside China about massive human rights violations, religious suppression and cultural genocide in Tibet. The PRC government has categorically rejected these accusations (The Tibetan Parliamentary and Policy Research Centre 2008). In addition, there has been a debate on the Tibet Question, which concerns Tibetan sovereignty, i.e., whether Tibet is subordinate to China (Goldstein 1999). On one hand, the Dalai Lama (1987) claims that 'Tibet was a fully independent state when the People's Liberation Army invaded the country in 1949/50' (see also Sperling 2004, p. 21). This claim has been used as a major justification for Tibetan independence from the PRC. On the other hand, the Republic of China (1912–49) maintained that Tibet was placed under the sovereignty of the Qing government in 1793 (Sperling 2004, pp. 6–7; Goldstein 1989, p. 72). The PRC claims that Tibet has been a part of China since the Yuan dynasty (1271–1368) (Wang and Nyima 1997, p. 20; Sperling 2004, p. 10). Who is telling the truth?

Historically, one of the earliest contacts between China and Tibet occurred during the Tang dynasty, when King Songtsen Gampo married a Chinese princess. This was the period at which the Tibetan Empire was at its height. China and Tibet both came under Mongol rule during the Yuan dynasty. Beijing considers the Yuan dynasty as a Chinese regime, and accordingly maintains that Tibet has been part of China since the Yuan dynasty. For example, Zhu Weiqun, executive deputy minister of the State Ethnic Commission, claims that the central authorities have had direct control over the Tibetan territory for the past 700 years (2011, p. 14). Some scholars in the West think differently, however. Goldstein (1999, p. 4) argues that the succeeding Ming dynasty (1368–1644), which was a Han regime, 'exerted no administrative authority' in Tibet. Elmer (2011, pp. 1–2) claims that it was not until the Qing dynasty that China expanded its effective control over Tibet. The Qing dynasty conquered Tibet in 1720 and turned it into a protectorate. In 1793, the Qing emperor issued the 'Twenty-Nine Regulations for Better Government in Tibet'. While Qing officials and soldiers were stationed in the territory, Tibetans were left to manage most of their internal affairs and Tibet's foreign policy (Dutt 1964, pp. 197–206; Heberer 1989, pp. 118–26; Goldstein 1999, pp. 1–36; Mackerras 2005b, p. 3). After the demise of the Qing dynasty in 1911, the 13th Dalai Lama declared Tibetan independence in 1913. He and the regents who succeeded him in the 1930s and 1940s governed Tibet enjoying de facto independence until 1950 (Elmer 2011, p. 2; Shakya 1999, p. 5; Wang and Nyima 2000, pp. 162–6; see also Kapstein 2006; Wang and Nyima 2009).

In 1950, the CCP and its People's Liberation Army (PLA) defeated Tibetan militia. Beijing negotiated the 17-Point Agreement with the government under the newly enthroned 14th Dalai Lama in 1951, by which Tibet was acknowledged as part of China, yet was allowed extensive autonomy, including the preservation of the Tibetan government with the Dalai Lama at its head, and of other Tibetan social institutions including the monastic system (Smith 2004, p. 3). However, in fact, Tibet was governed by the Tibetan administrative system, supervised by CCP officials between 1951 and 1956. From 1956 to 1959 it came under the authority of the Preparatory Committee of the Tibetan Autonomous Region (TAR), which was chaired by the Dalai Lama and composed of representatives of the Tibetan government, other collaborative bodies and CCP officials. But real authority resided in the CCP Tibet Work Committee (Smith 2004, p. 11). In 1959,

Tibetan aristocrats and monasteries launched a revolt against CCP rule because their properties and power had been undermined by the CCP's reform measures. The rebellions spread to Tibetan communities in other provinces. Beijing quickly crushed the revolt. The Dalai Lama fled to India (Elmer 2011, pp. 2–3; Goldstein 1999; Jian 2006; Kapstein 2006; Lyon 2008). Beijing wasted no time in promoting local elections until all 70 counties in Tibet formed people's congresses in 1965. These people's congresses in turn elected a total of 301 delegates (226 Tibetan, 59 Han Chinese, and 16 of other minority nationalities) to the People's Congress in Tibet, which convened on 1 September 1965 to establish the Tibet Autonomous Region (TAR) (Smith 2004, p. 12).

Some historical data suggest that the Tibetan population was 0.96 million in 1737 and grew to three million by 1910, and remained three million in 1950; other sources give different estimates (Ma 1996, pp. 30–2). However, according to the first PRC census in 1953, there were only 1.27 million Tibetans in Tibet. It is possible that previous estimates were not scientific, or they included Tibetans in the 'Greater Tibetan areas' of the Qinghai-Tibet Plateau that included Tibet, Qinghai, and parts of Sichuan, Gansu and Yunnan, whereas the first census surveyed in the region of the TAR only. The second census recorded 1.25 million Tibetans in the TAR in 1964, the third census 3.85 million in 1982, and the fourth census 4.59 million in 1990. Overall, birth rates among Tibetans were higher than the national average, and between 1982 and 1990 the population growth rate of the Tibetans in the TAR was 2.16, as compared with 1.48 nationwide (Ma 1996, pp. 30–42; Mackerras 2005b, pp. 20–1). By 2010, the Tibetan population in China had reached nearly 6.3 million (see table 1.1).

Xinjiang

Compared with Tibet, Xinjiang's engagement with China is much longer and its relations with China are closer. The Han dynasty

(206 BC–220 AD) set up the Office of Protector-General of the Western Regions in what is now Xinjiang, and the Tang dynasty (618–907) established the Anxi and Beiting Office of Protector-General in the region (Information Office of the State Council 2005). However, some Uyghurs and Western scholars have argued that

> until the eighteenth century no Chinese dynasty had continuously controlled for any length of time or governed in any thoroughgoing way the entire territory that is modern Xinjiang. The Han and Tang dynasties had settled the Turpan area and established isolated garrisons elsewhere. The Mongol Yuan in theory briefly kept all of China and Central Eurasia under one khan, though the fault lines of this empire are all too visible. (Millward and Perdue 2004, p. 48)

Some scholars have insisted that substantial Chinese rule over this region was established only after the Qing conquest of Xinjiang in 1759 (Millward 1998, pp. 25–33, 137–46; 2007, p. 24; Millward and Perdue 2004, p. 48; Tursun 2008, pp. 93, 95–6). Uyghur nationalist accounts have asserted that Uyghurs have been a unified nation since ancient times (Bovingdon 2004a, pp. 359, 363). Notwithstanding, it is a subject of debate whether Uyghurs are indigenous inhabitants of Xinjiang. Chinese sources claims that the origin of Uyghurs can be traced back to Dingling nomads in northern and north-western China and in areas that form today's Mongolia in the third century BC. Dingling was later called the Tiele, Tieli, Chile or Gaoche in Chinese historical documents. The Yuanhe tribe reigned among the Gaoche tribes during the fifth century AD, and the Weihe reigned among the Tiele during the seventh century (Chang 2003, p. 40; People's Daily Online n.d.). After 747, Bayan Chor (Moyan Chuo in Chinese) brought many tribes under Uyghur rule, including Sekiz Oghuz, Qïrghïz, Qarluqs, Türgish, Basmïls, Toquz Tatars and Chiks. After Bayan Chor died in 759, Bögü

Qaghan succeeded and converted to Manichaeism in 762, and Manichaeism became the official religion of the Uyghur Empire. The Uyghur Empire collapsed in 840 due to the combined forces of a domestic rebellion, a large-scale famine, and a foreign invasion. Uyghurs fled towards the south and south-west and settled down in Gansu and Turfan in northern Xinjiang (Mackerras 1972; Uyghur Empire n.d.).

It is claimed that Uyghurs practised Nestorian Christianity and shamanism in addition to Manichaeism before 932. Some Uyghurs became Buddhist afterwards; others were converted to Islam before the Mongol conquest of Xinjiang around 1200 (Fuller and Lipman 2004, p. 326; Koch 2006, p. 10). Some scholars argue that the massive Uyghur conversion to Islam was not completed until the mid-1400s. Others claim that the conversion was not concluded until the 1600s (Zang 2011c). The Qing Empire gradually gained control over Xinjiang after a series of successful military campaigns beginning in the seventeenth century against Dzunghars, who were Mongolian warriors and the rulers of the region at that time. Qing rule in Xinjiang was contested by repeated Muslim rebellions, and the most serious one was led by Yaqub Beg (1865–1877), a Tajik from Panjakent in Tajikistan, who conquered and ruled much of Southern Xinjiang, including Aksu, Kucha and Kashgar. The Qing's army put down these rebellions, and Xinjiang became a province of the Qing Empire in 1884. As mentioned in chapter 4, the Qing dynasty relied on a Beg (a generic term for chiefs of Turkic groups in various oases appointed by the central government) system to govern the region. Uyghur leaders were bound by salaries and titles to the Qing government. While Qing officials ran political and military affairs in Xinjiang, Uyghurs and other ethnic minorities were allowed to preserve their customs, cultures and social systems under their jurisdiction (Borei 2002, pp. 276–80; Clarke 2011, pp. 18–21; Kim 2004, p. 11; Ji 2002, pp. 95–162; see also Newby 1998).

After the Qing Empire collapsed in 1911, Xinjiang was ruled successively by three warlords: Yang Zengxin (1912–28), Jin Shuren

(1928–34), and Sheng Shicai (1934–44). General Sheng suppressed Uyghur nationalism and Islamic movements, was known for his extensive use of torture in his campaigns against pan-Turkic and pan-Islamic movements, and was regarded by Uyghurs as a ruthless mass-killer (Hao 2009; Hyer 2006, p. 81; see also Whiting and Sheng 1958; Forbes 1986). The central government of the Nationalist regime was not able to place Xinjiang under its direct control until 1944. It appointed four governors of Xinjiang between 1944 and 1949: Wu Zhongxin (1944–5), Zhang Zhizhong (1945–7), Masud Sabri (1947–9), and Burhan Shähidi (1949) (Clarke 2011, pp. 28–41).

It is necessary to mention that in 1933 Uyghur rebels formed the First East Turkestan Republic, which was suppressed by Chinese forces in 1934. With the support of the Soviet Union, Uyghur rebels established the Second East Turkestan Republic in 1944. It withstood the military campaigns by the Nationalist Army, but was eventually absorbed into the PRC when the CCP and its army entered Xinjiang in 1949 (Braker 1985, p. 109; Clarke 2011, pp. 37–9; see also Benson 1990; Ji 2002, pp. 252–78; S. Li 2003, pp. 145–57, 218–23; J. Huang 2003, pp. 79, 127, 144; Xinjiang Academy of Social Sciences, History Division 1997, Vol. 2, pp. 328–40; Vol. 3, pp. 92–165, 166–85, 329–34, 335–6, 435–48, 483–5, 495, 511–27; Bai and Ozawa 1992). At that time, some Uyghurs expected that they would soon enjoy full political independence in Xinjiang as they had been told by Mao Zedong a decade earlier. But 'CCP officials asked Uyghurs to be satisfied with autonomy' (Clarke 2011, pp. 40–1; Bovingdon 2004b, p. 5). The region became the Xinjiang Uyghur Autonomous Region (XUAR) on 1 October 1955.

According to historical sources, there were 3.29 million Uyghurs in Xinjiang in 1949 (Toops 2004, pp. 243–8; S. Li 2003, pp. 38–9). The first PRC census recorded 3.6 million Uyghurs in Xinjiang in 1953, the second PRC census more than 4 million in 1964, the third PRC census nearly 6 million in 1982, the fourth PRC census nearly

7.2 million in 1990, and the fifth PRC census more than 8.3 million in 2000 (Toops 2004, pp. 243–8; Editorial Team of Xinjiang Local Gazettes 2004, p. 1). The Uyghur population was estimated to be more than 8.8 million by 2003 and nearly 10.1 million by 2010. Over 82 per cent of them clustered in southern Xinjiang in places like Hotan and Kashgar. Nearly 12 per cent of them lived in northern Xinjiang, including in Ürümchi (Ji 2002, pp. 279–94).

THE SOCIALIST TRANSFORMATION OF TIBET AND XINJIANG: 1949–1966

The system of regional autonomy has been a major institutional framework with which Beijing has placed Tibet and Xinjiang under its control. Beijing also carried out socialist campaigns and class struggles to integrate Tibetans and Uyghurs into the Chinese nation before 1976. As noted, the Chinese army put down the armed rebellion in Tibet in 1959, and killed, wounded or captured some 5,600 Tibetans in the battles. An analyst put the number at 3,000 or more killed (Sautman 2006, p. 246). In Xinjiang, the CCP organized a Red Terror campaign, mercilessly handling ethnic and religious affairs and executing some Uyghurs with 'deviant' political or religious views in the 1950s (Braker 1985, pp. 153–4). Then, in both Tibet and Xinjiang, the ethnic elites, who had signed the pacts with the CCP around 1949, were gradually removed from the governments and replaced by politically reliable Tibetan or Uyghur cadres whom the CCP had recruited and trained after 1949 (Hess 2009, p. 86; Millward 2007, pp. 237–9; Shakya 2009). The CCP also replaced religious courts with people's courts, 'and secular state-run schools took the place of religious schools' (Hess 2009, p. 80).

Next, the Chinese government carried out the socialist transformation of the economic systems in Tibet and Xinjiang. The main sources of income for the ruling classes in Xinjiang before 1949 were Islamic taxes and income generated from a system called *waqfiya*, which included land and other endowment properties. Millward and Tursun (2004, pp. 88–9) state that the CCP 'eliminated Islamic taxes (1950–1951); then in the land reform and associated "Movement to Reduce Rents and Oppose Local Despots", it expropriated waqf lands and thus eliminated institutional Islam's main source of revenue . . . Authorities also pressured axuns into relinquishing their private wealth' (also Mackerras 1994, p. 199; Millward 2007, pp. 247–8). Adle et al. (2005, p. 389) think that before 1952,

> approximately 8 per cent of the rural population were landlords and between 40 and 50 per cent were rich peasants, but between them they owned over 80 per cent of the land. By the end of 1953, Xinjiang had completed its programme of land reform, encompassing more than 74.2 million ha of land, over 70,000 herds of livestocks, 60,000 farm tools, 200,000 homesteads and 70 million kg of grain distributed among 33.2 million peasants.

The CCP introduced the People's Commune system in 1958, in which nearly every Uyghur farmer, like Han farmers in China proper, had to surrender his land to, and work for, his commune (Clarke 2011, pp. 58–60; Dreyer 1976, p. 128; McMillen 1979, pp. 131–2).

In Tibet, during the early 1950s the CCP adopted a gradual approach that eschewed radical class struggle against the Tibetan establishment. However, 'democratic reforms' were forcibly introduced in 1958. The CCP abolished the bondage of the serfs and slaves to their masters, as well as privileges, corvée labour and high-interest loans (for a different account, see Fischer 2013, chapter 2). It spent 45 million yuan on the redemption of 60,000 hectares of land and over 820,000 head of livestock from more than 1,300 Tibetan serf-owners and agents who had not participated in the 1959 rebellion. Over 2.8 million mu of land was confiscated from Tibetan serf-owners who had participated in the 1959 rebellion, which were 'distributed to 800,000 former serfs or slaves of 200,000 households. Each of the former serfs and slaves got about 3.5 mu of land' (Elmer 2011, pp. 2–3; Mackerras 2005b, p. 5; see also Lyon 2008; Xinhua 2009a). The mutual aid team system and the commune system were implemented successively in Tibet afterwards.

Beijing's nationality policy and class struggle seemed to work in Tibet and Xinjiang before 1966. Indeed, there was fierce Tibetan resistance to Chinese rule in 1959 as noted above (Goldstein 1999; see also Dillon 2009, pp. 168–75; Fischer 2004, p. 5). In Xinjiang, 60,000 Uyghur and Kazak refugees fled to the Soviet Union in 1962 (Wheeler 1964, p. 176; see also Jun 2005; McMillen 1979). But overall, there were few if any reports of serious ethnic conflicts in Tibet and Xinjiang during the period 1949–66. In his fieldwork in Ürümchi, Clark (1999) reported undivided loyalty to the CCP and total commitment to socialist construction among Uyghur professionals and cadres before the Cultural Revolution of 1966–76. Uyghurs worked together with Han Chinese for the sake of socialist construction. So did Tibetans in Tibet (Goldstein et al. 1999; 2004).

Why did Beijing's nationality policy work relatively well during this period? Firstly, the Cold War put ethnic identity into the background and gave the CCP the moral high ground and political legitimacy in replacing the nationality issue with class struggle (Goldstein et al. 1999; 2004). The CCP suppressed ethnic consciousness, accusing anyone who referred to nationality issues of advocating ethnic separatism. Religious affiliation and ethnic customs were criticized as feudal and backward and to be removed from everyday life to ensure socialist transformation. Also, China was closed to the outside world and contact with people in a foreign country was forbidden; if it took place it would be treated as an act of treason or espionage and punished harshly.

Secondly, the CCP promoted socioeconomic development in Tibet and Xinjiang (and other minority areas). As noted in chapter 2, it adopted various measures such as flexibility in local economic practices, increased state funding for local development projects, and more local control over the distribution of tax revenues in the minority areas (Gladney 1998, p. 244). Beijing's financial support was a key factor for the well-being of the local populations in the minority areas. In 1981, the overall level of socioeconomic development in Tibet was substantially lower than that of China as a whole, but the annual average income of urban residents in Tibet was higher than that in China as a whole (Ma 1996, p. 240; Mackerras 1994, pp. 200–5), a direct outcome of heavy government subsidies. Schools and hospitals were set up and highways were built linking Lhasa to China and to the borders of India, Nepal and Pakistan (Smith 2004, p. 11; Lyon 2008). Similar infrastructure projects were carried out in Xinjiang (chapter 2). Living standards among Tibetans and Uyghurs were improved and there was little ethnic inequality as China was one of the most equal societies (in terms of the Gini coefficient) in the world at that time.

Thirdly, the CCP carried out the policy of divide and rule in Tibet and Xinjiang and raised new elite groups including government officials, professionals and the modern working class to replace old ruling groups. The new social groups enjoyed upward mobility, benefited from the modernization process the CCP had pursued, embraced socialist ideology, and were the main supporters of the CCP in the regions (Hess 2009, p. 76; see also Clark 1999; Goldstein et al. 1999; 2004). They served as role models and gave hope for upward mobility to their compatriots. In Xinjiang, for example, the CCP employed about 3,000 minority cadres in 1950 and 46,000 in 1955. By 1965, there were more than 100,000 non-Han government positions, constituting 56 per cent of all cadres in Xinjiang (Information Office of the State Council 1996).

THE CULTURAL REVOLUTION OF 1966–1976

However, during the Cultural Revolution of 1966–76, the principle of class struggle was excessively applied to ethnic minority groups in Tibet and Xinjiang (and other minority areas as well). Scholars have observed that while many Han Chinese were victimized, 'the Cultural Revolution's call to attack the "Four Olds" of old customs, ideas, culture and habits was ultimately more portentous for the ethnic minorities than it was for the Han' (Clarke 2011, p. 66; Dreyer 1994, p. 44; Heberer 1989, pp. 25–7; McMillen 1979, p. 186; see also Goldstein et al. 2009). In the pre-1966 era, the cultural differences and deviation from uniformity were defined as old customs and habits to be modified or removed gradually through socialization of socialist values and scientific education. Now they were regarded as a 'class contradiction', which had to be forcefully and immediately eradicated. Many special treatments for minority nationalities were abolished, clergymen were persecuted, monasteries, temples and mosques were demolished or shut down, and religious scripts were burnt in public in both Tibet (Mackerras 2005b, pp. 6–7; see also Goldstein et al. 2009) and Xinjiang (Barabantseva 2008, p. 580; Clarke 2011, pp. 65–70; Hess 2009, pp. 80–1; Millward 2007, pp. 275–6; see also Lyon 2008).

Furthermore, the pre-1966 policy of regional autonomy was condemned as creating independent tendencies and encouraging separatism among the ethnic minorities (see chapter 4), elite members among ethnic minorities were labelled, without any evidence or justification, as the agents of ethnic nationalism and separatism in minority areas and were hit hard. In Xinjiang, for example, some Uyghur cadres were humiliated in public meetings, others were tortured, killed or went missing. The Cultural Revolution appeared to be an all-out attack on ethnic cultures and religions in Tibet and Xinjiang by the CCP and Han Chinese (Clark 1999; Goldstein et al. 1999).

As a result, the differences among ethnic groups in these regions were aggravated. Dreyer (1976, p. 175) argues that 'the great effort to erase differences among nationalities resulted in heightening minorities' awareness of these differences and seemed to induce a stubborn desire to retain them'. The extremist and discriminatory nature of the Cultural Revolution policies led to the growth of resentment towards the CCP and ethnic consciousness among Uyghurs and Tibetans. In 1980, the then CCP Secretary General Hu Yaobang asserted that Tibet was worse off than before the Cultural Revolution, and that the CCP owed the Tibetan people an apology (Lyon 2008).

FROM SOCIALIST REVOLUTION TO ECONOMIC DEVELOPMENT IN THE POST-1978 ERA

After the Cultural Revolution, the CCP recognized the damage done to Tibetans, Uyghurs and other ethnic minority groups between 1966 and 1976. To reconcile with the ethnic minority groups, Beijing carried out a liberalization policy in the early 1980s, which meant more autonomy for minority areas, more equal opportunities for ethnic minorities, and fewer restrictions on ethnic and religious expression. In May 1980, Hu Yaobang proposed to enact 'ample autonomy' in Tibet: 'as a first step he ordered that two thirds of the cadre positions in Tibet be filled with Tibetans and a large number of the Han cadres be retired or transferred to China proper. There was a goal of increasing the proportion of the Tibetan cadres to more than two thirds of the total officials in Tibet from 1981 to 1983' (Huang 1995, pp. 195–6). After meeting the Xinjiang CCP Committee in July 1980, Hu approved a proposal along similar lines, mandating that the party appoint non-Hans as first party secretaries at various levels, and stipulating that the ratio of minority cadres in Xinjiang 'be raised to over 60 per cent' (Joseph 2010, pp. 347–8; see also Clarke 2011, p. 77).

Thus, a large number of Han cadres were withdrawn from Tibet and Xinjiang to make room for Tibetans and Uyghurs to fill government posts in these two regions. There appeared to be five large-scale withdrawals in Tibet during the 1980s: in 1980, 1981, 1982, 1983 and 1989. In 1980, 3,000 Han cadres were withdrawn from Tibet, and the corresponding figure was 2,705 for 1983, and 3,507 for 1989. In addition, 1,710 Han cadres retired and were resettled from Tibet to inland provinces in 1989. As a result, the proportion of Tibetan cadres to all cadres in Tibet rose from 44.5 per cent in 1978 to 54.5 per cent in 1981, 60.3 per cent in 1986, and 61.4 per cent in 1989 (Mackerras 2005b, p. 8; see also Huang 1995, pp. 190, 194–6). By 1996, there were some 37,000 Tibetan cadres, making up 66.6 per cent of the total number of cadres in the TAR (Information Office of the State Council 1996). The corresponding figures for 2004 were 49,752 Tibetan cadres and 74 per cent, with many leading posts in the people's congresses and governments being filled by Tibetans and other minority nationalities in the TAR (Chang 2004; Mackerras 2005b, p. 12; Xinhua 2005b). Sautman (2006, p. 256) argues that 'On an everyday basis, Tibetans probably play a larger role in running Tibet than does the TAR's Han party secretary, who devotes much of his time to liaising with Beijing.'

Similar efforts were made in Xinjiang. Many Uyghur cadres who had been purged during the Cultural Revolution were reinstated, and many non-Han cadres were recruited into the regional and local governments in Xinjiang, raising the total number of ethnic minority cadres to over 180,000 by 1983 (Information Office of the State Council 1996; see also Clarke 2011, pp. 74, 78). By 2009, 348,000 non-Han cadres constituted 52 per cent of the total cadres in Xinjiang. (Xinhua 2009b; see also US Congressional-Executive Commission on China 2005a, p. 11). In May 2010, then President Hu Jintao emphasized in a central work conference on Xinjiang's development that minority elites should be encouraged to take on more regional cadre roles (US Congressional-Executive Commission on China 2005a, p. 11; Rahman 2005, pp. 82–3; Dong 2010; Xinhua 2009b).

Other liberalization policies implemented in Tibet and Xinjiang included measures to give Tibetans and Uyghurs some degree of freedom in cultural and religious expression (Clarke 2011, pp. 73–80; Mackerras 2005b, pp. 7–8). In addition, Beijing has institutionalized minority entitlement policy that has given minority groups preferential considerations in birth control, college admission quotas, job place-ment and ethnic slots in leadership representation (chapter 2). It announced the 'two restraints and one leniency' policy to give minority suspects leniency in restraining and prosecuting in 1984 (Hess 2009, p. 82; Rudelson and Jankowiak 2004, p. 307; Sautman 2006, pp. 244, 256; see also Hao 2009), and opened up negotiations with the Dalai Lama (Smith 2004, p. 3). Tibet's population and range of cultural activities expanded. Although ethnically related problems existed in Tibet, they did not 'amount to genocide or colonialism' (Sautman 2006, p. 244).

More importantly, the CCP has reassessed and reoriented its policy towards the minority nationalities. It announced at the Third Plenum of the 11th Central Committee in December 1978 that class struggle was no longer the key factor in the development of its nationality policy (Clarke 2011, p. 73), acknowledging that the class underpinning of the nationality question was largely irrelevant for the emergent social reali-ties in the post-1978 era, and thus must be repudiated. The approach to the interpretation and handling of the nationality question would be put in line with the rules of the market economy the CCP has promoted since 1978 (Barabantseva 2008, pp. 581–2; Clarke 2011, p. 73), and the nationality question can no longer be regarded as an issue of class struggle (Hyer 2009, p. 271). In other words, the CCP gave up its practice of forced minority acculturation and has promoted ethnic unity and eventual *ronghe* through economic development. Beijing has accordingly stressed national cohesion and the idea of an all-inclusive (and classless) Chinese nation, which has been legitimized with terms such as the 'people of the dragon (龙的传人)'. All nationality groups in China have been defined as the 'descendants of Yan and Huang (炎黄子孙)'. These notions have been used to build ethnic solidarities for governance in Tibet and Xinjiang.

Beijing has in the post-1978 era defined ethnic issues mainly in terms of inter-group inequality in income, education, health, etc., but not in terms of cultural concerns, religious demands, language issues or political rights (see chapter 3). Correspondingly, in the post-1978 era, Beijing has focused on assisting Tibetans and Uyghurs to catch up with the economic development level of Han Chinese, hoping that economic growth would stimulate the development of other aspects of ethnic minorities such as politics and culture, which in turn would increasingly solidify a new type of socialist ethnic relations and strengthen national unity in Tibet and Xinjiang. Economic development has been placed at the centre of political rhetoric and been treated as a panacea for almost all diagnosed problems associated with ethnic relations in these two regions (Barabantseva 2008, pp. 583–7; Mackerras 2005b, p. ii; 2011a, p. 116; see also Koch 2006).

The CCP launched the Great Western Development policy in 2000 to boost economic growth in Western China including Tibet and Xinjiang. Acknowledging that ethnic minorities in western regions have not benefited from China's fast-paced economic growth as much as people living in eastern regions, Beijing has implemented policies including more tax exemptions and more state investment in infrastructure to allocate resources and benefits to China's west (Goodman 2004, pp. 319–20; Koch 2006, 14; Mackerras 2005b, p. 12; 2011a, p. 116). From 1994 to 2001, for example, 15 Han municipalities, provinces and central government organs supported the construction of 716 projects (costing 3.16 billion yuan) in Tibet. Between 2001 and

2005, Tibet received financial assistance (1.062 billion yuan) from Han regions for the construction of 71 projects (Information Office of the State Council 2005). As noted elsewhere in this book, similar assistance projects have also existed in Xinjiang, financially supported by Han regions (see chapter 2).

The economies in Tibet and Xinjiang have been developing rapidly in the post-1978 era. Xinjiang's GDP climbed from 105 billion yuan in 1997 to 220 billion yuan in 2004, 352 billion yuan in 2007, 420 billion yuan in 2008, and 657.4 billion yuan in 2011. Its GDP per capita increased from 1,680 yuan in 1997 to 16,820 yuan in 2007 and then to 19,798 yuan in 2009. In 2003, the annual income of urban citizens in Xinjiang reached 7,180 yuan, while income per capita of farmers and herdsmen in the region increased by 9.2 per cent, exceeding 2,000 yuan. In 2007, the income per capita of Xinjiang farmers reached 3,150 yuan (Xinjiang Demographic Analysis and Economy Overview n.d.; http://en.wikipedia.org/wiki/Xinjiang; Li 2013). Similarly, the output value of Tibet's agricultural and animal husbandry sector grew from 264 million yuan in 1965 to 6.27 billion yuan in 2004. The per capita GDP in Tibet averaged 7,779 yuan in 2004, about 33 times the corresponding figure in 1965. Tibet's GDP in 2004 topped 21.15 billion yuan, 65 times more than the corresponding figure in 1965 (Mackerras 2005b, p. 12; Xinhua 2005c). Of course, readers should read these data critically, as mentioned in the Preface.

RISING ETHNIC CONFLICTS IN TIBET AND XINJIANG SINCE THE 1990S

Surprisingly, rapid economic development in Tibet and Xinjiang has been accompanied by rising ethnic consciousness and inter-group tensions/conflicts in these two regions since the 1990s (Koch 2006, pp. 13–17; Smith Finley 2007a). This combination is contrary to Beijing's belief that economic growth would promote ethnic unity in Tibet and Xinjiang, which is a precondition for minority acculturation and assimilation into Han society. In particular, in Tibet, this combination has taken place since the Dalai Lama has become increasingly less confrontational in his dealings with the PRC. In 1992, he modified his previous demand for autonomy for Tibet similar to the privilege enjoyed by post-1997 Hong Kong, and asked for 'meaningful autonomy' instead. He has recently declared his concern for 'religious harmony', 'human values' and 'the well-being of the Tibetan people', by which he has referred to the resolution of the Tibetan issue through 'international norms' (Chung 2006, p. 82; Lai 2009a, p. 11; Mackerras 2005b, p. 15) rather than independence through violence. It seems that many Tibetan activists have supported the Dalai Lama's modified position. Others, however, have become increasingly militant, contrary to what the Dalai Lama desires for Tibet. A series of demonstrations in Tibet took place in the 1980s as some monks and nuns called for Tibetan independence and the return of the Dalai Lama. In the 1990s there were occasional small-scale bombings (Chung 2006, p. 77; Mackerras 2005b, pp. 8–9; Sautman 2005, p. 99; Smith 2004, p. 3). Then there were large-scale protests by Tibetans in March 2008. Barnett (2009, pp. 11–13) observed that the protests took place all across the Tibetan areas, not just in the TAR. The overwhelming majority of the protests in the late 1980s were led by Tibetan monks or nuns, with comparatively few lay Tibetans involved. In comparison, it was estimated that less than a quarter of the Tibetan protesters in 2008 were monks or nuns, while 17 per cent were Tibetan student protesters and others were mixed or lay groups, including Tibetan farmers and workers. Their compatriots in neighbouring Sichuan and Qinghai provinces have joined their cause after 2008. In 2011 alone, 11 Tibetan monks set fire to themselves in an unprecedented series of demonstrations in Sichuan (Burke and Branigan 2011). It is claimed that there was a total of 113 self-immolations in Tibet and Tibetan regions between February 2009 and

April 2013 (US Congressional-Executive Commission on China 2011; VOA Tibetan 2013).

In Xinjiang, similarly, Uyghur separatists have raised the levels of threatening rhetoric and violence since the 1990s (Mackerras 2011a, p. 121). A wave of demonstrations in Ürümchi and Yarkand in the late 1980s was followed by a major uprising in Baren during April 1990. Then there were large and violent demonstrations in Yining in February 1997. At the same time, several buses were bombed in Ürümchi. According to Bovingdon (2010, pp. 174–90), of all the 'organized protests and violent events' from 1949 to 2005, about half took place in the 1990s. In 2004, various Uyghur diasporic groups were united to form the World Uyghur Congress (http://www.uyghurcongress. org/en/). On 4 August 2008, four days before the Beijing Olympics, two Uyghur men armed with knives and explosives ambushed a military police unit and killed 16 Chinese police officers and wounded 16 others. The riot on 5 July 2009 in Ürümchi was the largest ethnic clash in Xinjiang, resulting in nearly 200 deaths and many injuries. In April 2013, 21 people were reported killed in a clash in Kashgar, Xinjiang (Blanchard 2013; McDonell, 2013). On 26 June 2013, some Uyghur extremists in Lukqun Township, Shanshan County in Xinjiang killed two Chinese policemen and 22 civilians. The Chinese police mounted a counterattack, killing 11 extremists and capturing four (Zhu 2013). On 28 October 2013, five people, including two tourists, were killed and dozens injured when a Uyghur family of three ploughed a jeep into pedestrians in Beijing's Tiananmen Square. It was quickly decided that this was a well-organized Uyghur terrorist attack. Five Uyghur suspects were detained in connection with the car crash and explosion in Tiananmen Square ten hours after the Tiananmen attack (Rajagopalan 2013). In comparison, 2013 was less violent than 2014. On 1 March 2014, eight knife-wielding Uyghur men and women attacked passengers at Kunming railway station, killing 29 people and wounding 143. In response, PRC President Xi Jinping made his first presidential visit in April 2014 to Xinjiang, which he called the 'front line against terrorism' in China. He urged strong steps to promote Uyghur integration and rapid economic growth but also demanded tough action against unrest in the region (Zhang 2014). On 30 April, the final day of President Xi's visit to the region, a pair of Uyghur assailants carried out an attack at the Ürümchi railway station, killing one civilian and wounding 79. President Xi promised 'decisive actions' against the 'terrorists' behind the attack (Blanchard 2014). On 22 May 2014, five Uyghur militants ploughed two SUVs into, and threw explosives into, a crowd in a market in Ürümchi. The SUVs then collided with each other and exploded. The attack killed 39 civilians and injured over 90. President Xi pledged to 'severely punish terrorists and spare no efforts in maintaining stability' (Connor 2014).

ETHNIC ISSUES AS A CHALLENGE TO GOVERNANCE IN TIBET AND XINJIANG

In response to escalating demands for independence in Tibet and Xinjiang, Beijing has used an iron fist to deal with ethnic protests in these two regions. The Chinese authorities have carried out a harsh crackdown of Uyghur and Tibetan separatists in Tibet and Xinjiang since the late 1990s (Chung 2006, p. 77; Clarke 2008, pp. 284–90; Hastings 2005, p. 32; Hierman 2007, pp. 49, 52, 54, 58–61; Hyer 2006, pp. 78–9; Smith Finley 2007a). Beijing has also used the carrot to reduce ethnic inequality and solicit support from Tibetans in Tibet and Uyghurs in Xinjiang. For example, after the 2009 ethnic riot in Ürümchi, Beijing has intensified its policy to support Xinjiang with financial and human resources assistance from Han regions (chapter 2), so that by 2015 the per capita GDP in Xinjiang would reach the national average, per capita income and levels of public services in Xinjiang would reach the average levels of China's western region, and infrastructure in Xinjiang would be greatly improved. Beijing hopes that economic development will lead to ethnic unity and enhance social stability in Xinjiang (Xinhua 2010a; 2011a).

Nevertheless, Beijing's ethnic policy has not adequately addressed the deep-seated frustrations felt by Tibetans and Uyghurs. Although Han Chinese and minority groups in both Tibet and Xinjiang have gained from rapid economic development, the social consequences are a strong feeling of relative deprivation and marginalization among some Tibetans and Uyghurs, who feel discontented when they compare their position to that of Han Chinese, and think that they have benefited far less from economic growth than Han Chinese. There are also feelings of political and social deprivation among Tibetans and Uyghurs due to the lack of religious freedom, threats to minority languages and customs, etc., in Tibet and Xinjiang.

Beijing's ethnic policy can cause serious problems when economic growth is not undertaken with sensitivity to promotion of minority rights, respect for religious freedom, preservation of ethnic culture, etc. (see chapter 7). These social and political issues cannot be addressed simply with economic growth, and have become an increasingly important concern for Tibetans and Uyghurs, given increased access to the outside world and global trends for human rights, multiculturalism and religious freedom. However, Beijing cannot afford to move towards the global trends because of their democratic nature, and has refused to admit that economic development alone does not work in the post-1978 era. It has instead blamed foreign interference for ethnic tensions and unrest in Tibet and Xinjiang, asserting that ethnic separatists have been funded by governments and religious organizations in the West, and that the ethnic riots are political rather than ethnic or cultural. It has depicted Han migrants and the PRC state as the victims of the violent extremism of ethnic separatists and foreign interference in Tibet and Xinjiang (Mackerras 2011a, p. 112). Beijing's target audience is Han Chinese, not the ethnic minority groups or people and the media outside the PRC. It has reached out to rally Han Chinese and harness Han nationalism and has refused to make compromises with the ethnic minority groups.

Beijing's approach has achieved some successes. Some Han Chinese have accepted this depiction of ethnic unrest wholeheartedly and demanded that Beijing re-examine its 'favouritist' nationality policy. They have criticized what they have perceived as the government's excessively benign stance towards the ethnic minorities, such as the 'two restraints and one leniency' policy mentioned above, claiming that this has treated minority peoples as being above Chinese law. Other Han Chinese have regarded the system of regional autonomy as a proven failure and have called for its cancellation (Hao 2009).

Beijing's approach has not alleviated the deep division along ethnic lines in Tibet and Xinjiang, and much more than cosmetic repairs and propaganda will be needed to cope with inter-group tensions in Tibet and Xinjiang. Beijing has not satisfactorily addressed the prejudices and stereotypes that have existed amongst the ethnic groups in Tibet and Xinjiang, and does not want to engage in a critical reflection on the negative effects of state nationality policy on ethnic relations. The way ethnic relations have been handled so far has prevented a fruitful rethinking of how the CCP can successfully involve minority nationalities in national reconciliation and ethnic unity, let alone minority acculturation and assimilation in Tibet and Xinjiang. In fact, Beijing's hands are tied because of its attachment to *ronghe* ideology, and its options are limited unless it starts to embrace diversity and multiculturalism at the expense of its ambition for minority acculturation and assimilation into Han society.

There are a few things Beijing can do to improve ethnic relations in Tibet and Xinjiang. One of the reasons for inter-group tensions in the two regions is Beijing's inability to reduce ethnic inequality between Han Chinese and Tibetans and between Han Chinese and Uyghurs. As noted, the CCP has placed economic development at the forefront of nationality policy making after 1978. This is not a new policy since similar approaches were already promoted in minority regions before the Cultural Revolution. But there is a key difference: economic growth took place in a relatively egalitarian society which benefited both the minority groups and Han Chinese and increased national unity and the legitimacy of the CCP in Mao's China. In post-1978 market reforms, however, Beijing has promoted efficiency and the 'survival of the fittest'. China has become one of the most unequal societies in the world as its Gini coefficient reached 0.47 in recent years (Chen 2010). Many scholars believe that China's Gini coefficient is more than 0.50. Market efficiency is gained at the expense of equality. In Tibet and Xinjiang, inequality has reflected itself mainly in terms of ethnic disparities in schooling, employment, income, etc. It is observed that the main beneficiaries of post-1978 economic growth have been Han Chinese rather than Tibetans or Uyghurs, since the former have the technology, capital and market connections to take advantage of the government policies (Hastings 2005, pp. 29–30). Minority entitlements from the government nationality policy in higher education and employment have become increasingly irrelevant in the post-1978 labour market, since job attainment has relied more and more on personal connections. Minority workers simply cannot compete with Han workers because of this. This may explain why some Uyghur job seekers have complained that Han Chinese have taken away good jobs in minority areas (Fuller and Lipman 2004, p. 325; Smith 2000, pp. 197, 200–1). Some Uyghurs have complained that the government has forsaken the preferential policy for national minorities'. Other Uyghurs have claimed that they encountered prejudice when seeking access to bank loans and administrative authorizations from government officials (Becquelin 2000, p. 85; Mackerras 2001, p. 299; Maurer-Fazio et al. 2007, p. 181; Yee 2003, p. 449). It has been observed that in Xinjiang, 'urban dissatisfaction stems from the fact that Uyghurs now have something to compare themselves with. It is socio-economic inequalities, there, which lie at the root of a rapidly strengthening

Uyghur national identity, an identity that did not emerge previously on the strength of religio-cultural differences alone' (Smith 2000, p. 201). Similarly, there has been growing Han–Tibetan inequality in income and employment in the TAR (Mackerras 2005b, pp. 13–14). Beijing can take some measures to narrow ethnic inequalities in Tibet and Xinjiang.

Beijing can also revisit its policy to support Han migration into Tibet and Xinjiang. It holds that Han migrants can help strengthen the CCP's control over the territory, develop the local economy, and better integrate minority areas into the PRC (see chapter 4). A well-known example is the Xinjiang Production and Construction Corps, which since 1954 has accommodated waves of Han migrants into Xinjiang. Large-scale Han migration has changed the ethnic population composition in Tibet and Xinjiang. The percentage of the Uyghur population in Xinjiang declined from over 75 per cent in 1949 to less than 46 per cent in 2004, whereas the Han population grew from under 10 per cent in 1949 to nearly 40 per cent in 2004 (Fischer 2004, p. 8; Rudelson and Jankowiak 2004, p. 306; also Becquelin 2000; Toops 2004). This in turn has intensified the social division between Uyghurs and Han. There is a similar pattern of Han migration into Tibet. Wong (2010; see also Woeser 2011) claims that Han Chinese workers, investors, merchants, teachers and soldiers are pouring into the region, and 'China's aim is to make Tibet wealthier – and more Chinese'. Han migration into Tibet and Xinjiang has created resentment against Han Chinese by Tibetans and Uyghurs. Some Uyghurs are afraid that 'they are quickly becoming a minority nationality within their own territory' (Rudelson and Jankowiak 2004, p. 310; Smith 2000, p. 200). Tibetans have developed a similar anxiety over Han migration into Tibet (Fischer 2004, pp. 1, 7; Mackerras 2005b, p. ii). It is in Beijing's interest to reassess its migration policy to protect ethnic interests in Tibet and Xinjiang, as this could alleviate the level of ethnic conflict in these two regions.

There are other things that are equally if not more fundamental and vital with regard to ethnic relations in Tibet and Xinjiang, but they are unachievable unless Beijing gives up its *ronghe* ideology. Firstly, the current nationality policy and its aggressive message about *ronghe* have produced a sense of insecurity among Tibetans and Uyghurs. The Chinese economy has grown rapidly since 1978, becoming the second biggest economy in the world in 2010. Its foreign exchange reserves, by far the largest in the world, rose to just shy of $4 trillion in the first quarter of 2014. At the same time, China has become an increasingly important player in international politics. The perception of a rising China is acutely felt at home, leading to national debates on how China can act as a superpower in the world. Some ethnic minority groups such as Hui and Zhuang who have been well acculturated have shared Han sentiments enthusiastically. Tibetans and Uyghurs have not, however. They have perceived their economic marginalization and possible cultural assimilation by Han Chinese (Mackerras 2011a, pp. 112, 118; Li 2013). It is a major challenge for Beijing to reconcile its *ronghe* ideology and the need of Tibetans and Uyghurs to survive economically and culturally admit a powerful Han society, in order to achieve some peace with these non-Han peoples.

Secondly, Tibetans and Uyghurs are religious peoples, and their religious beliefs are different from those of Han Chinese. Because of its *ronghe* ambition, Beijing has been unable to deal satisfactorily with the issue of religion in Tibet and Xinjiang. It has promised to preserve ethnic minority cultures in the PRC, but at the same time has artificially separated religion from ethnic cultures, viewing religion as a rival for political power and repressing religious activities in Tibet and Xinjiang. It is reported that 'practicing Muslims cannot find work in the state or state-sponsored sectors of the Xinjiang economy because of the strictures of official atheism.' It is also reported that 'anyone wishing to rise in the state-dominated sectors of society must avoid the mosque and any unseemly contact with Islamic teachers' (Fuller and Lipman 2004, pp. 324–5; Hess 2009, pp. 76–80). The issue is not Islam per se, as Hui Muslims are given the right to practise their religion. The difference between Hui Muslims and Uyghurs is how Islam is used by the two groups. As an acculturated minority group, Hui Muslims have no interest in using Islam to advance autonomy or independence. In contrast, Uyghurs have maintained the desire 'to retain those aspects of their culture, including Islam and the Uyghur language, that constitute the core of their personal and collective identities' (Fuller and Lipman 2004, pp. 324–6; Smith 2000, pp. 201, 214), and have relied on Islam and Uyghur nationalism to resist acculturation and assimilation. So have Tibetans. It is another major challenge for Beijing to figure out how to accommodate the religious issue in Tibet and Xinjiang since it has no desire to give up its *ronghe* ideology.

Thirdly, while there have been changes in the CCP's nationality rhetoric, some core ideas about Han Chinese and non-Han groups have persisted, and the dichotomy between Han Chinese and non-Han groups has been taken for granted by Han Chinese and the government. Minority groups have been ascribed the characteristics of insignificant numbers, backwardness, poverty and remoteness, and of being incapable of moving forward without help from Han Chinese and the government. This kind of discourse localizes ethnic minorities within the periphery of the Chinese state and ethnicizes their status in the notion of the inclusive Chinese nation (Barabantseva 2008). But if Han Chinese and the government continue to think this way, China's achievements will not be celebrated as the achievements of all the peoples in the PRC, including Tibetans and Uyghurs. The ethnic dichotomy would be a centrifugal force moving non-Han peoples away from the PRC. There seems to be an impasse here as Beijing cannot afford to give up the ethnic dichotomy between civilized Han Chinese and uncivilized non-Han groups, as it is part of the foundation of the Confucian hierarchy of different peoples in terms of Han civilization, *ronghe* ideology and the PRC nationality policy.

DISCUSSION

There have been frequent criticisms of Beijing's policies in Tibet and Xinjiang by NGOs, international organizations and governments in the West. Navanethem Pillay, the UN High Commissioner for Human Rights, claimed on 27 July 2009 that 'China's own law provides formal guarantees and minority protections for ethnic groups, as well as elements of self-governance. However, serious systemic violations of human rights are reported to be taking place at the same time as increasing exclusion of ethnic minorities from a top-down policy of economic development of the western portion of the country.' She asserted that Beijing had failed 'to protect minority rights' when commenting on ethnic conflicts in Tibet and Xinjiang in an 'update report' to the 12th session of the UN Human Rights on 15 September 2009 (Unrepresented Nations and Peoples Organization 2009; see also Mackerras 2005b, pp. 1–2).

A more eye-catching event is an open letter to the then PRC President Hu Jintao by 12 Nobel Peace laureates, published in *The New York Times* on 2 April 2012, urging him to engage in 'meaningful dialogue' with the Dalai Lama over Chinese policies in Tibet. The laureates, including Desmond Tutu, Jody Williams and Lech Walesa, expressed concern over 'the drastic expressions of resentment by the people of Tibet'. The letter calls for Mr Hu to open up Tibet to journalists and diplomats, stop the arbitrary detention of Tibetans and respect religious freedom (Wong 2012). The US Congressional-Executive Commission on China claims that the PRC government has failed to uphold the legal rights of minorities living in the Tibetan Autonomous Region and the Xinjiang Uighur Autonomous Region (US Congressional-Executive Commission on China 2005b, p. 2).

Apparently, Beijing has been unable to develop an effective policy towards its minority nationalities in the post-1978 era. In comparative perspective, the PRC did a better job in Mao's China. For example, there were far fewer ethnic riots in the pre-1978 era than in the post-1978 era. Rising ethnic consciousness among various ethnic minority groups has been a post-1978 phenomenon (Gladney 1996; Zang 2013) and the demand for Xinjiang independence has become a credible force only since 1978 (Rudelson 1997; Zang 2013). The difference was partly due to Cold War politics, the rapid improvement of living standards, the promotion of egalitarianism, and the rise of minority professionals and cadres in minority regions in Mao's China. In the post-1978 era, the Chinese government has focused on economic growth as a panacea for national unity in China. However, the current economic development strategy has favoured Han migrants at the expense of minority interests in Tibet and Xinjiang. If continued, this policy would in fact increase ethnic unrest and violence in these two regions. Other important causes of ethnic conflict in Tibet and Xinjiang include social and political marginalization and possible assimilation to Han society. Other minority groups in the PRC have faced similar challenges, but they have been less restless because they are either relatively weak or numerically small and have to live with discrimination and prejudice. Tibetans and Uyghurs are more empowered than these ethnic minority groups partly because of their population concentration and sizes and because they receive support and attention from the international community.

Why doesn't Beijing recognize that unrest in minority areas has more to do with ethnic and cultural issues than with foreign interference? Why doesn't Beijing do more to promote ethnic cultures and give more political power to the minority nationalities? Part of the answer to these questions is Beijing's attachment to *ronghe* ideology, which accounts for Beijing's inability to copy with the escalating ethnic tensions in Tibet and Xinjiang and to meet the international norms on minority rights in both China and abroad. This next chapter discusses this issue in some detail.

RECOMMENDED READING

Andrew Martin Fischer, *The Disempowered Development of Tibet in China: A Study in the Economics of Marginalization* (Lanham, MD: Lexington Books, 2013).

Colin Mackerras (ed.), *Ethnic Minorities in Modern China*, Vol. IV (London: Routledge, 2011).

Emily Yeh, *Taming Tibet: Landscape Transformation and the Gift of Chinese Development* (Ithaca, NY: Cornell University Press, 2013).

7 China's Nationality Policy and International Minority Rights

The previous chapters have discussed various aspects of China's nationality policy and its impacts on the ethnic minorities in the PRC. This chapter studies whether Beijing's nationality policy and *ronghe* ideology have contributed to a good minority rights regime in China. As shown below, opinions on this question from Beijing (and its supporters) and its critics vary greatly and are emotionally charged, and thus cannot be used to answer this question. A plausible approach is to examine whether the PRC has met its legal obligations to protect minority nationality groups from the perspective of the international norms on minority rights. Thus, this chapter asks: Has the Chinese state accepted the international standards of minority rights in designing its ethnic policy? Has it changed its ethnic policy to meet the international standards? What are the distinguishing features of Beijing's foreign policy towards minority rights in international politics? Has Beijing made progress in its socialization into the international norms on minority rights? Is the gap between Beijing's nationality policy and the international norms on minority rights likely to disappear in the near future?

There can be different international standards of minority rights. I use the European standards in this chapter. The European Union (EU) has developed and is a major champion of minority rights as a key norm in global governance, and has often gone beyond the international status quo on minority rights. Pentassuglia (2005, p. 19; see also Castellino and Redondo 2006, p. 10) writes that 'Specific regional minority standards beyond Europe are still virtually lacking, although some minority aspects are creeping into the indigenous rights discourse within the inter-American human rights protection system and attempts have been made recently to advance minority issues within the African human rights protection system as well.' The European approach towards minority rights is preferred over the US approach because the latter is distinguished by its equal opportunity programmes with a focus on individual rights, whereas the former promotes both individual rights and minority group guarantees including self-determination and even territorial secession.

Accordingly, this chapter first outlines the historical development of the minority rights regime since the seventeenth century, with emphasis on Europe. It then provides an account of a major paradigm shift in minority rights in global governance since 1989. Next, it puts emphasis on Beijing with the aim of examining some key aspects of its protection of minorities and of identifying the areas of improvement in the minority rights regime in the PRC. There is also a brief discussion of Beijing's foreign policy towards minority rights in international politics. It then reviews Beijing's progress in its socialization into the international norms on minority rights, and explains why there is a gap between Beijing's nationality policy and the international norms on minority rights. This chapter ends with an optimistic note that Beijing may move towards a universal human rights regime that celebrates and promotes diversity, multiculturalism, autonomy and self-determination.

MINORITY RIGHTS: A HISTORICAL PERSPECTIVE

Human rights mean equal enjoyment of basic rights for everybody, whereas minority rights are for the exclusive benefits of minority groups to compensate and mitigate discrimination they suffer, with the ultimate goal of establishing universal human rights in society (Human

Rights in China 2007, p. 11; Kymlicka 1995, p. 6; Sautman 1999, p. 286). The minority rights regime protects women, gays and lesbians, ethnic minorities and other minority groups. Scholars (Vermeersch 2003, p. 1; Kymlicka 1995, p. 10) point out that minority rights range from 'the introduction of minority self-governments, the granting of territorial or cultural autonomy to minority groups, the funding of activities and organisations of national minorities' to 'guaranteed representation, or consultation of minorities in government institutions' and 'funding of bilingual education or mother-tongue instruction'. Minority rights also include freedom of religion, the right to establish religious, social and educational institutions, and the right to preserve the distinctive characteristics of the ethnic minority including its customs. Minority rights are intended to remedy the structural imbalance between minorities and majorities (Pentassuglia 2005, pp. 11, 19; Vermeersch 2003, p. 1; Kymlicka 1995, p. 162), and are about cultural diversity and multiculturalism in society (Preece 1997, p. 348).

According to Koszorus (1982), the first direct attempts at minority protection appeared in the thirteenth century and grew in importance as a result of the Reformation. Examples included the Peace of Augsburg signed in 1555, the Pact of Warsaw signed in 1573, and the Edict of Nantes signed in 1598. Some bilateral treaties concluded during the seventeenth and eighteenth centuries contained provisions concerning religious minorities. The Treaty of Vienna of 1606, for example, guaranteed the right of the Hungarian Protestant minority to exercise its religion in Royal Hungary. The Peace of Westphalia, signed in Osnabrück and Münster in 1648, raised the importance of the protection of religious minorities as a matter of major international concern (Grossman 1984, p. 5; Castellino and Redondo 2006, p. 5; Preece 1998, pp. 55–66). By the end of the nineteenth century, some treaties protecting national minorities had emerged in the field of international law (Castellino and Redondo 2006, p. 12).

The 1919 League of Nations System of Minority Guarantees legitimated the formation of nation states on the Central, Eastern and

South-eastern European territories of the former Ottoman, Austrian and Russian empires (Koenig 2008, p. 102; Pentassuglia 2005, p. 9; Preece 1998, pp. 67–94) and extended protection to members of 'racial, linguistic and religious' minorities in these areas (Koszorus 1982). Both the US President Woodrow Wilson and the leader of the Bolsheviks in Russia Vladimir Ilyich Lenin advocated national self-determination. The 1923 Treaty of Lausanne established a minority rights protection system in Greece and Turkey, taking the principle of reciprocity as its basis, defining both countries 'as custodians that could monitor and intervene in the affairs of their kindred minority across the border'. Yet these treaties and rhetoric were not taken seriously until the 1960s (Wilson 2002, p. 6; Castellino and Redondo 2006, p. 11). Minority rights were instead used as an instrument for international rivalry after 1919. For example, national minority demands were used by Nazi Germany in its expansionist efforts before the Second World War.

There was no immediate improvement in minority rights straight after the Second World War. In 1948, the UN General Assembly proclaimed the Universal Declaration of Human Rights. Although it was a milestone in the global human rights movement and set up the framework for an international minority rights regime, it did not explicitly deal with national minority rights. This situation was partially addressed when the International Convention on the Elimination of All Forms of Racial Discrimination was promulgated in 1965 (Office of the High Commissioner for Human Rights 1965). The General Assembly of the UN adopted the International Covenant on Civil and Political Rights in 1966, setting up the global minimum standard on state conduct directed at national minorities (United Nations 1966; see also Pentassuglia 2005, pp. 10, 13–14; Preece 1997, p. 347).

Despite these advances, minority rights did not have an independent standing in international relations before the end of the Cold War (Pentassuglia 2005, pp. 9–10; Preece 1997, pp. 346–7, 356; Wilson

2002, p. 6; Stein 2003, p. 4). The efforts of the UN concerning the protection of minority rights have become increasingly unequivocal after 1989, partly because the demises of the former Soviet Union, Czechoslovakia and Yugoslavia led to ethnic, national and religious tensions in Central and Eastern Europe in the early 1990s. The post-1989 migrations by ethnic minority groups between European countries, the violent ethnic conflicts in former Yugoslavia, and possible further ethnic unrest in other Eastern European countries compelled the EU to contemplate the issue seriously (Preece 1997, p. 349; 1998, pp. 30–54; Wilson 2002, p. 6). Regarding the condition of ethnic minorities, both as a potential obstacle to the democratization of former communist states and as an economic and social problem in Western European states on the receiving end of minority migrations from Central and Eastern Europe, the Council of Europe (CoE), the European Court of Human Rights and the EU have together played a major role in developing a minority rights regime within the framework of human rights (Fleming 2002, pp. 533–4; Pentassuglia 2005, pp. 17–18; Preece, 1997, pp. 345, 351).

This development formed part of the background when the UN Declaration on the Rights of Persons Belonging to National or Ethnic, Religious and Linguistic Minorities was officially proclaimed in 1992. This document has been regarded as the first instrument devoted exclusively to minority rights concerns (Preece 1997, p. 348; Henrard 2001, pp. 53–4). It stipulates that 'Persons belonging to national or ethnic, religious and linguistic minorities . . . have the right to enjoy their own culture, to profess and practise their own religion, and to use their own language, in private and in public, freely and without interference or any form of discrimination' (United Nations 1992; see also Sautman 1999, p. 287). Nation states are required to adopt the provisions for the promotion of minority cultures and languages, and to take minority concerns into consideration in both domestic programmes and international cooperation. The 1992 declaration nevertheless reiterates the traditional international position, which holds that minority rights are not intended as a vehicle to further minority secession or irredentism (Human Rights in China 2007, pp. 10–11; Koenig 2008, p. 106; Pentassuglia 2005, pp. 14–15; Preece 1997, p. 348).

Also in 1992, a Charter for Regional or Minority Languages was adopted under the auspices of the CoE for 'the protection of the historical regional and minority languages' in Europe (Fortman 2011, p. 270). A year later, 'respect to and protection of minority rights' were included as a major political condition for EU membership in the 1993 Copenhagen Accession Criteria (Wilson 2002, pp. 6, 9; see also Copenhagen Criteria n.d.). Minority rights provisions have since been recognized as criteria for membership in the CoE, which is a tacit precondition for membership in the EU.

Since 1993, a series of policy reforms has occurred in the socioeconomic area and in relation to legal, political and cultural rights of minorities in the EU (Memisoglu 2007, pp. 2, 12; Preece 1997, pp. 349–51). The CoE encouraged its member states to sign the Framework Convention for the Protection of National Minorities in 1995 (Council of Europe 1995; Preece 1997, p. 351; Wilson 2002, pp. 13–14), which emphasizes the protection of ethnic minorities as an integral part of the universal human rights regime, thereby falling within the scope of international cooperation (Fortman 2011, p. 271; Henrard 2001, pp. 55–6; Wilson 2002, pp. 14–16). The European Council directive of 29 June 2000 reiterated the principle of equal treatment among persons irrespective of racial or ethnic origin (Pentassuglia 2005, p. 18).

The European initiatives have been followed by relevant international organizations. The International Commission on Intervention and State Sovereignty (2001) published a landmark report titled *The Responsibility to Protect* (R2P). Of the five distinct kinds of protection tasks it identifies, the first stands out as the protection of 'minorities'. In 2007, the UN General Assembly adopted a strongly worded Declaration on the Rights of Indigenous Peoples, which contains clear statements on vital issues such as self-determination and access to lands, territories and resources (United Nations 2007).

A PARADIGM SHIFT IN MINORITY RIGHTS

The background to the publication of the European reports and initiatives and the UN declarations has been a major paradigm shift in minority rights since the end of the Cold War in 1989, in which the Westphalian norms of state sovereignty and responsible international behaviour, such as non-aggression, non-intervention, and non-interference in internal affairs, have successively lost plausibility due to the global diffusion of human rights as a new vocabulary of international contestation and legitimacy. Regional movements, indigenous peoples, and ethnic, linguistic or religious minorities are making claims for full political and legal inclusion and demanding the public recognition of their distinctive collective identities (Koenig 2008, pp. 95–6, 101). The new actor-constellations and situations in international human rights discourse have demanded 'a further specification and differentiation of collective human rights and, paradoxically, resulted in the eventual delegitimization of national statehood and citizenship' (Koenig 2008, p. 108). As a result, the pressure on national governments has become significantly heavier, pushing them to accept the global standards set out in international treaties, conventions and declarations (Memisoglu 2007, p. 2; Vermeersch 2004, pp. 6–7, 17; Koenig 2008, p. 97). There has been a growing consensus on the new perimeters of minority rights despite on-going debates on this sensitive subject since 1992 (Wilson 2002, p. 10). Three closely related questions have been at the heart of the debates, as discussed below.

Individual Rights or Collective Rights?

The first major question in the debate is whether minority rights are individual, collective, or both. This issue is less controversial than the other two issues discussed below. In the 1992 UN declaration mentioned above, the bearers of minority rights are individuals (Pentassuglia 2005, p. 11; He 2004, p. 119; Koenig 2008, pp. 100, 103; Preece 1997, pp. 354–5; Stein 2003, pp. 3, 20). Individual minority rights often refer to freedom of expression, freedom of association and freedom from discrimination. Members of ethnic minority groups also have the right to protect and promote their languages and cultures, and are entitled to equal opportunity programmes in education and employment. These rights have been regarded as 'the global minimum standard of state conduct towards minorities' (Preece 1997, pp. 347, 355–7).

Importantly, there has since emerged a view in the international community on the need to pay attention to both individual minority rights and collective minority guarantees. This view is understandable since 'It is not only as citizens, but also as members of the imagined community of humankind that individuals are assigned legitimate agency and enjoy rights' (Koenig 2008, pp. 101, 104–5). Anything that can move beyond the global minimum standard on minority rights must include group guarantees, which in turn must include self-determination, autonomy or even secession, especially if minority groups are subject to majority tyranny and forced assimilation. This proposal has immediately led to the second major issue in the global debate on minority rights as discussed below.

Minority Rights vs. State Sovereignty

Are self-determination and national autonomy more important than state sovereignty and territorial integrity? In other words, can state sovereignty be superseded by minority rights? Some scholars and politicians have advocated both self-determination, justified by the principle of free association, and human rights to identity and existence to support national minority guarantees. In contrast, state sovereign rights advocates have supported the individual rights formulation and refused to accept any collective minority guarantees that might be used by a minority group to further its secessionist aspiration. State sovereign rights advocates have stressed territorial integrity and political stability and appealed to non-intervention in order to forestall or limit the recognition of international guarantees for minority rights (Farer 2003, p. 405; Preece 1997, pp. 352–3).

Indeed, in the 1990s, the majority opinion recognized individual rather than collective rights. The content of minority rights provisions largely reflected the post-1945 human rights status quo and acknowledged that such provisions were constrained by traditional statist tenets of international relations such as state sovereignty, territorial integrity and non-intervention. Yet the new norms regulating state conduct towards minorities have gradually established themselves since the 1990s and recommendations have emerged in favour of various forms of minority autonomy, self-government and the prohibition against forced assimilation. These new norms have increasingly become part of the international standards on minority rights (Preece 1997, pp. 351–5, 357–8).

These developments have been partly the outcome of the changes in the definitions of state sovereignty since the 1990s. Farer (2003, p. 395) argues that a sovereign state may be a constitutional nation for only a portion of its citizens. 'Others, like many Basques in Spain, may identify with a community of blood and feel in varying degrees alienated from the state.' It follows that the state is not immune to self-determination challenges as it may be felt by its constituent members to be a contingent cluster of institutions and legal norms. In other words, if it is not a community of choice, state sovereignty cannot rule out self-determination or secession. Thus, the oppressed minority nationalities are entitled to aspire to sovereignty and to the undisputed mastery of a determinate space and territory.

The obligations and public functions of modern states have also been redefined partly due to the international diffusion of human rights. The emerging notions of 'sovereignty as responsibility' and 'the responsibility to protect' are framed as radical departures from the traditional conception of sovereignty that entails only rights and not responsibilities on the state. Koenig (2008, p. 99, 107–8) points out that 'States are no longer expected to represent a homogeneous national community, but rather have to publicly recognize a variety of particularistic collective identities legitimated by universalistic human rights.' The sovereignty of a modern state must be seen to exist in the service of humanity, otherwise it would not be regarded as legitimate in the eyes of its citizens and the international community. The sovereignty of a humanized state implies responsibility for the protection of, and the state's accountability for, human rights including minority rights (Peters 2009, p. 513).

Thus, a modern state has both the responsibility to maintain sovereignty and territorial integrity and the obligation to protect human rights. If the state suppresses or fails to protect ethnic minorities, it loses its mandate to govern them and can no longer claim its sovereignty over the territory in which the minority groups live. Self-determination and secession can be a means for protecting a people from serious and sustained violation of political, civil and cultural rights, which can serve to deter the state from suppressing minority rights (Farer 2003, pp. 404–5). Self-determination was used to justify a 'remedial secession' in the Kosovo war, and the justification for NATO's military action was regarded as appropriate by the international community (Berg 2009, p. 219; Dietrich 2010, p. 123; Muharremi 2008, p. 401).

Finally, the state is more powerful than national minority groups and may use force to prevent self-determination from occurring (Farer 2003, p. 401). Examples include ethnic cleansing in Sudan and former Yugoslavia, resulting in a large number of casualties. How should the international community respond to this kind of humanitarian crisis? This question leads to the third issue in the global debate on minority rights: are minority rights an internal affair of a sovereign state or part of international relations?

Non-interference vs. International Intervention

There was no legal space for humanitarian interventions before 1989. For a long time, international intervention was seen as a game in which 'the powerful do what they will and the weak accept what they must'. National minority questions were regarded as strictly the province of domestic politics, and inadequate international attention was given to minority rights before 1989 (Castellino and Redondo 2006, pp. 10, 12–13; Farer 2003, pp. 383–4, 385–7). Since then, the international community has gradually come to the realization that minority rights are not always guaranteed by majoritarian politics, and thus can fall outside the borders of exclusively internal jurisdiction of a state (Castellino and Redondo 2006, p. 13; Wilson 2002, p. 5). Humanitarian interventions including criticisms, sanctions or even military action by international actors are required if a state suppresses or fails to protect minority nationalities. Humanitarian interventions are ethically justified because they assist oppressed people against majority tyranny in order to establish a democratic government. 'Intervention is not limited to facilitation of an already certain birth, just to reducing its pain and duration', and the reduction is, along with the intrinsic merit of self-determination, part of the ethical justification for humanitarian intervention (Farer 2003, pp. 383, 392–3, 400). This view has slowly but surely disempowered governmental bodies and reconfigured the international system of nation states.

Since the 1990s, because ethnic minorities are recognized to possess certain legitimate international rights, it has been increasingly difficult for a state, accused of mistreating its ethnic minorities, to defend itself against international criticisms or sanctions by arguing that minority matters were subjects of domestic politics (Preece 1997, pp. 358–60).

It has been realized that the failure to protect minority rights in a sovereign state has major ramifications for international relations and regional security and thus invites humanitarian interventions by the international community. Protection of minority rights has become a key component of regional or international security as evidenced by the Rwandan genocide and policies of ethnic cleansing in Sudan and former Yugoslavia. Thus, it is by the restriction of state sovereignty that individual human dignity is, along with peace, promoted as a universal value (Prantl and Nakano 2011, p. 207; Vermeersch 2004, p. 10).

International intervention is just also because of the above notions of 'sovereignty as responsibility' and 'the responsibility to protect'. The recognition of state sovereignty has been increasingly made conditional on the state's ability to protect human rights including minority rights (Castellino and Redondo 2006, p. 13; Koenig 2008, pp. 99, 107; Peters 2009, p. 513). International action without the consent of the target state is justified, and the justifying condition is gross violations of personal security rights (Farer 2003, p. 404; Prantl and Nakano 2011, p. 206). It is the obligation of the international community to intervene to remedy the state failure to protect minority rights and maintain a just international order (Glanville 2011a, p. 233; 2011b, p. 241).

These views have been increasingly accepted as part of global governance by a large group of nation states, especially after the Rwandan genocide, ethnic cleansing by the Croat Ustase and the Serb Cetniks, and the Darfur conflict. Enforcement of minority rights in a sovereign state can occur, or be facilitated, through international intervention employing a combination of carrots and sticks (Falk 1999, pp. 847–8; Koenig 2008, p. 100; Pentassuglia 2005, pp. 20–1), which according to Havel and many others is consistent with the principles and values of human rights (Falk 1999, p. 847; Russett 1993, p. 277). One example of humanitarian intervention is the Kosovo War. As another example, international and regional organizations, including the EU, have been an integral part of minority rights politics in Central and Eastern Europe (Vermeersch 2004, p. 6). There has been a steady movement away from the more traditional elements of international relations that has privileged nation states and defended their sovereign rights from incursions by rival, non-state claimants, including national minorities. Collective minority rights formulations, especially those which include rights to regional autonomy or self-government, have undercut the traditional concept of state sovereignty (Pentassuglia 2005, pp. 19–20; Preece 1997, p. 362; Vermeersch 2004, p. 7).

THE MINORITY RIGHTS REGIME IN CHINA

Beijing has had serious reservations about post-1992 international human rights treaties (Castellino and Redondo 2006, pp. 34, 40–1). It has been an outsider to the international human rights regime for most of the time (Foot 2001; Kent 1999), and its domestic record in minority rights and its positions in the Kosovo War and the Darfur conflict have turned it into a major target of international criticism. Why has Beijing acted this way? A short answer to this question is the gap between the current international standards on minority rights and China's policy towards ethnic minorities, underscored by *ronghe* ideology, which does not accommodate collective minority guarantees as discussed below.

Minority rights can be guaranteed by a state's constitution, by a particular law on minority protection, or by individual legislation in specific areas, e.g. laws on minority language, laws on minority education, etc. In the PRC, the 1982 Constitution elaborates a range of minority rights to be realized through national and local laws, and many new laws and policies on minority rights have been promulgated since 1982. Overall, it seems that Beijing's nationality policy meets the international standards of some, but probably not others (Mackerras 2011a, p. 124; Sautman 1999, pp. 283, 294).

As noted in chapter 2, Beijing has called for preferred hiring of minorities in the state sector in the PRC. Minority candidates are given preferred treatment for promotion to the political hierarchy, and some minority groups are exempted from China's one-child policy. Universities are required to give minority students 'priority over others with equal qualifications' and to set up preparatory courses for them (Sautman 1999, pp. 294–5; also US Congressional-Executive Commission on China 2005a, pp. 16–17; Mackerras 2011a, pp. 113–14). The affirmative action policy is consistent with the Confucian approach towards the paternal state responsibility for ethnic minorities. There are also political and practical considerations in implementation of minority entitlements because they can raise minority elites who can showcase China's nationality policy both domestically and internationally, and are a key stabilizing factor in minority–state relations. The political loyalty of minority elites is essential for Chinese governance in minority regions (chapter 5). However, the minimum hiring quotas for minorities are in danger of fading into oblivion because of the post-1978 decline of the state sector. The growth of the private sector, which is not required by law to implement affirmative action programmes, has been accompanied by ethnic discrimination in hiring (Human Rights in China 2007, pp. 2, 20–1; Zang 2010; 2011a).

Beijing has also promoted economic growth in minority areas (see chapter 2). However, the various measures promoted by the PRC have not offset the growth of the economic gap between Han areas and minority areas. Both Han areas and minority areas have grown rapidly in the post-1978 era, but the former have developed at a faster rate than the latter, and Han Chinese do better financially than minorities. 'Overall growth, however, masks a large and increasing income disparity' between minorities and Han Chinese (Barabantseva 2009, p. 244; US Congressional-Executive Commission on China 2005a, pp. 16–17; Dreyer 2005, p. 82; Hansen 2005, p. 117; Human Rights in China 2007, pp. 7, 11; Sautman 1999, p. 285).

As noted in chapter 3, Beijing has stated that minority languages and cultures are valued and respected, and that minority groups have the right to use their languages and practise their cultures and religions (Mackerras 1994; Wang and Phillion 2009, p. 2; Zuo 2007). Nevertheless, the nationwide promotion of Mandarin Chinese since 1956 and the popularity of Mandarin Chinese in the post-1978 era because of China's booming economy have created an unfavourable or even dangerous condition for some minority languages in China. Other factors that have had a detrimental effect on minority languages include the use of Mandarin as the teaching medium at universities and the policy that Mandarin is the official working language in the governments of minority areas (US Congressional-Executive Commission on China 2005a, pp. 19–20; Human Rights in China 2007, pp. 2, 26–9; Mackerras 2011a, pp. 117–18; Wang and Phillion 2009, p. 1). Overall, the promotion of minority languages and cultures has been less impressive and unequivocal than the promotion of affirmative action and regional economic growth. This is partly because the former has not always served Beijing's *ronghe* policy and may lead to rising ethnic consciousness and demands for more autonomy, or even independence, among ethnic minorities in the PRC. Finally, freedom of religion in Tibet and Xinjiang has been a main concern in relation to China's minority rights.

As noted in chapter 4, the PRC Constitution proclaims that regional autonomy is practised by minority nationalities living in compact communities, who are free to 'preserve or reform their own ways and customs'. In other words, ethnic regional autonomy is mainly cultural, for example by allowing the official use of language in minority regions. This is puzzling because Beijing is not enthusiastic about the protection of minority cultures, as noted above. Furthermore, regional autonomy should be mainly about power to the minority nationalities, and there is no evidence that regional autonomy has indeed promoted minority cultures. As noted, autonomous regions have very limited power in legislation and judiciary, and are firmly controlled by the central government (US Congressional-Executive Commission on China 2005a, p. 17; Human Rights in China 2007, pp. 2, 14–15; Ghai and Woodman 2009, pp. 29, 32–3; Mackerras 1994, pp. 153–66, 264–5; 2003, p. 26; Moneyhon 2002, pp. 10–11; Sautman 2000, p. 73).

Finally, Article 1 of the PRC Constitution states that 'it is necessary to combat big-nation chauvinism, mainly Han chauvinism'. Article 4 proclaims the equality of nationalities and prohibits acts based on 'great nation chauvinism' and 'local nationalism'. However, Han chauvinism is treated by government officials today as if it were basically a pre-1949 phenomenon. Deng Xiaoping allegedly stated in 1987 that since 1949 'there had never been any ethnic discrimination in the country'. In 1988, Zhao Ziyang, the former CCP chief, claimed that racial discrimination was common 'everywhere in the world except China' (Ku 2008; see also Stein 2003, pp. 20–1). Yet studies have shown that disparaging attitudes towards minorities are common among Han Chinese, and few Han Chinese if any have been punished for remarks or discriminatory deeds against ethnic minorities (Brown 2009, pp. 83–6; US Congressional-Executive Commission on China 2005a, pp. 20–1; Human Rights in China 2007, p. 8; Kaltman 2007, pp. 115–16; Sautman 2012, p. 16). After the 2008 Lhasa unrest and the 2009 Ürümchi riot, Han resentment of minorities has become more vocal, with complaints that minorities are ungrateful and that leniency towards them spurs separatism (Ghai and Woodman 2009, p. 45; Ma 2007b; Sautman 2010; 2012).

The above brief review shows clearly that the issues of poverty, education and economic development have remained at the core of Beijing's nationality policy (Ghai and Woodman 2009, pp. 44–5), whereas matters related to ethnic cultural protection and autonomy are marginalized in policy making. In other words, what the CCP has done is part of the minimum standards for the state conduct towards ethnic minorities, and includes few thoughts or actions related to group guarantees. Beijing's nationality policy is lagging behind the global trend with regard to the protection of minority rights, and there is a major gap between Beijing's nationality policy and its execution on the ground (US Congressional-Executive Commission on China 2005b, pp. 15–16; Human Rights in China 2007, pp. 2, 13; Ghai and Woodman 2009, p. 29; Sautman 1999, p. 283). Some of the laws and directives on minority rights that were promulgated before or during the 1990s and have not been updated are incapable of coping with the demands from national minorities today. China has changed drastically since it opened to the world in 1978. Yet Beijing has been slow to observe the changes in the international minority rights regime and continues to put a premium on the rights and interests of the state rather than national minorities (Chin and Thakur 2010, p. 122).

MINORITY RIGHTS AND CHINA'S FOREIGN POLICY

Some scholars in the West have developed two versions of China's foreign policy on minority rights in international politics. The first version portrays Beijing as a calculative player in international relations, who is allegedly driven by its political interests and disregards minority rights in relevant countries. This version is supported by the veto Beijing used in February 1999 on extending a peacekeeping force in Macedonia (because of Macedonia's diplomatic ties with Taiwan, over which China claims sovereignty), Beijing's opposition to the use of force by the UN to resolve the Kosovo crisis despite escalating violence against ethnic Albanian civilians (BBC News 1999; Bowman 2003), and Beijing's veto on a US resolution in 2007 calling on Myanmar's military junta, who were China's allies, to stop persecution of minority and opposition groups in that country (Leopold 2007; Iliopoulos 2011). Beijing's votes were motivated either by its ideology or its obsession with non-interference in international politics. Of course, by no means does this suggest that other countries have not selectively supported minority rights in particular countries for various reasons. Thus, this version appears to be a weak attack on Beijing's foreign policy on minority rights.

The second version asserts that China's foreign policy is inspired partly by a desire to maximize its rights and interests and to minimize its responsibilities and normative costs (Mushkat 2011, pp. 53–4). For example, China's role in providing weapons and aircraft to Sudan has been portrayed as an attempt to obtain oil from that country. In addition, Beijing threatened to use its veto in the UN Security Council to protect Khartoum from sanctions and watered down resolutions on Darfur in order to protect its interests in Sudan. Beijing has been accused of putting oil interests over minority rights (Prantl and Nakano 2011, pp. 213–14; see also Herbst 2008; Human Rights Watch 2003; Sudan Divestment Task Force 2007). Of course, by no means does this suggest that other countries have not selectively supported minority rights in particular countries for self-interest. Thus, this version also appears to be a weak attack on Beijing's foreign policy on minority rights.

Notwithstanding, Beijing has not been portrayed as a responsible power in terms of safeguarding international minority rights norms in global governance. Yet from Beijing's perspective, its stance has served its interests: it does not support secessionist movements in other countries for fear that it would erode its own attempt to maintain national unity and stop Taiwan and Tibet from seceding. Nor does Beijing have the intention to grant its minority nationalities the rights that are inconsistent with its *ronghe* policy. Similar to its domestic policy towards the minority nationalities, Beijing's foreign policy has emphasized economic interests over rights in the protection of minority cultures and self-determination. Given its *ronghe* ideology, the similarity between China's domestic nationality policy and its foreign policy towards minority rights is an expected behavioural pattern rather than a surprise.

CHANGES IN CHINA'S POLICY TOWARDS MINORITY RIGHTS

In light of the post-1992 international minority rights regime, Beijing's nationality policy is apparently inadequate and outmoded. Nevertheless, since 1978 Beijing has shown a growing movement towards global norms on minority rights (Chin and Thakur 2010, pp. 119–21, 129; Human Rights in China 2007, p. 11; Kent 2002, pp. 344–5, 358; Mushkat 2011, p. 68). Senior Chinese leaders have publicly reiterated the need to rethink China's international strategy (Chin and Thakur 2010, p. 121). In recent decades, Beijing's once rigid understanding of sovereignty has become somewhat flexible, especially in those situations where a country is confronted by the possible breakdown of law and order. In particular, the PRC endorsed the key properties of R2P – first at the 2005 World Summit, and subsequently in UN Security Council Resolution 1674 (2006) on the protection of civilians in armed conflict, as well as in the 2009 UN General Assembly Informal Debate and the subsequent UN resolution on the implementation of R2P (Chin and Thakur 2010, p. 129; Prantl and Nakano 2011, pp. 212–14). By 2010, China had deployed more than 2,000 troops, military observers and police on the ground in UN operations for security control and nation building throughout the world, becoming the largest contributor to such operations among the five permanent members of the UN Security Council (Chin and Thakur 2010, p. 128; see also United Nations 2010).

There have also been some noticeable efforts to improve minority rights in China: in a 2005 speech, the then PRC President Hu Jintao called for more freedom of religion, higher degrees of ethnic regional autonomy, Han officials learning minority languages, greater quotas for hiring minority cadres, and more recognition of their contributions (Sautman 2012, p. 16). Human Rights in China (2007, p. 32) claims that 'China has acknowledged some of its problems' in the protection of minority rights. That means that efforts to resolve these problems are likely to be made. Since the 2009 Ürümchi riot, for example, Beijing has implemented measures to reduce the income gap between Han Chinese and Uyghurs in Xinjiang (chapter 2), and required Han officials in Xinjiang to acquire Uyghur language skills so that they can 'serve' Uyghurs better. Beijing has intensified its effort to support economic growth in Xinjiang after the attack on Ürümqi on 22 May 2014.

The changes discussed above are an inevitable product of liberalization at home and engagement with the international community in the post-1978 era (Mushkat 2011, p. 43). The increasing exchange between China and the rest of the world has begun to promote awareness of the international minority rights regime among Chinese officials and scholars. Beijing has found it fruitful to accommodate international norms as much as possible as it will gain prestige abroad and better integrate the PRC into the international community. More and more people in China have realized that if Beijing does not take steps to improve its minority rights regime, it will continue to be a major target of international criticism regarding minority rights abuses. Some Chinese citizens have accepted human rights as a guiding principle in handling ethnic relations in the PRC, arguing strongly that the foundation of national unity and the harmony of all nationalities must be based on respect for human rights, and that the reunification of China is not the highest goal if it does not promote human rights. It seems that the human rights discourse has formed a new framework with which Chinese scholars have examined government nationality policy. 'It thus seems that Chinese scholars have "rightized" every official policy towards the minority, grouping them under the "minority right" umbrella' (He 2003, p. 232; 2004, p. 117; Leibold 2010, p. 20; Prantl and Nakano 2011, p. 213; Sautman 2012, p. 11).

Another major vehicle for the changes is the pressure from Western countries to promote human rights in the PRC. Many foreign dignitaries have raised issues related to ethnic minorities in meetings with Chinese officials (Public and Cultural Diplomacy E 2011), and there are also institutional arrangements as a major platform for the discourse on minority rights in China. For example, China and the EU have exchanged views regularly during the EU–China Dialogues on Human Rights including minority rights (Bi 2011; Delegation of the European Union to China 2011). Beijing has tried to enhance the life chances for members of the ethnic minorities, hoping that these measures would alleviate the criticisms from the West and improve its image abroad (Ma 2007a, p. 17; Leibold 2010, p. 3). Some Chinese laws are drafted in an apparent effort to accommodate international standards (US Congressional-Executive Commission on China 2005b, pp. 15–16). Beijing has adopted, albeit limited and selective, international norms and practices that would make its ethnic minority policy more participatory and accommodating. Beijing's foreign policy considerations have encouraged changes in China's treatment of minority groups (Cultural Survival 1997).

Finally, the Chinese state's paradoxical enlistment of international development actors in the task of modernizing its minority areas, such as Tibet (Mackerras 2005b, pp. 28–30), has allowed these NGOs to adopt international norms on minority rights and emphasize the importance of transparency, accountability, 'local' consent and participation in approving and devising development projects (Williams 2008). In other words, these norms and practices are essential elements for the future development of a Chinese minority rights regime in line with new global trends, although they are not necessarily consistent with Beijing's nationality policy.

RIGIDITIES AND INERTIA IN BEIJING'S MINORITY RIGHTS REGIME

Notwithstanding, Beijing's variant of minority rights is still highly selective in nature, and the changes mentioned above may reflect utilitarian considerations rather than a major cognitive adjustment 'culminating in the formation of benign worldview' (Chin and Thakur 2010, p. 122; Mushkat 2011, pp. 43, 54; see also Foot 2001; Kent 1999). The scope for new global normative preferences to be introduced into the national discourse in China is limited (Cultural Survival 1997; He 2004, p. 117). Beijing has not been hesitant to water down or veto UN resolutions on minority rights if it needs to. More importantly, the changes in official attitudes towards minority rights have occurred mainly in the realm of China's foreign relations but not in that of domestic politics (Chin and Thakur 2010, p. 120; Mushkat 2011, pp. 65, 67). For example, Beijing has championed multilateralism, mutual respect, tolerance and dialogues in international relations, yet its approach to policy making on minority rights in China is highly centralized and paternal in nature. Maintaining a fairly strong Leninist impulse, it has thwarted any form of pluralism or organization outside the state's control and precluded the adoption of international norms through societal pressure (Cultural Survival 1997; He 2004, p. 117).

Beijing has maintained its policy towards national minorities in China by insisting on the supremacy of state sovereignty and territorial integrity over individual rights and collective minority guarantees (Castellino and Redondo 2006, pp. 20–1; He 2003, p. 234; Kent 2002, p. 358). It has defined nationality issues strictly as part of its internal affairs that are not subject to foreign criticism (Zhu and Blachford 2005, p. 243). Mr Li Baodong, China's Ambassador to the UN in Geneva, criticized Ms Navanethem Pillay, the United Nations High Commissioner for Human Rights, for ignoring facts in China and asked her to respect the principles of neutrality, objectivity and impartiality and strictly adhere to the mandate given by the General Assembly after she raised issues of minority rights in China (Unrepresented Nations and Peoples Organization 2009; see also Leibold 2010, p. 15). As another example, Chinese officials laughed off Australia's concerns on minority rights in the PRC and questioned Australia's own human rights record (Dorling 2011). Foreign criticisms of Beijing's minority rights regime have generally been labelled as an attempt to disintegrate China and thus are not acceptable. Beijing has also attributed the origins of ethnic unrest in China to the activities of hostile forces in the West, and has asserted that the nationality issue has become a political problem because the West wants to use ethnic and religious issues as a weapon to interfere in China's internal affairs and prevent the rise of a unified, powerful China. The Chinese official Zhu Weiqun (2012) said that there was 'an antagonistic contradiction between us and them and the CCP will deal with it uncompromisingly'.

Finally, Beijing has rejected 'Western' human rights standards and argued that human rights (including minority rights) issues must be contextualized with regard to a country's history and culture. Thus, human rights standards are based on Western values stressing civil liberalities (Castellino and Redondo 2006, pp. 18–24) and so are not suitable for China. According to Beijing, economic modernization is an equivalent to human rights, including minority rights, in China. Nevertheless, Beijing's approach is outdated according to international standards and dilutes the original and authentic meaning of human rights including minority rights, redirects attention from civic and political rights to economic growth, and implies that civic and political rights can be sacrificed for the sake of economic development (He 2003, p. 233; Mushkat 2011, pp. 60–1).

DISCUSSION

The internationalization of minority rights gained significant momentum towards the end of the twentieth century. International institutions and Western countries have become major actors in this process by pushing non-Western states including China to accept new global standards in the area of minority rights (Memisoglu 2007, p. 7; Vermeersch 2004, pp. 6–7; Castellino and Redondo 2006, p. 10). There has been a paradigm shift in the definition of minority rights, as they are seen as both individual and group rights, self-determination is increasingly considered to be more important than state sovereignty and territorial integrity, and humanitarian interventions are acceptable for the protection of minority rights (Farer 2003, pp. 403–4). Forming a good policy in the area of minority rights is becoming a global imperative. Under the umbrella of global governance in which minority rights are an integral part, each nation state, including the PRC, is subject to close scrutiny in terms of its nationality policy because minority rights can no longer be viewed exclusively as a domestic issue (Kent 1999; Zhu and Blachford 2005).

The PRC cannot become or be respected as a responsible power if its policy towards its minority nationalities does not meet international standards on minority rights. Beijing has made some efforts to narrow socioeconomic gaps between Han Chinese and ethnic minorities, but these efforts have been insufficient to reduce ethnic inequality in the post-1978 era. It has a lot to do to build up a respectful record on, and become a leading advocate for, minority rights. China's domestic policy towards ethnic minorities has international implications. For example, China has one of the world's largest Muslim populations – more than 20 million, which is more than the United Arab Emirates, Iraq, Libya or Syria – and has increasing contacts with trade partners in the Middle East and new Muslim nations created on its borders in Central Asia. China has provided the Middle East and Central Asia with consumer goods, weaponry and increasing numbers of Muslim pilgrims to Mecca. These relations could be jeopardized if discontent among Uyghurs continues over such issues as limitations on Islamic activities, uncontrolled mineral and energy development, etc. in Xinjiang (Cultural Survival 1997).

Moreover, Beijing has legal and moral obligations to improve its domestic policy and foreign policy on minority rights because minority rights have become an integral part of the international human rights regime and global governance (He 2004, p. 103; Castellino and Redondo 2006, p. 10). Human Rights in China (2007, p. 10) states that 'As a state party to numerous international treaties and conventions, and as a result of developing international legal norms, the PRC has obligations to respect, protect, promote and fulfill the human rights of all its citizens, and has additional obligations to protect the rights of ethnic minorities' (see also Lundberg 2009, p. 400; Peerenboom 2002, p. 536). It is in Beijing's interest to make sure that its policy towards minority rights meets the demands of global norms.

So far, Beijing has been a fan of the Westphalian norms on state sovereignty and shown little interest in national autonomy and self-determination. The *ronghe* ideology has effectively prevented Beijing from accepting international norms on minority rights: it has sponsored acculturation and assimilation, whereas the global norms on minority rights have promoted self-determination and multiculturalism. The latter has recognized group rights, whereas the former has nothing to do with collective guarantees. The international norms on minority rights are based on group equality, whereas the *ronghe* policy is hierarchical in nature, placing Han Chinese above ethnic minorities. Fundamentally, minority rights are associated with individual freedom, pluralism, state responsibility and democracy, and none of these are found in the dictionary of *ronghe* ideology. There is an intrinsic contradiction between the international minority rights regime and *ronghe* ideology.

It is doubtful that Beijing will give up *ronghe* ideology because its nationality policy is consistent with the overall principle with which the CCP governs China: promoting economic growth while maintaining one-party rule. In the foreseeable future, Beijing will face a dilemma between the need to improve its minority rights regime (because of international pressure and its desire to enhance its international image and better integrate China into the international community) and the need to maintain territorial integrity, Chinese nationalism and political legitimacy. The latter need seems to outweigh the former in determining Beijing's future nationality policy because, for Chinese leaders, political power is more important than a good international image for China.

But an overhaul of Beijing's nationality policy in the foreseeable future cannot be ruled out. *Ronghe* owes its origin to Confucianism, is an outmoded ideology if measured by current global norms on minority rights, and will become outdated eventually. It is possible that Beijing will move towards the universal human rights regime that celebrates and promotes diversity, multiculturalism, autonomy and self-determination as the PRC is further integrated into the international community, that extreme Han nationalism will lose its appeal to Han people in the face of growing concerns about individual liberality and well-being, and that the ideas of human rights and democracy will become everyday words in China.

RECOMMENDED READING

Rosemary Foot, *Rights beyond Borders: The Global Community and the Struggle over Human Rights in China* (Oxford: Oxford University Press, 2001).

Ann Kent, *China, the United Nations and Human Rights: The Limits of Compliance* (Philadelphia, PA: University of Pennsylvania Press, 1999).

References

Adle, Chahryar, Madhavan K. Palat and Anara Tabyshalieva (eds). 2005. *History of Civilizations of Central Asia, Volume VI: Towards the Contemporary Period: From the Mid-nineteenth to the End of the Twentieth Century.* Paris: UNESCO.

Alberts, Eli. 2007. *A History of Daoism and the Yao People of South China.* Amherst, NY: Cambria Press.

Amnesty International. 2009. *Uighur Ethnic Identity under Threat in China,* available at http://www.amnesty.org/en/library/asset/ASA17/010/2009/en/e952496e-57bb-48eb-9741-e6b7fed2a7d4/asa170102009en.pdf.

Anaya, S. James. 1995. 'The Capacity of International Law to Advance Ethnic or Nationality Rights Claims'. In Will Kymlicka (ed.), *The Rights of Minority Cultures.* Oxford: Oxford University Press, pp. 321–30.

Bai, Zhensheng and Shigeo Ozawa. 1992. *A Brief History of Society and Politics in Modern Xinjiang, 1912–1949* [新疆現代政治社会史略，1912–1949年]. Beijing: China Social Science Press [in Chinese].

Bai, Zhihong. 2007. 'Ethnic Identities under the Tourist Gaze'. *Asian Ethnicity* 8/3, 245–59.

Banister, Judith. 1992. 'Ethnic Diversity and Distribution'. In Dudley L. Poston and David Yaukey (eds), *The Population of Modern China.* New York: Plenum Press, pp. 553–70.

Barabantseva, Elena. 2008. 'From the Language of Class to the Rhetoric of Development: Discourses of "Nationality" and "Ethnicity" in China'. *Journal of Contemporary China* 17/56, 565–89.

Barabantseva, Elena. 2009. 'Development as Localization: Ethnic Minorities in China's Official Discourse on the Western Development Project'. *Critical Asian Studies* 41/2, 225–54.

Baranovitch, Nimrod. 2001. 'Between Alterity and Identity: New Voices of Minority People in China'. *Modern China* 27/3, 359–401.

Baranovitch, Nimrod. 2007. 'Inverted Exile: Uyghur Writers and Artists in Beijing and the Political Implications of Their Work'. *Modern China* 33/4, 462–504.

Barbour, Brandon and Reece Jones. 2013. 'Criminals, Terrorists, and Outside Agitators: Representational Tropes of the "Other" in the 5 July Xinjiang, China Riots'. *Geopolitics* 18/1, pp. 95–114.

Barnett, Robert. 2009. 'The Tibet Protests of Spring, 2008: Conflict between the Nation and the State'. *China Perspectives* 3, 6–23.

BBC News. 1999. 'World: Europe UN peacekeepers prepare to leave Macedonia', 1 March, available at http://news.bbc.co.uk/1/hi/world/europe/288402.stm.

Becquelin, Nicolas. 1997. 'Trouble on the Marches: Interethnic Tensions and Endemic Poverty in the National Minority Areas'. *China Perspectives* 10, 19–28.

Becquelin, Nicolas. 2000. 'Xinjiang in the Nineties'. *The China Journal* 44, 65–90.

Bennett, Michael T. 2008. 'China's Sloping Land Conversion Program: Institutional Innovation or Business as Usual?' *Ecological Economics* 65, 699–711.

Benson, Linda. 1990. *The Ili Rebellion, The Moslem Challenge to Chinese Authority in Xinjiang*. Armonk, NY: M.E. Sharpe.

Benson, Linda. 2004. 'Education and Social Mobility among Minority Populations in Xinjiang'. In S. Frederick Starr (ed.), *Xinjiang: China's Muslim Borderland*. Armonk, NY: M.E. Sharpe, pp. 190–215.

Berg, Eiki. 2009. 'Re-examining Sovereignty Claims in Changing Territorialities: Reflections from Kosovo Syndrome'. *Geopolitics* 14/2, 219–34.

Bhalla, Ajit S. and Shufang Qiu. 2006. *Poverty and Inequality among Chinese Minorities*. London: Routledge.

Bi, Mingxin. 2011. 'China, EU Hold Human-Rights Dialogue in Beijing', 17 June, available at http://news.xinhuanet.com/english2010/china/2011-06/17/c_13936067.htm.

Blanchard, Ben. 2013. 'China Says Xinjiang Minorities Too Busy Dancing to Make Trouble'. *Reuters*, 28 May, available at http://www.reuters.com/article/2013/05/28/us-china-xinjiang-idUSBRE94R03Z20130528.

Blanchard, Ben. 2014. 'China Says Three Killed in Attack at Xinjiang Train Station'. *Reuters*, 30 April, available at http://www.reuters.com/article/2014/04/30/us-china-xinjiang-blast-idUSBREA3T0HX20140430.

Blanton, Robert T., David Mason and Brian Athow. 2001. 'Colonial Style and Post-Colonial Ethnic Conflict in Africa'. *Journal of Peace Research* 38/4, 473–91.

Blondeau, Anne-Marie, Katia Buffetrille and Donald Lopez. 2008. *Authenticating Tibet: Answers to China's 100 Questions*. Berkeley: University of California Press.

Borei, Dorothy V. 2002. 'Ethnic Conflict and Qing Land Policy in Southern Xinjiang, 1760–1840'. In Robert J. Antony and Jane Kate Leonard (eds), *Dragons, Tigers, and Dogs: Qing Crisis Management and the Boundaries of State Power in Late Imperial China*. Ithaca, NY: Cornell University, pp. 273–301.

Bovingdon, Gardner. 2002. 'The Not-so-Silent Majority'. *Modern China* 28/1, 39–78.

Bovingdon, Gardner. 2004a. 'Contested Histories'. In S. Frederick Starr, *Xinjiang: China's Muslim Borderland*. Armonk, NY: M.E. Sharpe, pp. 353–74.

Bovingdon, Gardner. 2004b. *Autonomy in Xinjiang: Han Nationalist Imperatives and Uyghur Discontent*. Washington, DC: East-West Center in Washington, Policy Studies 11.

Bovingdon, Gardner. 2010. *The Uyghurs: Strangers in Their Own Land*. New York: Columbia University Press.

Bowman, Steve. 2003. 'Kosovo and Macedonia: U.S. and Allied Military Operations'. Congressional Research Service, 8 July, available at http://www.au.af.mil/au/awc/awcgate/crs/ib10027.pdf.

Bradley, David. 2005. 'Language Policy and Language Endangerment in China'. *International Journal of the Sociology of Language* 173, 1–21.

Bradley, David. 2009. 'Language Policy for China's Minorities: Orthography Development for the Yi'. *Written Language and Literacy* 12/2, 170–87.

Braker, Hans. 1985. 'Nationality Dynamics in Sino-Soviet Relations'. In S. Enders Wimbush (ed.), *Soviet Nationalities and Strategic Perspective*. London: Croom Helm, pp. 101–57.

Briney, Amanda. n.d. China's Autonomous Regions: List of the Five Autonomous Regions of China. Available at http://geography.about.com/od/chinamaps/tp/china-autonomous-Regions.htm.

Brown, Melissa J. 2001. 'Ethnic Classification and Culture: The Case of the Tujia in Hubei, China'. *Asian Ethnicity* 2/1, 55–72.

Brown, Melissa J. 2002. 'Local Government Agency'. *Modern China* 28/3, 362–95.

Brown, Melissa J. 2007. 'Ethnic Identity, Cultural Variation, and Processes of Change: Rethinking the Insights of Standardization and Orthopraxy'. *Modern China* 33/1, 91–124.

Brown, Ronald. 2009. *Understanding Labor and Employment Law in China*. Cambridge: Cambridge University Press.

Bruhn, Daniel. 2008. 'Minority Language Policy in China, with Observations on the *She* Ethnic Group', 20 May, available at http://linguistics.berkeley.edu/~dwbruhn/dwbruhn_250E-paper.pdf.

Bulag, Uradyn E. 2002. *The Mongols at China's Edge: History and Politics of National Unity*. Lanham, MD: Rowman & Littlefield.

Bulag, Uradyn E. 2003. 'Mongolian Ethnicity and Linguistic Anxiety in China'. *American Anthropologist* 105/4, 753–63.

Bulag, Uradyn E. 2004. 'The Dialectics of Colonialization and Ethnicity Building'. In Morris Rossabi (ed.), *Governing China's Multiethnic Frontiers*. Seattle, WA: University of Washington Press, pp. 84–116.

Burke, Jason and Tania Branigan. 2011. '"Burning martyrs": the wave of Tibetan monks setting themselves on fire'. *The Guardian*, 10 November, available at http://www.guardian.co.uk/world/2011/nov/10/burning-martyrs-tibetan -monks-fire.

Caffrey, Kevin. 2004. 'Who "Who" Is, and Other Local Poetics of National Policy'. *China Information* 18/2, 243–74.

Casas, Roger. 2011. 'Linguistic Policy and "Minority" Languages in the People's Republic of China', available at http://anu.academia.edu/RogerCasas/Papers/ 985139/Linguistic_Policy_and_Minority_Languages_in_the_Peoples _Republic_of_China_The_Case_of_the_Tai_Lue_of_Sipsong_Panna.

Castellino, Joshua and Elvira Domínguez Redondo. 2006. *Minority Rights in Asia: A Comparative Legal Analysis*. Oxford: Oxford University Press.

CCP Politburo. 1941. Policy Platform on the Governance of the Shanganning Region (陕甘宁边区施政纲领), 11 May, available at http://baike.baidu. com/view/461815.html?fromTaglist [in Chinese].

Chang, Chiung-Fang. 2003. *Fertility Patterns among the Minority Populations of China: A Multilevel Analysis*. PhD dissertation, Texas A&M University.

Chang, Wei Min. 2004. 'Ethnic Regional Autonomy System and Its Practice in the Tibet Autonomous Region', available at http://zt.tibet.cn/tibetzt-en/ zyfy/zyfy_5_2.htm.

Chen, Jia. 2010. 'Country's Wealth Divide Past Warning Level'. *China Daily*, 12 May, available at http://www.chinadaily.com.cn/china/2010-05/12/ content_9837073.htm.

Chiang, Kai-shek. 1943. *China's Future* (中国之命运), available at http://www. zgsf.com.cn/viewthread.php?tid=8500 [in Chinese].

Childs, Geoff. 2008. *Tibetan Transitions: Historical and Contemporary Perspectives on Fertility, Family Planning, and Demographic Change*. Leiden: Brill.

Chin, Gregory and Ramesh Thakur. 2010. 'Will China Change the Rules of Global Order?' *The Washington Quarterly* 33/4, 119–38.

China.biz, The. 2011. 'News Digest: China Endeavors to Protect, Foster Ethnic Minorities' Traditional Cultures', January, available at http://thechina.biz/ china-economy/china-endeavors-to-protect-foster-ethnic-minorities -traditional-cultures/.

China's Ethnic Unity Textbook Compiling Team (ed.) (民族团结教育教材编写组). 2009. *A General Introduction to Theory on Nationality* (民族理论常识). Beijing: China Central Radio and TV University Press [in Chinese].

Chinese Soviet Republic, The. 1931. *Communist Constitution*, available at http://sites.google.com/site/legalmaterialsontibet/home/communist-constitution-1931.

Ching, Julia. 1993. *Chinese Religions.* Maryknoll, NY: Orbis Books.

Chow, Chun-Shing. 2005. 'Cultural Diversity and Tourism Development in Yunnan Province, China'. *Geography* 90/3, 294–303.

Chung, Chien-peng. 2006. 'Confronting Terrorism and Other Evils in China: All Quiet on the Western Front?' *China and Eurasia Forum Quarterly* 4/2, 75–87.

Clark, William Carl. 1999. *Convergence or Divergence: Uighur Family Change in Urumqi.* PhD dissertation, University of Washington.

Clarke, Michael E. 2008. 'China's "War on Terror" in Xinjiang'. *Terrorism and Political Violence* 20/2, 271–301.

Clarke, Michael E. 2011. *Xinjiang and China's Rise in Central Asia: A History.* London: Routledge.

Claude, Richard Pierre and Burns H. Weston. 1992. *Human Rights in the World Community.* Philadelphia, PA: University of Pennsylvania Press.

Clothey, Rebecca. 2001. 'China's Minorities and State Preferential Politics'. Paper presented at the 45th Annual Meeting of the Comparative and International Education Society (Washington, DC, March), available at http://files.eric.ed.gov/fulltext/ED453139.pdf.

Common Program of the Chinese People's Political Consultative Conference, The, 29 September 1949, available at http://www.fordham.edu/halsall/mod/1949-ccp-program.html.

Connor, Neil. 2014. '31 Dead in Attack in China's Xinjiang'. *The Australian,* 22 May, available at http://www.theaustralian.com.au/news/latest-news/blast-near-park-in-chinas-xinjiang-region/story-fn3dxix6-1226926796740.

Constable, Nichole (ed.). 1996. *Guest People: Hakka Identity in China and Abroad.* Seattle, WA: University of Washington Press.

Constitution of the People's Republic of China (adopted on 4 December 1982), available at http://english.peopledaily.com.cn/constitution/constitution.html.

Copenhagen Criteria. n.d. Available at http://www.euro-dollar-currency.com/copenhagen_criteria.htm.

Council of Europe. 1995. *Framework Convention for the Protection of National Minorities,* 1 February, available at http://conventions.coe.int/Treaty/Commun/QueVoulezVous.asp?NT=157&CL=ENG.

CSCE Conference on the Human Dimension, The. 1990. *Document of the Copenhagen Meeting of the Conference on the Human Dimension of the CSCE*, 5–29 June, available at http://www.osce.org/odihr/elections/14304.

Cultural Survival. 1997. 'The Question of Minority Identity and Indigeneity in Post-Colonial China', 21 October, available at http://www.culturalsurvival.org/publications/cultural-survival-quarterly/china/question-minority-identity-and-indigeneity-post-colon.

Dalai Lama. 1987. 'Five Point Peace Plan: Address to the U.S. Congressional Human Right's Caucus', 21 September. http://www.dalailama.com/messages/tibet/five-point-peace-plan.

Dautcher, Jay Todd. 1999. *Folklore and Identity in a Uighur Community in Xinjiang, China*. PhD dissertation, University of California, Berkeley.

Dayton, D. 2006. *Big Country, Subtle Voices: Three Ethnic Poets from China's Southwest*. MA thesis, Department of Chinese Studies, University of Sydney. Available at http://ses.library.usyd.edu.au/bitstream/2123/1630/6/02whole Dayton.pdf.

Deal, David and Laura Hostetler. 2006. *The Art of Ethnography: A Chinese 'Miao Album'*. Seattle, WA: University of Washington Press.

Decree from the State Ethnic Affairs Commission and the Ministry of Public Security to Verify and Confirm a Citizen's Nationality Status (家民委公安部关于中国公民确定民族成份的规定). 1990. 10 May, available at http://www.mzb.com.cn/html/report/174493-1.htm [in Chinese].

Delegation of the European Union to China. 2011. 'EU-China Dialogue on Human Rights', 16 June, available at http://eeas.europa.eu/delegations/china/press_corner/all_news/news/2011/20110616_01_en.htm.

di Sarsina, Paolo Roberti, Luigi Ottaviani and Joey Mella. 2011. 'Tibetan Medicine: A Unique Heritage of Person-Centered Medicine'. *EPMA Journal* 2/4, 385–9.

Dietrich, Frank. 2010. 'The Status of Kosovo – Reflections on the Legitimacy of Secession'. *Ethics & Global Politics* 3/2, 123–42.

Dillon, Michael. 2004. *Xinjiang: China's Muslim Far North West*. New York: RoutledgeCurzon.

Dillon, Michael. 2009. *Contemporary China*. London: Routledge.

Directive from the State Ethnic Affairs Commission and the Ministry of Public Security to Impose a Moratorium on Nationality Status Shift (国家民委、公安部关于暂停更改民族成份工作的通知). 1989. 11 November, available at http://www.chinabaike.com/law/zy/bw/gw/mz/1340681.html [in Chinese].

Dong, Shasha. 2010. 'Xinjiang Recruits More Ethnic Minorities for Municipal-Level Cadre Positions', 11 October, available at http://news.xinhuanet.com/english2010/china/2010-10/11/c_13552146.htm.

Dorling, Philip. 2011. 'Beijing Officials "Laughed off" Australian Concerns', *Sydney Morning Herald*, 27 April, available at http://m.smh.com.au/national/beijing-officials-laughed-off-australian-concerns-20110426-1dv7a.html.

Dreyer, June Teufel. 1976. *China's Forty Millions*. Cambridge, MA: Harvard University Press.

Dreyer, June Teufel. 1994. 'The PLA and Regionalism in Xinjiang'. *Pacific Review* 7/1, 41–55.

Dreyer, June Teufel. 2005. 'China's Vulnerability to Minority Separatism'. *Asian Affairs: An American Review* 31/2, 69–85.

Durrant, Stephen. 1979. 'The Nišan Shaman Caught in Cultural Contradiction'. *Sings* 5/2, 338–47.

Dutt, Vidya Prakash. 1964. *China's Foreign Policy, 1958–1962*. New York: Asia Publishing.

Dwyer, Arienne. 2005. *The Xinjiang Conflict*. East-West Center in Washington: Policy Studies 15, available at http://www.eastwestcenter.org/fileadmin/stored/pdfs/PS015.pdf.

Eberhard, Wolfram. 1982. *China's Minorities: Yesterday and Today*. Belmont, CA: Wadsworth.

Editorial Team of Xinjiang Local Gazettes (新疆维吾尔自治区地方志编纂委员会). 2004. *Xinjiang Yearbook 2004 (新疆年鉴 2004)*. Urumchi (乌鲁木齐市): Xinjiang Yearbook Press (新疆年鉴社).

Elmer, Franziska. 2011. 'Tibet and Xinjiang: Their Fourfold Value to China'. *Culture Mandala: Bulletin of the Centre for East-West Cultural & Economic Studies* 9/2, 1–14.

Fairbank, John K. 1942. 'Tributary Trade and China's Relations with the West'. *Far Eastern Quarterly* 1/2, 129–49.

Falk, Richard. 1999. 'Kosovo, World Order, and the Future of International Law'. *American Journal of International Law* 93/4, 847–57.

Fan, Ruiping and Ian Holliday. 2006. 'Policies for Traditional Medicine in Peripheral China'. *Journal of Alternative and Complementary Medicine* 12/5, 483–7.

Farer, Tom J. 2003. 'The Ethics of Intervention in Self-Determination Struggles'. *Human Rights Quarterly* 25/2, 382–406.

Fei, Hsiao-tung. 1980. 'Ethnic Identification in China'. *Social Sciences in China* 1, 94–107.

Feng, Jianhua. 2007. 'Endangered Ethnic Culture', 31 May, available at http://www.bjreview.com/nation/txt/2007-05/28/content_64791.htm.

Fischer, Andrew Martin. 2004. *Urban Fault Lines in Shangri-La*, CSRC Working Papers 1/421 available at http://www.isn.ethz.ch/isn/Digital-Library/Publications/Detail/?ots591=0c54e3b3-1e9c-be1e-2c24-a6a8c7060233&lng=en&id=57493.

Fischer, Andrew Martin. 2013. *The Disempowered Development of Tibet in China: A Study in the Economics of Marginalization*. Lanham, MD: Lexington Books.

Fitzgerald, Charles Patrick. 1941. *The Tower of Five Glories: a Study of the Min Chia of Ta Li, Yunnan*. London: Cresset.

Fleming, Michael. 2002. 'The New Minority Rights Regime in Poland'. *Nations and Nationalism* 8/4, 531–48.

Foot, Rosemary. 2001. *Rights beyond Borders: The Global Community and the Struggle over Human Rights in China*. Oxford: Oxford University Press.

Forbes, Andrew. 1986. *Warlords and Muslims in Chinese Central Asia: A Political History of Republican Sinkiang, 1911–1949*. Cambridge: Cambridge University Press.

Fortman, Bas de Gaay. 2011.'Minority Rights: A Major Misconception?' *Human Rights Quarterly* 33/2, 265–303.

Fuller, Graham E. and Jonathan N. Lipman. 2004. 'Islam in Xinjiang'. In S. Frederick Starr (ed.), *Xinjiang: China's Muslim Borderland*. Armonk, NY: M.E. Sharpe, pp. 320–52.

Gao, Fang. 2009.'Model Minority, Self-perception and Schooling: Multiple Voices of Korean Students in China'. *Asia Pacific Journal of Education*, 29/1, 17–27.

Gao, Fang. 2010. 'A Comparative Analysis of the Meaning of Model Minority among Ethnic Koreans in China and the United States'. *Comparative Education* 46/2, 207–22.

Gerin, Roseanne. 2011. 'Ethnic Minority Games Come to Guizhou'. *Beijing Review*, 7 July, available at http://www.bjreview.com.cn/eye/txt/2011-07/01/content_373841.htm.

Ghai, Yash (ed.). 2000. *Autonomy and Ethnicity*. Cambridge: Cambridge University Press.

Ghai, Yash and Sophia Woodman. 2009. 'Unused Powers: Contestation over Autonomy Legislation in the PRC'. *Pacific Affairs* 82/1, 29–46.

Gillette, Maris. 2000. *Between Mecca and Beijing*. Stanford, CA: Stanford University Press.

Gladney, Dru C. 1991. *Muslim Chinese*, 1st edn. Cambridge, MA: Harvard University Press.

Gladney, Dru C. 1994.'Representing Nationality in China: Refiguring Majority/Minority Identities'. *Journal of Asian Studies* 53/1, 92–123.

Gladney, Dru C. 1995. 'Tian Zhuangzhuang, the "Fifth Generation", and "Minorities Film" in China'. *Public Culture* 8/1, 161–75.

Gladney, Dru C. 1996. *Muslim Chinese*, 2nd edn. Cambridge, MA: Harvard University Press.

Gladney, Dru C. 1998. *Ethnic Identity in China*. Belmont, CA: Wadsworth.

Gladney, Dru C. 2004a. 'The Chinese Program of Development and Control: 1978–2001'. In S. Frederick Starr (ed.), *Xinjiang: China's Muslim Borderland*. Armonk, NY: M.E. Sharpe, pp. 101–19.

Gladney, Dru C. 2004b. 'Responses to Chinese Rule: Patterns of Cooperation and Opposition'. In S. Frederick Starr (ed.), *Xinjiang: China's Muslim Borderland*. Armonk, NY: M.E. Sharpe, pp. 375–96.

Glanville, Luke. 2011a. 'The Antecedents of "Sovereignty as Responsibility"'. *European Journal of International Relations* 17/2, 233–55.

Glanville, Luke. 2011b. 'Ellery Stowell and the Enduring Dilemmas of Humanitarian Intervention'. *International Studies Review* 13/2, 241–58.

Goldstein, Melvyn C. 1989. *A History of Modern Tibet, Volume 1: 1913–1951*. Berkeley, CA: University of California Press.

Goldstein, Melvyn C. 1999. *The Snow Lion and the Dragon*. Berkeley, CA: University of California Press.

Goldstein, Melvyn C., Ben Jiao, Cynthia M. Beall and Phuntsog Tsering. 2002. 'Fertility and Family Planning in Rural Tibet'. *The China Journal* 47, 19–39.

Goldstein, Melvyn C., Ben Jiao, Cynthia M. Beall, and Phuntsog Tsering. 2003. 'Development and Change in Rural Tibet: Problems and Adaptations'. *Asian Survey* 43/5, 758–99.

Goldstein, Melvyn C., Ben Jiao and Tanzen Lhundrup. 2009. *On the Cultural Revolution in Tibet*. Berkeley, CA: University of California Press.

Goldstein, Melvyn C., Dawei Sherap and William R. Siebenschuh. 2004. *A Tibetan Revolutionary: The Political Life and Times of Bapa Phüntso Wangye*. Berkeley, CA: University of California Press.

Goldstein, Melvyn C., William R. Siebenschuh and Tashi Tsering. 1999. *The Struggle for Modern Tibet: The Autobiography of Tashi Tsering*. Armonk, NY: East Gate Book/M.E. Sharpe.

Goodman, David. 2004. 'The Campaign to "Open up the West"'. *China Quarterly* 178, 318–34.

Government of the Chinese Soviet Republic. 1935. A Declaration to People in Inner Mongolia (对内蒙古人民宣言), 20 December, available at http://hi.baidu.com/cjsh001/blog/item/c3726308adf2d0910b7b8209.html [in Chinese].

Government of the Chinese Soviet Republic. 1936. A Declaration to Hui People (对回族人民的宣言), 25 May, available at http://www.norislam.com/?viewnews-6561 [in Chinese].

Gros, Stéphane. 2004. 'The Politics of Names: The Identification of the Dulong (Drung) of Northwest Yunnan'. *China Information* 18/2, 275–302.

Grossman, Leo. 1984. *Essays on International Law and Organization*. Leiden: Brill.

Guo, Jingfu, Jingtao Wang and Jianbin Wang. 2010. 'Study on Development Policies of the Special Industries in Ethnic Minority Areas of China'. *International Journal of Business and Management* 5/2, 201–4.

Gustafsson, Bjorn and Li Shi. 2003. 'The Ethnic Minority–Majority Income Gap in Rural China during Transition'. *Economic Development and Cultural Change* 51/4, 805–22.

Hance, Jeremy. 2011. 'Reforestation Program in China Preventing Future Disasters', 13 May, available at http://news.mongabay.com/2011/0512 -hance_china_slcp.html.

Hannum, Emily. 2002. 'Educational Stratification by Ethnicity in China'. *Demography* 39/1, 95–117.

Hannum, Emily and Yu Xie. 1998. 'Ethnic Stratification in Northwest China'. *Demography* 35/3, 323–33.

Hansen, Mette Halskov. 2005. *Frontier People*. Vancouver: University of British Columbia Press.

Hao, Temtsel. 2009. 'Xinjiang, Tibet, Beyond', *Open Democracy*, 27 July, available at http://www.opendemocracy.net/article/xinjiang-tibet-beyond-china-s -ethnic-relations.

Harrell, Stevan. 1995a. 'Introduction: Civilizing Projects and the Reaction to Them'. In Stevan Harrell (ed.), *Cultural Encounters on China's Ethnic Frontiers*. Seattle, WA: University of Washington Press, pp. 3–27.

Harrell, Stevan. 1995b. 'The History of the History of the Yi'. In Stevan Harrell (ed.), *Cultural Encounters on China's Ethnic Frontiers*. Seattle, WA: University of Washington Press, pp. 63–91.

Harrell, Stevan (ed.). 2001. *Ways of Being Ethnic in Southwest China*. Seattle, WA: University of Washington Press.

Harrell, Stevan. 2007. 'L'état, c'est nous, or We Have Met the Oppressor and He Is Us: The Predicament of Minority Cadres in the PRC'. In Diana Lary (ed.), *The Chinese State at the Borders*. Vancouver: University of British Columbia Press, pp. 221–39.

Hasmath, Reza. 2007. 'The Paradox of Ethnic Minority Development in Beijing'. *Comparative Sociology* 6/4, 464–80.

Hasmath, Reza. 2008. 'The Big Payoff? Educational and Occupational Attainments of Ethnic Minorities in Beijing'. *European Journal of Development Research* 20/1, 104–16.

Hastings, Justin P. 2005. 'Perceiving a Single Chinese State: Escalation and Violence in Uighur Protests'. *Problems of Post-Communism* 52/1, 28–38.

Hays, Jeffrey. 2012. 'Deforestation and Desertification in China', available at http://factsanddetails.com/china/cat10/sub66/item389.html.

He, Baogang. 2003. 'Minority Rights: A Confucian Critique of Kymlicka's Theory of Nonassimilation'. In Kim-chong Chong, Sor-hoon Tan and C.L. Ten (eds), *The Moral Circle and the Self: Chinese and Western Approaches*. Chicago, IL: Open Court Publishing, pp. 219–45.

He, Baogang. 2004. 'Confucianism versus Liberalism over Minority Rights'. *Journal of Chinese Philosophy* 31/1, 103–23.

Heberer, Thomas. 1989. *China and Its National Minorities*. Armonk, NY: M.E. Sharpe.

Henrard, Kristin. 2000. *Devising an Adequate System of Minority Protection*. The Hague: Kluwer Law International.

Henrard, Kristin. 2001. 'The Interrelationship between Individual Human Rights, Minority Rights and the Right to Self-Determination and Its Importance for the Adequate Protection of Linguistic Minorities'. *Global Review of Ethnopolitics* 1/1, 41–61.

Henry, Gary T. 2001. *Islam in Tibet*. Louisville, KY: Fons Vitae.

Herbst, Moira. 2008. 'Oil for China, Guns for Darfur', *Businessweek*, 14 March, available at http://www.businessweek.com/globalbiz/content/mar2008/gb20080314_430126.htm.

Hess, Stephen E. 2009. 'Islam, Local Elites, and China's Missteps in Integrating the Uyghur Nation'. *OAKA: Journal of Central Asian and Caucasian Studies* 4/7, 75–96.

Hesterman, Donna. 2011. 'Reforesting Rural Lands in Western China Pays Big Dividends, Stanford Researchers Say', *Stanford News*, 11 May, available at http://news.stanford.edu/news/2011/may/reforesting-rural-china-051111.html.

Hierman, Brent. 2007. 'The Pacification of Xinjiang: Uighur Protest and the Chinese State, 1988–2002'. *Problems of Post-Communism* 54/3, 48–62.

Hillman, Ben. 2003. 'Paradise under Construction: Minorities, Myths and Modernity in Northwest Yunnan'. *Asian Ethnicity* 4/2, 175–88.

Hofer, Theresia. 2008. 'Socio-Economic Dimensions of Tibetan Medicine in the Tibet Autonomous Region, China'. *Asian Medicine* 4/1, 174–200.

Horowitz, Donald L. 2000. *Ethnic Groups in Conflict*. Berkeley, CA: University of California Press.

Howland, Douglas. 2011. 'The Dialectics of Chauvinism'. *Modern China* 37/2, 1–32.

Hsu, Francis. 1971. *Under the Ancestor's Shadow: Kinship, Personality, and Social Mobility in Village China*. Stanford, CA: Stanford University Press.

Hsu, Mei-Ling. 1993. 'The Growth of Chinese Minority Populations'. *GeoJournal* 30/3, 279–82.

Hua, Cai. 2001. *A Society without Fathers or Husbands*. New York: Zone Books.

Huang, Jianhua. 2003. *A Study of the Policies on Xinjiang by the Nationalist Government* [国民党政府的新疆政策研究]. Beijing: Nationality Press [in Chinese].

Huang, Pei. 1990. 'New Light on the Origins of the Manchu'. *Harvard Journal of Asiatic Studies* 50/1, 239–82.

Huang, Xing. 2003. 'Minority Language Planning of China in Relation to Use and Development', available at http://www.sil.org/asia/ldc/parallel_papers/huang_xing.pdf.

Huang, Xingtao. 2002. 'Ethnic Consciousness and Identity: A Historical Study of the Evolution of Han Nationalism in Modern China' (民族自觉与符号认同：'中华民族'观念萌生与确立史察). *Chinese Social Sciences Reviews* (中国社会科学评论), Hong Kong, available at http://jds.cass.cn/UploadFiles/ztsjk/2010/11/201011041511494945.pdf [in Chinese].

Huang, Yasheng. 1995. 'China's Cadre Transfer Policy toward Tibet in the 1980s'. *Modern China* 21/2, 184–204.

Human Rights in China. 2007. *China: Minority Exclusion, Marginalization and Rising Tensions*. London: Minority Rights Group International, available at http://www.hrichina.org/en/publications/hric-report/china-minority-exclusion-marginalization-and-rising-tensions.

Human Rights Watch. 2003. 'China's Involvement in Sudan: Arms and Oil', available at http://www.hrw.org/reports/2003/sudan1103/26.htm.

Hutcheon, Stephen. 2008. 'More Ceremony Fakes Unearthed'. *The Sydney Morning Herald*, 15 August, available at http://www.smh.com.au/news/off-the-field/additional-ceremony-fakes-unearthed/2008/08/15/1218307191766.html.

Hyer, Eric. 2006. 'China's Policy towards Uighur Nationalism'. *Journal of Muslim Minority Affairs* 26/1, 75–86.

Hyer, Eric. 2009. 'Sinocentrism and the National Question in China'. In Susana Carvalho and François Gemenne (eds), *Nations and Their Histories*. Basingstoke: Palgrave Macmillan, pp. 255–73.

Iliopoulos, Katherine. 2011. 'Jurists Call for Commission of Inquiry into Burma War Crimes', available at http://www.crimesofwar.org/commentary/jurists-call-for-commission-of-inquiry-into-burma-war-crimes/.

Information Office of the State Council of the PRC. 1996. *White Paper: Progress in China's Human Rights Cause*, 'VII: Guarantee of the Rights of the Minority Nationality', available at http://www.china.org.cn/e-white/prhumanrights1996/15-7.htm.

Information Office of the State Council of the PRC. 1999a. *National Minorities Policy and Its Practice in China*, 'III: Regional Autonomy for Ethnic Minorities', available at http://chineseculture.about.com/library/china/whitepaper/blsminority.htm.

Information Office of the State Council of the PRC. 1999b. *National Minorities Policy and Its Practice in China,* 'V: Preservation and Development of the Cultures of Ethnic Minorities', available at http://chineseculture.about.com/library/china/whitepaper/blsminority.htm.

Information Office of the State Council of the PRC. 2005. *White Paper 2005: Regional Autonomy for Ethnic Minorities in China,* 28 February, available at http://www.china.org.cn/e-white/20050301/index.htm.

Information Office of the State Council of the PRC. 2009. *China's Ethnic Policy and Common Prosperity and Development of All Ethnic Groups,* available at http://www.china.org.cn/government/whitepaper/node_7078073.htm.

Information Office of the State Council of the PRC. 2010a. 'China's Ethnic Policy and Common Prosperity and Development of All Ethnic Groups'. *Chinese Journal of International Law* 9/1, 221–59.

Information Office of the State Council of the PRC. 2010b. *Progress in China's Human Rights in 2009,* available at http://news.xinhuanet.com/english2010/china/2010-09/26/c_13529921.htm.

Ingram, Catherine. 2011. 'Echoing the Environment in Kam Big Song'. *Asian Studies Review* 35/4, 439–55.

International Commission on Intervention and State Sovereignty. 2001. *The Responsibility to Protect,* available at http://responsibilitytoprotect.org/ICISS%20Report.pdf.

Jacobs, David and Daniel Tope. 2008. 'The Politics of Resentment in the Post Civil-Rights Era: Minority Threat, Homicide, and Ideological Voting in Congress'. *American Journal of Sociology* 112/5, 1458–94.

Janes, Craig R. 1995. 'The Transformations of Tibetan Medicine'. *Medical Anthropology Quarterly* 9/1, 6–31.

Jankowiak, William. 1993. *Sex, Death, and Hierarchy in a Chinese City.* New York: Columbia University Press.

Ji, Dachun. 2002. *A Collection of Papers on the Modern History of Xinjiang* (新疆近世史论稿). Harbin: Heilongjiang Education Press [in Chinese].

Jian, Chen. 2006. 'The Tibetan Rebellion of 1959 and China's Changing Relations with India and the Soviet Union'. *Journal of Cold War Studies* 8/3, 54–101.

Johnson, Bonnie and Nalini Chhetri. 2002. 'Exclusionary Policies and Practices in Chinese Minority Education'. *Current Issues in Comparative Education* 2/2, 142–53.

Johnson, Emily and Gregory Chow. 1997. 'Rates of Return to Schooling in China'. *Pacific Economic Review* 2/2, 101–13.

Johnson, Nan E. and Kao-Ti Zhang. 1991. 'Matriarchy, Polyandry, and Fertility amongst the Mosuos in China'. *Journal of Biosocial Science* 23, 499–505.

Jonsson, Hjorleifur. 2000. 'Yao Minority Identity and the Location of Difference in the South China Borderlands'. *Ethnos* 65/1, 56–82.

Joseph, William (ed.). 2010. *Politics in China: An Introduction.* New York: Oxford University Press.

Jun, Hu and Kevin Stuart. 1992. 'The Guanting Tu (Monguor) Wedding Ceremonies and Songs'. *Anthropos* 87/1–3, 109–32.

Jun, Niu. 2005. *1962: The Eve of the Left Turn in China's Foreign Policy.* CWIHP Working Paper No. 48, Woodrow Wilson International Center for Scholars, Washington, DC.

Kaltman, Blaine. 2007. *Under the Heel of the Dragon: Islam, Racism, Crime, and the Uighur in China.* Athens, OH: Ohio University Press.

Kang, David C. 2010. *East Asia before the West: Five Centuries of Trade and Tribute.* New York: Columbia University Press.

Kapstein, Matthew T. 2006. *The Tibetans.* Malden, MA: Blackwell.

Kaup, Katherine Palmer. 2000. *Creating the Zhuang.* Boulder, CO: Lynne Rienner.

Kaup, Katherine Palmer. 2002. 'Regionalism versus Ethnicnationalism in the People's Republic of China'. *The China Quarterly* 172, 863–84.

Kent, Ann. 1999. *China, the United Nations and Human Rights: The Limits of Compliance.* Philadelphia, PA: University of Pennsylvania Press.

Kent, Ann. 2002. 'China's International Socialization: The Role of International Organizations'. *Global Governance* 8/3, 343–64.

Khan, Almaz. 1995. 'Chinggis Khan: From Imperial Ancestor to Ethnic Hero'. In Stevan Harrell (ed.), *Cultural Encounters on China's Ethnic Frontiers.* Seattle, WA: University of Washington Press, pp. 248–77.

Khan, Almaz. 1996. 'Who are the Mongols? State, Ethnicity, and the Politics of Representation in the PRC'. In Melissa Brown (ed.), *Negotiating Ethnicities in China and Taiwan.* Berkeley, CA: Institute of East Asian Studies, University of California, pp. 125–59.

Kim, Ho-Dong. 2004. *Holy War in China: The Muslim Rebellion and State in Chinese Central Asia.* Stanford, CA: Stanford University Press.

Kim, Wang-Bae. 2010. 'Nostalgia, Anxiety and Hope: Migration and Ethnic Identity of Chosonjok in China'. *Pacific Affairs* 83/1, 95–114.

King, Ryan D. and Darren Wheelock. 2007. 'Group Threat and Social Control: Race, Perceptions of Minorities, and the Desire to Punish'. *Social Forces* 85/3, 1255–80.

Koch, Jessica. 2006. *Economic Development and Ethnic Separatism in Western China.* Working Paper No. 134, Asia Research Centre, Murdoch University.

Koenig, Matthias. 2008. 'Institutional Change in the World Polity'. *International Sociology* 23/1, 95–114.

Koszorus, Frank. 1982. 'The Forgotten Legacy of the League of Nations Minority Protection System'. In Bela K. Kiraly, Peter Pastor and Ivan Sanders (eds), *Essays on World War I: Total War and Peacemaking, A Case Study on Trianon*. New York: Social Science Monographs, Brooklyn College Press, distributed by Columbia University Press, pp. 547–73, available at http://www.hungarianhistory.com/lib/tria/tria41.htm.

Ku, Teddy. 2008. 'Race & Patriotism …', 27 March, available at http://www.icubed.us/node/887.

Kunovich, Robert M. 2004. 'Social Structural Position and Prejudice'. *Social Science Research* 33/1, 20–44.

Kymlicka, Will. 1995. *Multicultural Citizenship: A Liberal Theory of Minority Rights*. Oxford: Clarendon Press.

Lai, Hongyi. 2009a. 'China's Ethnic Policies and Challenges'. *East Asian Policy* 1/3, 5–13.

Lai, Hongyi. 2009b. 'The Evolution of China's Ethnic Policies'. Background Brief No. 440, East Asian Institute, National University of Singapore, 12 March, available at http://www.eai.nus.edu.sg/BB440.pdf.

Lai, Hongyi. 2010. 'Ethnic Autonomous Regions: A Formula for a Unitary Multiethnic State'. In Jae Ho Chung and Lam Tao-Chiu (eds), *China's Local Administration: Traditions and Changes in the Sub-National Hierarchy*. London: Routledge, pp. 62–85.

Lary, Diana. 1996. 'The Tomb of the King of Nanyue – The Contemporary Agenda of History: Scholarship and Identity'. *Modern China* 22/1, 3–27.

Law of the People's Republic of China on Regional National Autonomy. 1984. Available at http://www.novexcn.com/regional_nation_autonomy.html.

Leibold, James. 2008. *Reconfiguring Chinese Nationalism: How the Qing Frontier and its Indigenes Became Chinese*. Basingstoke: Palgrave Macmillan.

Leibold, James. 2010. 'The Beijing Olympics and China's Conflicted National Form'. *The China Journal* 63, 1–24.

Lenin, Vladimir Ilyich. 1972. 'The Right of Nations to Self-Determination'. In Vladimir Ilyich Lenin, *Collected Works*, Vol. 20. Moscow: Progress Publishers, pp. 393–454.

Leopold, Evelyn. 2007. 'China, Russia Cast Rare Veto against U.S. on Myanmar', 12 January, available at http://www.militaryphotos.net/forums/archive/index.php/t-104527.html.

Li, Chengwu. 2009. From Self-Determination to Regional Autonomy – A History of How the CCP Has Developed Policies to Address the National

Question (从'民族自决'到'区域自治'–中国共产党解决中国民族问题的历史考), 28 June, available at http://www.hprc.org.cn/gsyj/yjjg/zggsyjxh_1/gsnhlw_1/erguoshixslwj/200906/t20090628_12807_1.html [in Chinese].

Li, Haizheng. 2003. 'Economic Transition and Returns to Education in China'. *Economics of Education Review* 22/3, 317–28.

Li, Shen (ed.). 2003. *Xinjiang, China: Past and Present* (中国新疆: 历史与现状). Urumchi: Xinjiang People's Press [in Chinese].

Li, Tao and Hongying Jiang. 2003. *Tibetan Customs*. Beijing: China Intercontinental Press.

Li, Xiaoxia. 2013. How to Maintain Effective Governance and Long-Term Stability amid Rapid Developments in Xinjiang (新疆跨越式发展下如何实现长治久安), 25 January, available at http://www.360doc.com/content/13/0125/12/111031_262303982.shtml [in Chinese].

Lin, Jing. 1997. 'Policies and Practices of Bilingual Education for the Minorities in China'. *Journal of Multilingual and Multicultural Development* 18/3, 193–205.

Lipman, Jonathan. 1997. *Familiar Strangers*. Seattle, WA: University of Washington Press.

Lipman, Jonathan. 2004. 'White Hats, Oil Cakes, and Common Blood'. In Morris Rossabi (ed.), *Governing China's Multiethnic Frontiers*. Seattle, WA: University of Washington Press, pp. 19–52.

Litzinger, Ralph. 1998. 'Memory Work: Reconstituting the Ethnic in Post-Mao China'. *Cultural Anthropology* 13/2, 224–55.

Litzinger, Ralph. 2000. *Other Chinas: The Yao and the Politics of National Belonging*. Durham, NC: Duke University Press.

Liu, Xingwu and Alatan. 1988. 'China's Policy towards Her Minority Nationalities'. *Social Scientist* 16/1, 136–59.

Lundberg, Maria. 2009. 'Regional National Autonomy and Minority Language Rights in the PRC'. *International Journal on Minority and Group Rights* 16/3, 399–422.

Lundberg, Maria and Yong Zhou. 2009. 'Regional National Autonomy under Challenge: Law, Practice and Recommendations'. *International Journal on Minority and Group Rights* 16/3, 269–327.

Lyon, Rob. 2008. 'China, Tibet and the World Economy', *In Defence of Marxism*, 1 April, available at http://www.marxist.com/china-tibet-world-economy.htm.

Ma, Rong. 1996. *Society and Population in Tibet* (西藏的人口与社会). Beijing: Unity Press [in Chinese].

Ma, Rong. 2007a. 'A New Perspective in Guiding Ethnic Relations in the 21st Century'. Discussion Paper 21, China Policy Institute, University of

Nottingham, July, available at http://www.nottingham.ac.uk/cpi/documents/ discussion-papers/discussion-paper-21-ethnic-relations.pdf.

Ma, Rong. 2007b. 'A New Perspective in Guiding Ethnic Relations in the Twenty-First Century: "De-politicization" of Ethnicity in China'. *Asian Ethnicity* 8/3, 199–217.

Ma, Rong. 2009. 'The Key to Understanding and Interpreting Ethnic Relations in Contemporary China'. *DevelopmentISSues* 11/1, 18–20.

Ma, Xiaoyi. 2009. 'The Function and Significance of Newly Created Ethnic Minority Writing Systems during Cultural Transition: Taking the Hani, Lisu, and Naxi Ethnic Minorities as Examples'. *Frontiers of Education in China* 4/3, 435–52.

Mackerras, Colin. 1972. *The Uighur Empire According to the T'ang Dynastic Histories: A Study in Sino-Uighur Relations 744–840.* Canberra: Australian National University Press.

Mackerras, Colin. 1984. 'Folksongs and Dances of China's Minority Nationalities: Policy, Tradition, and Professionalization'. *Modern China* 10/2, 187–226.

Mackerras, Colin. 1988. 'Aspects of Bai Culture: Change and Continuity in a Yunnan Nationality'. *Modern China* 14/1, 51–84.

Mackerras, Colin. 1992. 'Integration and the Dramas of China's Minorities'. *Asian Theatre Journal* 9/1, 1–37.

Mackerras, Colin. 1994. *China's Minorities: Integration and Modernization in the Twentieth Century.* Hong Kong: Oxford University Press.

Mackerras, Colin. 1995. *China's Minority Cultures.* New York: St. Martin's Press.

Mackerras, Colin. 2001. 'Xinjiang at the Turn of the Century'. *Central Asia Survey* 20/3, 289–303.

Mackerras, Colin. 2003. *China's Ethnic Minorities and Globalization.* London: RoutledgeCurzon.

Mackerras, Colin. 2004a. 'Conclusion: Some Major Issues in Ethnic Classification'. *China Information* 18/2, 303–13.

Mackerras, Colin. 2004b. 'What is China? Who is Chinese?' In Peter Hays Gries and Stanley Rosen (eds), *State and Society in 21st Century China.* London: Routledge, pp. 216–34.

Mackerras, Colin. 2005a. 'China's Ethnic Minorities and the Middle Classes'. *International Journal of Social Economics* 32/9, 814–26.

Mackerras, Colin. 2005b. People's Republic of China: Background Paper on the Situation of the Tibetan Population. A Writenet report, available at http://www.unhcr.org/refworld/pdfid/423ea9094.pdf.

Mackerras, Colin. 2011a. 'Ethnic Minorities'. In Xiaowei Zang (ed.), *Understanding Chinese Society.* London: Routledge, pp. 111–26.

Mackerras, Colin (ed.). 2011b. *Ethnic Minorities in Modern China*, 4 vols. London: Routledge.

Mamet, Rizvan, Cardell Jacobson and Tim Heaton. 2005. 'Ethnic Intermarriage in Beijing and Xinjiang'. *Journal of Comparative Family Studies* 36/1, 187–201.

Mao, Zedong, 1953. *Selected Works of Mao Zedong, Vol. III* (毛泽东选集第3卷). Beijing: People's Press [in Chinese].

Martin, Terry. 2001. *Affirmative Action Empire: Nations and Nationalism in the Soviet Union, 1923–1939*. Ithaca, NY: Cornell University Press.

Mason, T. David. 2003. 'Structures of Ethnic Conflict: Revolution versus Secession in Rwanda and Sri Lanka'. *Terrorism and Political Violence* 15/4, 83–113.

Maurer-Fazio, Margaret, James Hughes and Dandan Zhang. 2007. 'An Ocean Formed from One Hundred Rivers'. *Feminist Economics* 13/3–4, 159–87.

McCarthy, Susan K. 2009. *Communist Multiculturalism: Ethnic Revival in Southwest China*. Seattle, WA: University of Washington Press.

McDonell, Stephen. 2013. '21 killed in Uighur clashes in China'. Australia Network News, 25 April, available at http://www.abc.net.au/news/2013-04-24/21-people-killed-after-unrest-in-xinjiang/4650024.

McKhann, Charles. 1995. 'The Naxi and the Nationalities Question'. In Steven Harrell (ed.), *Cultural Encounters on China's Ethnic Frontiers*. Seattle, WA: University of Washington Press, pp. 39–62.

McMillen, Donald. 1979. *Chinese Communist Power and Policy in Xinjiang, 1949–1977*. Boulder, CO: Westview.

Memisoglu, Fulya. 2007. 'The European Union's Minority Rights Policy and Its Impact on the Development of Minority Rights Protection in Greece'. Paper prepared for the 3rd Hellenic Observatory PhD Symposium on Contemporary Greece: Structures, Context and Challenges. Hellenic Observatory, European Institute, LSE, 14–15 June, available at http://www2.lse.ac.uk/european Institute/research/hellenicObservatory/pdf/3rd_Symposium/PAPERS/MEMISOGLOU_FULYA.pdf.

Miao, Xiaoyang. 2011. 'Splendid Gala'. *Beijing Review*, 28 September, available at www.bjreview.com.cn/special/2011-09/28/content_395273.htm.

Millward, James. 1998. *An Historical Perspective on the Crisis in Chinese Turkestan: The Forgotten Legacy of the Qing Dynasty*. Woodrow Wilson International Center, Asia Program Occasional Papers #79.

Millward, James. 2007. *Eurasian Crossroads*. New York: Columbia University Press.

Millward, James and Peter Perdue. 2004. 'Political and Cultural History of the Xinjiang Region through the Late 19th Century'. In S. Frederick Starr (ed.), *Xinjiang: China's Muslim Borderland*. Armonk, NY: M.E. Sharpe, pp. 27–62.

Millward, James and Nabijan Tursun. 2004. 'Political History and Strategies of Control, 1884–1978'. In S. Frederick Starr (ed.), *Xinjiang: China's Muslim Borderland*. Armonk, NY: M.E. Sharpe, pp. 63–98.

Mishra, Vinod and Russell Smyth. 2010. 'Economic Returns to Schooling for China's Korean Minority'. Discussion Paper 37/10, Department of Economics, Monash University, available at http://www.buseco.monash.edu.au/eco/research/papers/2010/3710economicmishrasmyth.pdf.

Mofcom. 2009. 'Spoken and Written Languages of the People's Republic of China', 22 March, available at http://no2.mofcom.gov.cn/aarticle/aboutchina/population/200903/20090306117656.html.

Moneyhon, Matthew. 2002. 'Controlling Xinjiang: Autonomy on China's "New Frontier"'. *Asian-Pacific Law & Policy Journal* 3/1, 120–52.

Moseley, George. 1973. *The Consolidation of the South China Frontier*. Berkeley, CA: University of California Press.

Moukala, Edmond. 2003. 'Language Revitalization in China', available at http://www.sil.org/asia/ldc/parallel_papers/edmond_moukala.pdf.

Muharremi, Robert. 2008. 'Kosovo's Declaration of Independence: Self-Determination and Sovereignty Revisited'. *Review of Central and East European Law* 33/4, 401–35.

Mullaney, Thomas. 2004. 'Ethnic Classification Writ Large'. *China Information* 18/2, 207–41.

Mullaney, Thomas. 2010a. 'Seeing for the State: The Role of Social Scientists in China's Ethnic Classification Project'. *Asian Ethnicity* 11/3, 325–42.

Mullaney, Thomas. 2010b. *Coming to Terms with the Nation: Ethnic Classification in Modern China*. Berkeley, CA: University of California Press.

Murphy, Rachel, Ran Tao and Xi Lu. 2011. 'Son Preference in Rural China: Patrilineal Families and Socioeconomic Change'. *Population and Development Review* 37/4, 665–90.

Mushkat, Roda. 2011. 'China's Compliance with International Law: What Has Been Learned and the Gaps Remaining'. *Pacific Rim Law & Policy Journal* 20/1, 41–69.

Naquin, Susan and Evelyn Rawski. 1987. *Chinese Society in the Eighteenth Century*. New Haven, CT: Yale University Press.

Nelson, Keely. 2005. 'Language Policies and Minority Resistance in China'. *Languages, Communities, and Education* 25, 25–30.

Newby, L. J. 1998. 'The Begs of Xinjiang: Between Two Worlds'. *Bulletin of the School of Oriental and African Studies* 61/2, 278–97.

Office of the High Commissioner for Human Rights. 1965. *International Convention on the Elimination of All Forms of Racial Discrimination*. Available at http://www.ohchr.org/EN/ProfessionalInterest/Pages/CERD.aspx.

Olson, James Stuart. 1998. *An Ethnohistorical Dictionary of China*. Westport, CT: Greenwood.

Park, Chai Bin and Jing-Qing Han. 1990. 'A Minority Group and China's One-Child Policy: The Case of the Koreans'. *Studies in Family Planning* 21/3, 161–70.

Pasternak, Burton and Janet Salaff. 1993. *Cowboys and Cultivators: The Chinese of Inner Mongolia*. Boulder, CO: Westview.

Peerenboom, Randall. 2002. *China's Long March toward the Rule of Law*. Cambridge: Cambridge University Press.

Pentassuglia, Gaetano. 2005. 'Minority Rights, Human Rights: A Review of Concepts, Entitlements and Procedures under International Law'. In Council of Europe and European Centre for Minority Issues, *Mechanisms for the Implementation of Minority Rights Standards*. Strasbourg: Council of Europe Publishing, pp. 9–25.

People's Daily Online. n.d. 'The Uygur Ethnic Minority', available at http://english.people.com.cn/data/minorities/Uygur.html.

Peters, Anne. 2009. 'Humanity as the A and Ω of Sovereignty'. *European Journal of International Law* 20/3, 513–44.

Phan, Binh G. 1996. 'How Autonomous Are the National Autonomous Areas of the PRC? An Analysis of Documents and Cases'. *Issues & Studies* 32/7, 83–108.

Postiglione, Gerard A. (ed.). 1999. *China's National Minority Education: Culture, Schooling, and Development*. London: Routledge.

Poston, Dudley and Michael Micklin. 1993. 'Spatial Segregation and Social Differentiation of the Minority Nationalities from the Han Majority in the People's Republic of China'. *Sociological Inquiry* 6/2, 150–65.

Poston, Dudley and Jing Shu. 1987. 'The Demographic and Socioeconomic Composition of China's Ethnic Minorities'. *Population and Development Review* 13/4, 703–22.

Poston, Dudley, Chiung-Fang Chang and Hong Dan. 2006. 'Fertility Differences between the Majority and Minority Nationality Groups in China'. *Population Research and Policy Review* 25/1, 67–101.

Potter, Pitman B. 2011. *Law, Policy, and Practice on China's Periphery: Selective Adaptation and Institutional Capacity*. London and New York: Routledge.

Prantl, Jochen and Ryoko Nakano. 2011. 'Global Norm Diffusion in East Asia: How China and Japan Implement the Responsibility to Protect'. *International Relations* 25/2, 204–23.

Preece, Jennifer Jackson. 1997. 'National Minority Rights vs. State Sovereignty in Europe: Changing Norms in International Relations?' *Nations and Nationalism* 3/3, 345–64.

Preece, Jennifer Jackson. 1998. *National Minorities and the European Nation-States System*. Oxford: Clarendon Press.

Public and Cultural Diplomacy E. 2011. 'Report Review: US State Department's Annual Report on Tibet Negotiations, March 2009–February 2010', 16 April, available at http://publicandculturaldiplomacye.blogspot.com/2011/04/report-review-us-state-departments.html.

Qarluq, Abduresit Jelil and Donald Hugh McMillen. 2011. 'Towards a "Harmonious Society"? A Brief Case Study of the Post-Liberation Settlement in Beijing of Uyghur Intellectuals and Their Relations with the Majority Society'. *Asian Ethnicity* 12/1, 1–31.

Quillian, Lincoln. 1995. 'Prejudice as a Response to Perceived Group Threat'. *American Sociological Review* 60/4, 586–611.

Rahman, Anwar. 2005. *Sinicization beyond the Great Wall*. Leicester: Troubador Publishing.

Rajagopalan, Megha. 2013. 'China Security Chief Blames Uighur Islamists for Tiananmen Attack', *Reuters*, 1 November, available at http://www.reuters.com/article/2013/11/01/us-china-tiananmen-idUSBRE9A003L20131101.

Ramsey, S. Robert. 1987. *The Languages of China*. Princeton, NJ: Princeton University Press.

Ratchnevsky, Paul and Thomas Nivison Haining. 1993. *Genghis Khan: His Life and Legacy*. Oxford: Blackwell.

Rees, Helen. 1995–96. 'The Many Musics of a Chinese County Town: A Case-Study of Co-existence in Lijiang, Yunnan Province'. *Asian Music* 27/1, 63–102.

Rhoads, Edward (ed.). 2000. *Manchus & Han: Ethnic Relations and Political Power in Late Qing and Early Republican China*. Seattle, WA: University of Washington Press.

Riek, Blake M., Eric W. Mania and Samuel L. Gaertner. 2006. 'Intergroup Threat and Outgroup Attitudes'. *Personality and Social Psychology Review* 10/4, 336–53.

Rossett, Arthur. 1991. 'Legal Structures for Special Treatment of Minorities in the People's Republic of China'. *Notre Dame Law Review* 66/5, 1503–29.

Rudelson, Justin. 1997. *Oasis Identities*. New York: Columbia University Press.

Rudelson, Justin and William Jankowiak. 2004. 'Acculturation and Resistance'. In S. Frederick Starr (ed.), *Xinjiang: China's Muslim Borderland*. Armonk, NY: M.E. Sharpe, pp. 299–319.

Russett, Bruce. 1993. 'Can a Democratic Peace Be Built?' *International Interactions* 18/3, 277–82.

Sautman, Barry. 1997. 'Preferential Policies for Ethnic Minorities in China'. Working Papers in the Social Sciences, No. 32, Division of Social Science,

HKUST, available at http://repository.ust.hk/dspace/bitstream/1783.1/1152/1/sosc32.pdf.

Sautman, Barry. 1999. 'Ethnic Law and Minority Rights in China: Progress and Constraints'. *Law & Policy* 21/3, 283–314.

Sautman, Barry. 2000. 'Legal Reform and Minority Rights in China'. In Stuart S. Nagel (ed.), *Handbook of Global Legal Policy*. New York: Marcel Dekker, pp. 71–102.

Sautman, Barry. 2005. 'China's Strategic Vulnerability to Minority Separatism in Tibet'. *Asian Affairs: An American Review* 32/2, 87–118.

Sautman, Barry. 2006. 'Colonialism, Genocide, and Tibet'. *Asian Ethnicity* 7/3, 243–65.

Sautman, Barry. 2010. 'Scaling Back Ethnic Minority Rights? The Debate about China's Ethnic Policies'. *Stanford International Law Journal* 46/3, 51–120.

Sautman, Barry. 2012. 'Paved with Good Intentions: Proposals to Curb Minority Rights and their Consequences for China'. *Modern China* 38/1, 10–39.

Schein, Louisa. 2000. *Minority Rules: The Miao and the Feminine in China's Cultural Politics*. Durham, NC: Duke University Press.

Schluessel, Eric T. 2007. '"Bilingual" Education and Discontent in Xinjiang'. *Central Asian Survey* 26/2, 251–77.

Schwarz, Henry G. 1962. 'Communist Language Policies for China's Ethnic Minorities: The First Decade'. *The China Quarterly* 12, 170–82.

Semyonov, Moshe, Rebecca Raijman and Anastasia Gorodzeisky. 2006. 'The Rise of Anti-Foreigner Sentiment in European Societies, 1988–2000'. *American Sociological Review* 71/3, 426–49.

Semyonov, Moshe, Rebecca Raijman and Anat Yom Tov. 2002. 'Labor Market Competition, Perceived Threat, and Endorsement of Economic Discrimination against Foreign Workers in Israel'. *Social Problems* 49/3, 416–31.

Semyonov, Moshe, Rebecca Raijman, Anat Yom Tov and Peter Schmidt. 2004. 'Population Size, Perceived Threat, and Exclusion'. *Social Science Research* 33/4, 681–701.

Shakya, Tsering. 1999. *The Dragon in the Land of Snows*. New York: Columbia University Press.

Shakya, Tsering. 2009. 'Tibet and China: The Past in the Present'. *Open Democracy*, 29 March, available at http://www.opendemocracy.net/article/tibet-and-china-the-past-in-the-present.

Shan, Wei. 2010. 'Comparing Ethnic Minorities and Han Chinese in China: Life Satisfaction, Economic Well Being and Political Attitudes'. *East Asian Policy* 2/2, 13–22.

Shan, Wei and Chen Gang. 2009. 'The Urumqi Riots and China's Ethnic Policy in Xinjiang'. *East Asian Policy* 1/3, 14–22.

Shichor, Yitzhak. 2005. 'Blow Up: Internal and External Challenges of Uyghur Separatism and Islamic Radicalism to Chinese Rule in Xinjiang'. *Asian Affairs: An American Review* 32/2, 119–35.

Shih, Chih-yu. 2001. 'Ethnicity as Policy Expedience: Clan Confucianism in Ethnic Tujia-Miao Yongshun'. *Asian Ethnicity* 2/1, 73–88.

Shih, Chih-yu. 2002. 'Ethnic Economy of Citizenship in China'. In Merle Goldman and Elizabeth J. Perry (eds), *Changing Meanings of Citizenship in Modern China*. Cambridge, MA: Harvard University Press, pp. 232–54.

Shih, Chuan-kang. 2010. *Quest for Harmony: The Moso Traditions of Sexual Union and Family Life*. Stanford, CA: Stanford University Press.

Smith, Joanne. 2000. 'Four Generations of Uyghurs'. *Inner Asia* 2/2, 195–224.

Smith, Joanne. 2002. 'Making Culture Matter'. *Asian Ethnicity* 3/2, 153–74.

Smith Finley, Joanne. 2007a. 'Chinese Oppression in Xinjiang, Middle Eastern Conflicts and Global Islamic Solidarities among the Uyghurs'. *Journal of Contemporary China* 16/53, 627–54.

Smith Finley, Joanne. 2007b. '"Ethnic Anomaly" or Modern Uyghur Survivor?' In Ildikó Bellér-Hann, M. Cristina Cesàro, Rachel Harris and Joanne Smith Finley (eds), *Situating the Uyghurs Between China and Central Asia*. Aldershot: Ashgate, pp. 219–37.

Smith, Warren. 2004. *China's Policy on Tibetan Autonomy*. Washington, DC: East-West Center in Washington Working Papers No. 2, October, available at http://www.eastwestcenter.org/sites/default/files/private/EWCWwp002.pdf.

Sperling, Elliot. 2004. *The Tibet–China Conflict: History and Polemics*. Washington, DC: East-West Center.

Stacey, Judith. 2009. 'Unhitching the Horse from the Carriage: Love without Marriage among the Mosuo'. *Utah Law Review* 2, 287–321.

Stalin, Joseph V. 1953. 'Marxism and the National Question.' In *Works, Volume 2: 1907–1913*. Moscow: Foreign Languages Publishing House, pp. 300–81.

State Ethnic Affairs Commission of the PRC. 2006. 'Preservation and Development of National Minority Cultures in China', 21 September, available at http://chinagate.cn/english/reports/48941.htm.

Stein, Justin J. 2003. 'Taking the Deliberative Turn in China'. *Journal of Public and International Affairs* 14, 1–25.

Stein, Rolf Alfred. 1972. *Tibetan Civilization*. Stanford, CA: Stanford University Press.

Steiner, Nicholas. 2010. 'Negotiating Policy and Identity in Uyghur China: Realizing a Uyghur Community Policy'. *Wittenberg University East Asian Studies Journal* 35, 43–56.

Studley, John. 1999. 'Ecotourism in China: Endogenous Paradigms for South-west China's Indigenous Minority Peoples', May, available at http://lib.icimod.org/record/10345.

Sudan Divestment Task Force. 2007. *PetroChina, CNPC, and Sudan: Perpetuating Genocide*, 15 April, available at http://home.comcast.net/~berkshire_hathaway/reports/PetroChina_CNPC_Sudan.pdf.

Swain, Margaret Byrne. 1989. 'Developing Ethnic Tourism in Yunnan, China'. *Tourism Recreation Research* 14/1, 33–9.

Tapp, Nicholas. 2002a. 'In Defence of the Archaic: A Reconsideration of the 1950s Ethnic Classification Project in China'. *Asian Ethnicity* 3/1, 63–84.

Tapp, Nicholas. 2002b. 'Cultural Accommodations in Southwest China: The "Han Miao" and Problems in the Ethnography of the Hmong'. *Asian Folklore Studies* 61/1, 77–104.

Tapp, Nicholas. 2002c. *The Hmong of China: Context, Agency, and the Imaginary*. Boston, MA: Brill Academic Publishers.

Tapp, Nicholas. 2010. 'Yunnan: Ethnicity and Economies – Markets and Mobility'. *Asia Pacific Journal of Anthropology* 11/2, 97–110.

Taynen, Jennifer. 2006. 'Interpreters, Arbiters or Outsiders'. *Journal of Muslim Minority Affairs* 26/1, 45–62.

Thierry, François. 1989. 'Empire and Minority in China'. In Gérard Chaliand (ed.), *Minority Peoples in the Age of Nation-States*. London: Pluto Press, pp. 76–99.

Tibetan Parliamentary and Policy Research Centre. 2008. 'Open Debate on Five Questions on Tibet', 3 November, available at http://www.tpprc.org/component/content/article/1-tpprc-news/77-open-debate-on-five-questions-tibet.html.

TibetTrip. n.d. 'Funeral Custom', available at http://www.tibettrip.com/funeral-customs.htm.

Took, Jennifer. 2005. *A Native Chieftaincy in Southwest China*. Leiden: Brill.

Toops, Stanley. 2004. 'The Demography of Xinjiang'. In S. Frederick Starr (ed.), *Xinjiang: China's Muslim Borderland*. Armonk, NY: M.E. Sharpe, pp. 241–63.

Trac, Christine Jane, Stevan Harrell, Thomas M. Hinckley and Amanda C. Henck. 2007. 'Reforestation Programs in Southwest China'. *Journal of Mountain Science* 4/4, 275–92.

Tsung, Linda T. H. 2009. *Minority Languages, Education and Communities in China*. Basingstoke: Palgrave Macmillan.

Tursun, Nabijan. 2008. 'The Formation of Modern Uyghur Historiography and Competing Perspectives toward Uyghur History'. *China and Eurasia Forum Quarterly* 6/3, 87–100.

United Nations Office of the High Commissioner for Human Rights. 1966. *International Covenant on Civil and Political Rights*, General Assembly resolution 2200A, 16 December, available at http://www.ohchr.org/en/professionalinterest/pages/ccpr.aspx.

United Nations. 1992. *Declaration on the Rights of Persons Belonging to National or Ethnic, Religious and Linguistic Minorities*, General Assembly resolution 47/135, 18 December, available at http://www.un.org/documents/ga/res/47/a47r135.htm.

United Nations. 2007. *United Nations Declaration on the Rights of Indigenous Peoples*, General Assembly resolution 61/295, 13 September, available at http://www.un.org/esa/socdev/unpfii/documents/DRIPS_en.pdf.

United Nations. 2010. 'Contributors to United Nations Peacekeeping Operations', available at www.un.org/en/peacekeeping/contributors/2010/oct10_1.pdf.

Unrepresented Nations and Peoples Organization. 2009. 'UN Human Rights Chief: China Fails to Protect Minority Rights', 16 September, available at http://www.unpo.org/article/10063.

Upton, Janet L. 1996. 'Home on the Grassland?' In Melissa J. Brown (ed.), *Negotiating Ethnicities in China and Taiwan*. Berkeley, CA: Institute for East Asian Studies, University of California, pp. 98–124.

US Congressional-Executive Commission on China. 2005a. *Annual Report 2005*. Washington, DC: US Government Printing Office, available at http://www.cecc.gov/pages/annualRpt/annualRpt05/CECCannRpt2005.pdf.

US Congressional-Executive Commission on China. 2005b. *China's Regional Ethnic Autonomy Law: Does it Protect Minority Rights?* 11 April, available at http://www.gpo.gov/fdsys/pkg/CHRG-109hhrg21045/pdf/CHRG-109hhrg21045.pdf.

US Congressional-Executive Commission on China. 2011. *Special Report: Tibetan Monastic Self-Immolations Appear to Correlate with Increasing Repression of Freedom of Religion*, 23 December, available at http://permanent.access.gpo.gov/gpo19336/CECC-Special-Report-Tibetan-Monastic-Self-Immolations-12-23-11.pdf.

'Uyghur Empire, The'. n.d. *All Empires*, available at http://allempires.com/article/index.php?q=The_Uyghur_Empire.

Vermeersch, Peter. 2003. 'EU Enlargement and Minority Rights Policies in Central Europe'. *Journal of Ethnopolitics and Minority Issues in Europe* 1, 1–32.

Vermeersch, Peter. 2004. 'Minority Policy in Central Europe: Exploring the Impact of the EU's Enlargement Strategy'. *Global Review of Ethnopolitics* 3/2, 3–19.

VOA (Voice of America) Tibetan. 2013. 'Two Tibetan Monks Set Themselves on Fire'. 24 April, available at http://m.voatibetanenglish.com/a/1648129.html

Walder, Andrew. 1986. *Communist Neo-traditionalism*. Berkeley, CA: University of California Press.

Wang, Cuntong. 2012. 'Trends in Contraceptive Use and Determinants of Choice in China: 1980–2010'. *Contraception* 85/6, 570–9.

Wang, Hui, Zhaoping Yang, Li Chen, Jingjing Yang and Rui Li. 2010. 'Minority Community Participation in Tourism'. *Tourism Management* 31/6, 759–64.

Wang, Jia Wei and Nyima Gyaincain. 1997. *The Historical Status of China's Tibet*. Beijing: China Intercontinental Press.

Wang, Jia Wei and Nyima Gyaincain. 2000. *The Historical Status of China's Tibet*. Beijing: China Intercontinental Press.

Wang, Jia Wei and Nyima Gyaincain. 2009. 'The Historical Status of China's Tibet'. *Journal of the Washington Institute of China Studies* 4/3, 18–66.

Wang, Tiezhi. 2007. 'Preferential Policies for Ethnic Minority Students in China's College/University Admission'. *Asian Ethnicity* 8/2, 149–63.

Wang, Yuxiang and JoAnn Phillion. 2009. 'Minority Language Policy and Practice in China'. *International Journal of Multicultural Education* 11/1, 1–14.

Wang, Zhenping. 2005. *Ambassadors from the Islands of Immortals: China–Japan Relations in the Han-Tang Period*. Honolulu, HI: University of Hawai'i Press.

West, Jennifer J. 2009. *Perceptions of Ecological Migration in Inner Mongolia, China*. Oslo: Center for International Climate and Environmental Research, July, available at http://www.cicero.uio.no/media/7543.pdf.

Wheeler, Geoffrey. 1964. *The Modern History of Soviet Central Asia*. New York: Greenwood Press.

White, Chris. 2008. 'Understanding China's Minorities through Learning Chinese: The Portrayal of Minorities in Chinese-as-a-Second-Language Textbooks'. *Journal of Multicultural Discourses* 3/2, 79–97.

Whiting, Allen and Sheng Shih-ts'ai. 1958. *Sinkiang: Pawn or Pivot?* East Lansing, MI: Michigan State University Press.

Wickeri, Philip L. and Yik-fai Tam. 2011. 'The Religious Life of Ethnic Minority Communities'. In David A. Palmer, Glenn Shive and Philip L. Wickeri (eds), *Chinese Religious Life*. Oxford: Oxford University Press, pp. 50–66.

Williams, Erin Elizabeth. 2008. 'Ethnic Minorities and the State in China', available at http://www.cpsa-acsp.ca/papers-2008/Williams,%20Erin.pdf.

Wilson, Duncan. 2002. Minority Rights in Education: Lessons for the European Union from Estonia, Latvia, Romania and the former Yugoslav Republic of Macedonia, available at http://r2e.gn.apc.org/sites/r2e.gn.apc.org/files/Duncan%281%29.pdf.

Woeser. 2009. 'Does This Kind of Special Policy Really Exist?', 30 June, available at http://highpeakspureearth.com/2009/does-this-kind-of-special -policy-really-exist-by-woeser/.

Woeser. 2011. 'Is Migration to Tibet Unrelated to Government Policies?', 27 April, available at http://highpeakspureearth.com/2011/is-migration -to-tibet-unrelated-to-government-policies-by-woeser/.

Wong, David W.S. 2000. 'Ethnic Integration and Spatial Segregation of the Chinese Population'. *Asian Ethnicity* 1/1, 53–72.

Wong, Edward. 2010. 'China's Money and Migrants Pour into Tibet', *New York Times*, 24 July, available at http://www.nytimes.com/2010/07/25/world/ asia/25tibet.html?pagewanted=all.

Wong, Edward. 2012. 'China: Nobel Winners Urge Tibet Talks', *New York Times*, 2 April, available at http://www.nytimes.com/2012/04/03/world/asia/ china-nobel-winners-urge-tibet-talks.html.

Wu, Shimin (ed.). 1998. *Zhongguo Minzu Zhengce Duben* [Collection on China's Ethnic Minority Policies]. Beijing: Central University of Nationalities Press.

Xie, Philip Feifan. 2003. 'Managing Aboriginal Tourism in Hainan, China: Government Perspectives'. *Annals of Leisure Research* 6/2, 278–99.

Xinhua. 2005a. 'China Improves Education Level, Medical Services in Ethnic Autonomous Areas', 28 February, available at http://english.sina.com/ china/1/2005/0228/22640.html.

Xinhua. 2005b. 'Ethnic Regional Autonomy System and Its Practice in the Tibet Autonomous Region', *China View*, 29 August, available at http://news.xin- huanet.com/english/2005-08/29/content_3417312.htm.

Xinhua. 2005c. 'Changes in Tibet: Facts & Figures', *SINA English*, 1 September, available at http://english.sina.com/china/1/2005/0901/44440.html.

Xinhua. 2008. 'Backgrounder: Regional Autonomy for China's Ethnic Minorities', *China View*, 30 April, available at http://news.xinhuanet.com/english/2008- 04/30/content_8080235.htm.

Xinhua. 2009a. 'Fifty Years of Democratic Reform in Tibet', *China Daily*, 2 March, available at http://www.chinadaily.com.cn/60th/2009-03/02/ content_8635852_2.htm.

Xinhua. 2009b. 'Ethnic Minority Officials Active in China's Politics', *People's Daily Online*, 21 July, available at http://english.people.com.cn/90001/90776/ 90882/6705156.html.

Xinhua. 2010a. National Counterpart Support Network Conference held in Xinjiang (全国对口支援新疆工作会议在北京召开), 30 March, available at http://www.btjx.gov.cn/publish/portal24/tab1843/info84918.htm [in Chinese].

Xinhua. 2010b. 'Ethnic Minorities Enjoy Equal Rights in China', 26 September, available at http://news.xinhuanet.com/english2010/china/2010-09/26/c_13530003.htm.

Xinhua. 2011a. Hu Jintao Gives Important Instructions to 2nd National Counterpart Support Network Conference in Xinjiang (第二次全国对口支援新疆工作会议在京召开 胡锦涛作出重要批示), 29 May, available at http://cpc.people.com.cn/GB/64093/64094/14767576.html [in Chinese].

Xinhua. 2011b. 'China Has Over 2.9 Million Ethnic Minority Cadres', 14 July, available at http://english.peopledaily.com.cn/90001/90776/90785/7439871.html.

Xinhua. 2012. 'Minority Writers Encouraged to Help Boost China's "Soft Power"', 20 September, available at http://english.people.com.cn/90785/7954509.html.

Xinjiang Academy of Social Sciences, History Division. 1997. *A Short History of Xinjiang* (新疆简史). Urumchi: Xinjiang People's Press [in Chinese].

Xinjiang Demographic Analysis and Economy Overview. n.d. Available at http://www.china-marketresearch.com/market-review/provincial-overview/xinjiang-demographic-economy.htm.

Xinjiang Education Press. 2009. *Fifty 'Whys' – A Book on the Fight against Separatism and Promotion of Ethnic Unity in China* (50个'为什么' – 维护国家统一，反对民族分裂，加强民族团结读本). Urumchi: Xinjiang Education Press [in Chinese].

Xu, Jianchu, Erzi Ma, Duojie Tashi, Yongshou Fu, Zhi Lu and David Melick. 2006. 'Integrating Sacred Knowledge for Conservation: Cultures and Landscapes in Southwest China'. *Ecology and Society* 10/2, article 7.

Xu, Shuhua, et al. 2009. 'Genomic Dissection of Population Substructure of Han Chinese and Its Implication in Association Studies'. *American Journal of Human Genetics* 85/6, 762–74.

Yan, Ruxian. 1989. 'Marriage, Family and Social Progress of China's Minority Nationalities'. In Chien Chiao and Nicholas Tapp (eds), *Ethnicity and Ethnic Groups in China*. Hong Kong: New Asia College, Chinese University of Hong Kong, pp. 79–87.

Yang, Li. 2011. 'Minorities, Tourism and Ethnic Theme Parks: Employees' Perspectives from Yunnan, China'. *Journal of Cultural Geography* 28/2, 311–38.

Yang, Li and Geoffrey Wall. 2009. 'Minorities and Tourism: Community Perspectives from Yunnan, China'. *Journal of Tourism and Cultural Change* 7/2, 77–98.

Yang, Rui and Mei Wu. 2009. 'Education for Ethnic Minorities in China'. *SAeDUC Journal* 6/2, 117–31.

Yee, Herbert. 2003. 'Ethnic Relations in Xinjiang: A Survey of Uygur–Han Relations in Urumqi'. *Journal of Contemporary China* 12/36, 431–52.

Yeh, Emily. 2013. *Taming Tibet: Landscape Transformation and the Gift of Chinese Development*. Ithaca, NY: Cornell University Press.

Yi, Lin. 2008. *Cultural Exclusion in China: State Education, Social Mobility and Cultural Difference*. New York: Taylor & Francis.

Yin, Pumin. 2011. 'Helping Xinjiang Catch Up', *Beijing Review*, 17 June, available at http://www.bjreview.com.cn/print/txt/2011-06/17/content_369507.htm.

Yin, Zhuguang and Yongfu Mao (eds). 1995. *Research on Ethnic Relationships in Xinjiang*. Urumqi: Xinjiang People's Press.

Yue, Hu. 2010. 'Hand in Hand', *Beijing Review*, 7 June, available at http://www.bjreview.com.cn/business/txt/2010-06/07/content_277403.htm.

Zang, Xiaowei. 2007. *Ethnicity and Urban Life in China: A Comparative Study of Hui Muslims and Han Chinese*. London: Routledge.

Zang, Xiaowei. 2008a. 'Market Reforms and Han–Hui Variation in Employment in the State Sector in a Chinese City'. *World Development* 36/11, 2341–52.

Zang, Xiaowei. 2008b. 'Gender and Ethnic Variation in Arranged Marriages in a Chinese City'. *Journal of Family Issues* 29/5, 615–38.

Zang, Xiaowei. 2010. 'Affirmative Action, Economic Reforms, and Han-Uyghur Variation in Job Attainment in the State Sector in Ürümchi'. *China Quarterly* 202, 344–61.

Zang, Xiaowei. 2011a. 'Uyghur–Han Earnings Differentials in Ürümchi'. *China Journal* 65, 141–55.

Zang, Xiaowei. 2011b. *Islam, Family Life, and Gender Inequality in Urban China*. London: Routledge.

Zang, Xiaowei. 2011c. 'Gender Roles and Ethnic Income Inequality in Ürümchi'. *Ethnic and Racial Studies* 35/2, 238–58.

Zang, Xiaowei. 2012. 'Minority Threat and Ethnic Variation in Party Membership Attainment in China'. *Journal of Contemporary China* 21/75, 519–30.

Zang, Xiaowei. 2013. 'Major Determinants of Uyghur Ethnic Consciousness in Ürümchi'. *Modern Asian Studies* 47/6, 2046–71.

Zeng, Xun. 2007. 'Enforcing Equal Employment Opportunities in China'. *University of Pennsylvania Journal of Labor & Employment Law* 9/4, 991–1025.

Zhang, Hong. 2014. 'President Xi Jinping Delivers Tough Message to "Frontline of Terror" on Visit to Xinjiang'. *South China Morning Post*, 29 April, available at http://www.scmp.com/news/china/article/1499803/xi-makes-rare-visit-xinjiangs-restive-south-bolster-anti-terror-campaign?page=all.

Zhang, Yingjin. 1997. 'From "Minority Film" to "Minority Discourse": Questions of Nationhood and Ethnicity in Chinese Cinema'. *Cinema Journal* 36/3, 73–90.

Zhao, Wuxing. 1991. *The Chinese Ethnic Minority Literature*. Beijing: China Intercontinental Press.

Zhao, Ying and Li Huaiyan. 2009. 'Endangered Ethnic Languages – Reviving or Archiving?', 29 July, available at http://news.xinhuanet.com/english/2009-07/29/content_11793112.htm.

Zhao, Zhenzhou. 2010. *China's Mongols at University*. Idaho Falls, ID: Lexington Books.

Zheng, Wei. 2009. 'Social Security and Minority Economic Development'. *Asian Social Science* 5/7, 41–3.

Zhou, Minglang. 2000. 'Language Policy and Illiteracy in Ethnic Minority Communities in China'. *Journal of Multilingual and Multicultural Development* 21/2, 129–48.

Zhou, Minglang. 2003. *Multilingualism in China: The Politics of Writing Reforms for Minority Languages, 1949–2002*. Berlin: Walter de Gruyter.

Zhou, Minglang. 2004. 'Minority Language Policy in China: Equality in Theory and Inequality in Practice'. *Language Policy* 4/1, 71–95.

Zhou, Minglang and Ann Maxwell Hill. 2009. *Affirmative Action in China and the U.S.: A Dialogue on Inequality and Minority Education*. Basingstoke: Palgrave Macmillan.

Zhou, Yong. 2009. 'Legal Predicament of Combining "Regional" and "National" Autonomy: A Group Rights Perspective'. *International Journal on Minority and Group Rights* 16/3, 329–48.

Zhu, Guobing and Yu Lingyun. 2000. 'Regional Minority Autonomy in the PRC'. *International Journal on Minority and Group Rights* 7/1, 39–57.

Zhu, Ningzhu, 2013. 'Rioters Kill 24 in Xinjiang', 27 June, available at http://news.xinhuanet.com/english/china/2013-06/27/c_132492895.htm.

Zhu, Weiqun (朱维群). 2011. 'Promote and Develop Tibetan Culture (努力推动西藏文化的保护及发展)', *China's Tibet* (中国西藏), No. 6, pp. 12–17 [in Chinese].

Zhu, Weiqun (朱维群). 2012. 'Thoughts on Current Nationality Issues (对当前民族领域问题的几点思考)', *Study Daily* (学习时报), 15 February, available at http://www.cpcnews.cn/BIG5/64093/64102/17122242.html [in Chinese].

Zhu, Yuchao and Dongyan Blachford. 2005. 'Ethnic Minority Issues in China's Foreign Policy: Perspectives and Implications'. *Pacific Review* 18/2, 243–64.

Zuo, Xiulan. 2007. 'China's Policy towards Minority Languages in a Globalizing Age'. *Transnational Curriculum Inquiry* 4/1, 80–91.

Index